Albert Bushnell Hart, Marion Gleason McDougall

Fugitive Slaves

(1619-1865)

Albert Bushnell Hart, Marion Gleason McDougall

Fugitive Slaves
(1619-1865)

ISBN/EAN: 9783744722544

Printed in Europe, USA, Canada, Australia, Japan

Cover: Foto ©ninafisch / pixelio.de

More available books at **www.hansebooks.com**

PUBLICATIONS OF THE SOCIETY FOR THE COLLEGIATE INSTRUCTION
OF WOMEN

Fay House Monographs

No. 3

FUGITIVE SLAVES

(1619–1865)

BY

MARION GLEASON McDOUGALL

PREPARED UNDER THE DIRECTION OF

ALBERT BUSHNELL HART, Ph. D.
ASSISTANT PROFESSOR OF HISTORY IN HARVARD UNIVERSITY

BOSTON, U.S.A.
PUBLISHED BY GINN & COMPANY
1891

Copyright, 1891,
BY THE SOCIETY FOR THE COLLEGIATE INSTRUCTION OF WOMEN.

University Press:
JOHN WILSON AND SON, CAMBRIDGE.

EDITOR'S PREFACE.

EVERY careful student of history is aware that it is no longer possible to write the general history of any important country from the original sources ; on any period, the materials which accumulate in a year are more than can be assimilated by one mind in three years. The general historian must use the results of others' work. It is therefore essential that the great phases of political and constitutional development be treated in monographs, each devoted to a single, limited subject and each prepared on a careful and scientific method.

This first number of the historical series of the Fay House Monographs aims to discuss the single topic of Fugitive Slaves. Mrs. McDougall has drawn together and compared many cases found in obscure sources, and has perhaps been able to correct some commonly received impressions on this neglected subject.

Even in its limited range this does not pretend to be a complete work in the sense that all the available cases are discussed or recorded. The effort has been made to use the cases as illustrations of principles, and to add such bibliography as may direct the reader to further details. The appendix of laws is as full as it was possible to make it from the collections in the Boston Public and Massachusetts State Libraries. If the monograph prove useful to the student of American history, it will meet the expectations of author and editor.

ALBERT BUSHNELL HART.

CAMBRIDGE, April 2, 1891.

AUTHOR'S PREFACE.

The following monograph was written while the author was a student in the "Harvard Annex" as a study in the Seminary course given by Professor Albert Bushnell Hart. The work has continued during parts of the four years since 1887. The effort has been to trace in some measure the development of public sentiment upon the subject, to prepare an outline of Colonial legislation and of the work of Congress during the entire period, and to give accounts of typical cases illustrative of conditions and opinions. Only a few of the more important cases are described minutely, but a critical list of the authorities may be found in the bibliographical appendix.

The thanks of the author are due first to Professor Hart, under whose direction and with whose assistance and encouragement the monograph has been prepared; then to Miss Anna B. Thompson, without whose careful training in the Thayer Academy and continued sympathy, the work could not have been undertaken. Many thanks are due also to the authorities of the Library of Harvard College for the use, in the alcoves, of their large and conveniently arranged collection of books and pamphlets on United States History, and to the assistants in the Boston Public and Massachusetts State Libraries for courteous aid. Colonel T. W. Higginson has kindly examined the chapter on the cases from 1850 to 1860, suggesting some interesting details; and Mr. Arthur Gilman has read the whole in proof, and made many valuable suggestions.

MARION GLEASON McDOUGALL.

Rockland, Mass., April 2, 1891.

CONTENTS.

CHAPTER I.

LEGISLATION AND CASES BEFORE THE CONSTITUTION.

	PAGE
§ 1. Elements of colonial slavery	1
§ 2. Regulations as to fugitives (1640–1700)	2
§ 3. Treatment of fugitives	3
§ 4. Regulations in New England colonies	4
§ 5. Escapes in New England: Attucks case	5
§ 6. Dutch regulations in New Netherlands	6
§ 7. Escapes from New Amsterdam	6
§ 8. Intercolonial regulations	7
§ 9. Intercolonial cases	8
§ 10. International relations	9
§ 11. International cases	10
§ 12. Relations with the mother country	11
§ 13. Regulation under the Articles of Confederation (1781–1788)	12
§ 14. Ordinance for the Northwest Territory (1787)	13
§ 15. The Fugitive question in the Constitutional Conventions	14

CHAPTER II.

LEGISLATION FROM 1789 TO 1850.

§ 16. Effect of the fugitive slave clause in the Constitution	16
§ 17. The first Fugitive Slave Act (1793)	16
§ 18. Discussion of the first act	18
§ 19. Propositions of 1797 and 1802	19
§ 20. Propositions from 1817 to 1822	21
§ 21. Period of the Missouri Compromise (1819–1822)	23
§ 22. Status of the question from 1823 to 1847	24
§ 23. Canada and Mexico places of refuge	25
§ 24. Status of fugitives on the high seas	26
§ 25. Kidnapping from 1793 to 1850: Prigg case	27
§ 26. Necessity of more stringent fugitive slave provisions	28
§ 27. Action of Congress from 1847 to 1850	28
§ 28. Slavery in the District of Columbia	29
§ 29. The second Fugitive Slave Act (1850)	29
§ 30. Provisions of the second Fugitive Slave Act	30
§ 31. Arguments for the bill	31
§ 32. Arguments against the bill	32

[v]

CHAPTER III.

PRINCIPAL CASES FROM 1789 TO 1860.

	PAGE
§ 33. Change in character of cases	34
§ 34. The first case of rescue (1793)	35
§ 35. President Washington's demand for a fugitive (1796)	35
§ 36. Kidnapping cases	36
§ 37. Jones case (1836)	36
§ 38. Solomon Northup case (about 1830)	37
§ 39. Washington case (between 1840 and 1850)	38
§ 40. Oberlin case (1841)	38
§ 41. Interference and rescues	38
§ 42. Chickasaw rescue (1836)	38
§ 43. Philadelphia case (1838)	39
§ 44. Latimer case (1842)	39
§ 45. Ottoman case (1846)	40
§ 46. Interstate relations	41
§ 47. Boston and Isaac cases (1837, 1839)	41
§ 48. Ohio and Kentucky cases (1848)	41
§ 49. Prosecutions	42
§ 50. Van Zandt, Pearl, and Walker cases (1840, 1844)	42
§ 51. Unpopularity of the Fugitive Slave Act of 1850	43
§ 52. Principle of the selection of cases	43
§ 53. Hamlet case (1850)	43
§ 54. Sims case (1851)	44
§ 55. Burns case (1854)	45
§ 56. Garner case (1856)	46
§ 57. Shadrach case (1851)	47
§ 58. Jerry McHenry case (1851)	48
§ 59. Oberlin-Wellington case (1858)	49
§ 60. Christiana case (1851)	50
§ 61. Miller case (1851)	51
§ 62. John Brown in Kansas (1858)	51

CHAPTER IV.

FUGITIVES AND THEIR FRIENDS.

§ 63. Methods of escape	53
§ 64. Reasons for escape	54
§ 65. Conditions of slave life	55
§ 66. Escapes to the woods	56
§ 67. Escapes to the North	57
§ 68. Use of protection papers	58
§ 69. Fugitives disguised as whites: Craft case	58

Contents. vii

	PAGE
§ 70. Underground Railroad	60
§ 71. Rise and growth of the system	60
§ 72. Methods pursued	61
§ 73. Colored agents of the Underground Railroad	62
§ 74. Prosecutions of agents	63
§ 75. Formal organization	63
§ 76. General effect of escapes	64

CHAPTER V.

PERSONAL LIBERTY LAWS.

§ 77. Character of the personal liberty laws	65
§ 78. Acts passed before the Prigg decision (1793-1842)	65
§ 79. Acts passed between the Prigg decision and the second Fugitive Slave Law (1842-1850)	66
§ 80. Acts occasioned by the law of 1850 (1850-1860)	66
§ 81. Massachusetts acts	67
§ 82. Review of the acts by States	69
§ 83. Effect of the personal liberty laws	70

CHAPTER VI.

THE END OF THE FUGITIVE SLAVE QUESTION (1860-1865).

§ 85. The Fugitive Slave Law in the crisis of 1860-61	71
§ 86. Proposition to enforce the Fugitive Slave Law	72
§ 87. Propositions to repeal or amend the law	73
§ 88. The question of slaves of rebels	73
§ 89. Slavery attacked in Congress	74
§ 90. Confiscation bills	75
§ 91. Confiscation provisions extended	75
§ 92. Effect of the Emancipation Proclamation (1863)	77
§ 93. Fugitives in loyal slave States	77
§ 94. Typical cases	78
§ 95. Question discussed in Congress	78
§ 96. Arrests by civil officers	80
§ 97. Denial of the use of jails in the District of Columbia	80
§ 98. Abolition of slavery in the District of Columbia	82
§ 99. Regulations against kidnapping	82
§ 100. Repeal of the Fugitive Slave Acts	83
§ 101. Early propositions to repeal the acts	83
§ 102. Discussion of the repeal bill in the House	84
§ 103. Repeal bills in the Senate	85
§ 104. The repeal act and the thirteenth amendment	86
§ 105. Educating effect of the controversy	87

APPENDICES.

APPENDIX A.
                                                                    PAGE
Colonial laws relative to fugitives.. 89

APPENDIX B.
National acts and propositions relative to fugitive slaves (1778-1854) 104

APPENDIX C.
National acts and propositions relating to fugitive slaves (1860-1864) 117

APPENDIX D.
List of important fugitive slave cases... 124

APPENDIX E.
Bibliography of fugitive slave cases and fugitive slave legislation 129

INDEX... 139

CHAPTER I.

LEGISLATION AND CASES BEFORE THE CONSTITUTION.

§ 1. Elements of colonial slavery.
§ 2. Regulations as to fugitives (1640-1700).
§ 3. Treatment of fugitives.
§ 4. Regulations in New England colonies.
  § 5. Escapes in New England; Attucks case.
§ 6. Dutch regulations in New Netherlands.
  § 7. Escapes from New Amsterdam.
§ 8. Intercolonial regulations.
  § 9. Intercolonial cases.
§ 10. International relations.
  § 11. International cases.
§ 12. Relations with the mother country.
§ 13. Regulation under the Articles of Confederation (1781-1788).
  § 14. Ordinance for the Northwest Territory (1787).
§ 15. The Fugitive question in the Constitutional Conventions.

§ 1. **Elements of colonial slavery.** — By the middle of the seventeenth century, the settlements made in America by the English, Dutch, and Swedes were arranged for the most part in a line of little colonies closely following the Atlantic coast. To the west, wide forests and plains, broken only by the paths of the Indian, stretched on to the Pacific; while long intervals of unpopulated country separated the colonists on the north from the French in Canada, and on the south from the Spaniards in Florida.

In all the colonies thus grouped together, the system of slavery had already become well established, and with its institution the question of the escape and return of the slaves had necessarily arisen. The conditions of the country, both physical and social, gave unusual facilities for flight. The wild woods, the Indian settlements, or the next colony, peopled by a foreign race, and perhaps as yet without firmly established government, offered to the slave a refuge and possibly protection. Escape, therefore, as a peculiar danger, demanded peculiar remedies. Though it is the purpose of this monograph not so much to study the detail of legislation or escape in the colonies as to deal with the period from 1789 to 1865, a slight sketch of the intercolonial laws and provisions which preceded and in part suggested later legislation will first be necessary.

Almost immediately after the introduction of slavery, in 1619, we begin to find regulations made by the colonists upon this subject. At first they applied solely to their own territory, but soon agreements were entered into among several colonies, or between a colony and the Indians or the French in Canada. These acts and agreements recognized not only the negro, as at a later period, but also the white and the Indian slave. There existed in some of the colonies of this time a peculiar class of white people, who received no wages, and were bound to their masters.[1] Usually these redemptioners were laborers or handicraftsmen, but sometimes they were persons of education who had committed a crime, and were sold according to law for a term of years, or for life. One of the class is curiously connected with the education of no less a person than George Washington. An unpublished autobiography of the Reverend John Boucher, who from 1760 to the Revolution was a teacher and preacher in Virginia, contains the following paragraph noticing the fact: —

"Mr. Washington was the second of five sons, of parents distinguished neither for their rank nor fortune. . . . George, who, like most people thereabouts at that time, had no other education than reading, writing, and accounts, which he was taught by a convict servant whom his father bought for a schoolmaster, first set out in the world as a surveyor of Orange County."[2]

§ 2. **Regulations as to fugitives.** — The earliest regulation upon this subject is found among the freedoms and exemptions granted by the West India Company, in 1629, "to all Patroons, Masters, or Private Persons" who would agree to settle in New Netherlands. The authorities promised to do all in their power to return to their masters any slaves or colonists fleeing from service.[3]

A little later, the Swedish colonists in Pennsylvania asked from their government the same privilege of reclaiming fugitives.[4] The preamble of an act against fugitives in East Jersey, in 1686, explains these provisions. They found that "the securing of such

---

[1] Hurd, Law of Freedom and Bondage, I. 295.
[2] Nation, April 18, 1889.
[3] Appendix A, No. 1.
[4] N. Y. Colonial Manuscripts, XIII. 211.

persons as Run away, or otherwise absent themselves from their master's lawfull Occasion," was "a material encouragement to such Persons as come into this country to settle Plantations and Populate the Province."[1] In many of the Southern colonies, as Maryland and South Carolina, so severe were the acts against this class of bound colonists that a runaway might be declared outlawed, and might rightfully be killed by any person.[2]

§ 3. **Treatment of fugitives.** — From 1640 to 1700, laws were also passed in New Jersey, Maryland, South Carolina, and Virginia. It is not necessary to follow out the provisions here,[3] but each of the Southern colonies, as in later regulations, provided most minutely for all possible cases. By a Virginia law of 1642, all persons who entertained runaways, whether slaves or hired freemen, were to be fined twenty pounds of tobacco for each night's hospitality. The fugitives were to add to their tenure of service double their time of absence, and on a second offence to be branded with the letter R.[4]

A curious regulation in 1660-1, in Virginia, provided that if a negro and white bound servant ran away together, since the negro's time of servitude was for life, and he was therefore incapable of making up his lost time, the white servant's punishment should be doubled by adding the negro's sentence to his own.[5] Another regulation, entitled "How to Know a Runaway," commanded that all recovered fugitives have their hair "cutt" close about their ears.[6]

Sometimes the penalties were even more severe, but the processes were much the same. A person who found a slave or vagabond without a pass usually took him before the next justice, who took cognizance of the captor's good service, and certified it in the next Assembly: the runaway was then delivered from constable to constable, until he was returned to his master.

After 1700 the process grows yet more elaborate; for example, take a North Carolina law of 1741. The securer of a runaway was to have seven shillings and sixpence proclamation money, and for every mile over ten which he conducted the fugitive threepence extra. When seized, runaways were to be whipped and

[1] Appendix A, No. 45.
[2] Hurd, Law of Freedom and Bondage, I. 295.
[3] The texts will be found *post*, Appendix A.   [4] Appendix A, No. 6.
[5] Appendix A, No. 23.   [6] Appendix A, No. 20.

placed in the county gaol. If the owner was known, he was notified and went for his slave; if not, a notice describing the runaway must be placed upon the door of the court-house, and sent to the clerk or reader of each church or chapel within the county. They were required to post all such notices every Lord's day for two months in some convenient place near the church. At the end of this time, should no claimant appear, the slave must be sent from constable to constable, till the public gaol of the government was reached. There, upon consent of the court or of two justices, he might be sold to hire by the gaoler.[1] The Maryland Archives record that in 1669 ten thousand pounds of tobacco were appropriated to build one of these log-house gaols wherein fugitive servants might be lodged.[2]

§ 4. **Regulations in New England colonies.**—Let us turn now to the New England colonies. Here we must expect to find but few provisions, since the class of slaves and bound servants was so small that it could easily be controlled. The first law in Massachusetts Bay was passed in 1630, and was entitled, "An Act respecting Masters, Servants, and Laborers." In accordance with the arbitrary methods of government then pursued, it included not only runaway servants, but also any persons who should "privily go away with suspicion of evil intention," and ordered the magistrate "to press men, boats, or pinnaces," and "to bring them back by force of arms." A humane provision, usually wanting in Southern laws, though also found in New Netherlands, declared that, whenever servants fled on account of the tyranny of their masters, they should be protected until measures for their relief could be taken.[3]

In Connecticut and New Hampshire similar laws were passed, and in 1707 Massachusetts Bay, in regulating the free negro population, enacted that every freeman or mulatto who should harbor a negro servant in his house without his owner's consent should pay five shillings for the use of the poor of the town.[4]

In those days, when bridges were few, the ferrymen were apparently much relied upon as agents to detect and apprehend runaways. In 1714 we find that several negro slaves had been carried over ferries, and thus escaped out of Rhode Island. The Assembly therefore enacted that "no ferryman or boatman what-

[1] Iredell, 90; Appendix A, No. 73.   [2] Maryland Archives, II. 224.
[3] Appendix A, No. 2.   [4] Appendix A, No. 53.

soever, within this colony, shall carry or bring any slave as aforesaid over their ferries, without a certificate under the hands of their masters or mistresses, or some person in authority, upon the penalty of paying all costs and damages their said masters or mistresses shall sustain thereby: and to pay a fine of twenty shillings for the use of the colony for each offence, as aforesaid." All persons were also commanded to take up any slave they might find travelling about without a pass.[1]

§ 5. **Escapes in New England: Attucks case.** — Although we do not find records of fugitive slave cases tried at this time within the New England colonies, advertisements of runaways exist in sufficient numbers to prove that escapes were common. It seems probable, therefore, that the return of a slave when within his own colony was taken as a matter of course, and roused so little opposition, and required so simple a process at law, that matters concerning it would seldom find mention in the chronicles of the time. Here is a typical advertisement: —

"Ran away from Samuel Gilbert of Littleton, an indentured Servant Boy, named Samuel Gilson, about 17 years old, of a middling Stature for his Age, and wears black curled Hair, he carried away with him a blue cloth Coat, a light colored Jacket with sleeves, one pair of worsted Stockings, two striped woolen Shirts, and one good linnen Shirt. He went away in company with a short thick set Fellow, who wore a green coat and a green Jacket double breasted, also a pair Indian green Stockings. Whoever shall take up and secure, or give information of said runaway, so that his master may find him again, shall receive a Reward of two dollars and all necessary charges from

SAMUEL GILBERT.

"All masters of vessels and others are cautioned against harboring," etc.[2]

Again a case interesting not only as an illustration of the customs of the time, but also because the fugitive himself bears a name known to history in another connection, is noticed in the Boston Gazette of 1750. Here is advertised as escaping, October 2, 1750, from his master, William Browne of Framingham, Massachusetts, "A molatto fellow about twenty-seven years of age, named Crispus." After describing his clothing and appearance, a reward of ten pounds, old tenor, is offered for his return, and "all masters of vessels and others are cautioned against

---

[1] Appendix A, No. 57; Appendix D, No. 6.   [2] Boston Gazette, Jan. 1, 1770.

concealing said servant on penalty of law."[1] Tradition has it, however, that he was never arrested, but returned of his own accord after a short time, and was for the next twenty years a faithful servant.[2] Then, in 1770, presumably while in town upon one of the expeditions he often undertook to buy and sell cattle for his master, he was drawn into the Boston Massacre of March 5.[3]

A somewhat famous case, which also occurred in Massachusetts, though many years later, may here be mentioned. About 1769 one Rotch, a Quaker, and therefore probably opposed to slavery, received on board the whaler Friendship a young negro boy named Boston, belonging to the heirs of William Swain. At the end of the voyage his master, John Swain, brought action in the court of Nantucket against Captain Folger for the recovery of the slave; the jury, whether from lack of evidence or from sympathy cannot be determined, returned a verdict in favor of the defendant.[4]

§ 6. **Dutch regulations in New Netherlands.** — The early New Netherlands regulations furnish many interesting provisions concerning fugitive servants. Apparently the servile class was numerous, and hard to govern. In the words of the ordinance of 1640, " many servants daily run away from their masters, whereby the latter are put to great inconvenience and expense; the corn and tobacco rot in the field, and the whole harvest is at a standstill, which tends to the serious injury of this country, to their masters' ruin, and to bring the magistracy into contempt." It was therefore ordained that runaways must, at the end of their term of indenture, serve double the time of their absence, and make good all loss and damage to their masters; while persons harboring fugitives were obliged to pay a fine of fifty guilders.[5]

§ 7. **Escapes from New Amsterdam.** — Within these Dutch colonies there is recorded a case of escape as early as 1659. Four menservants of Cornelis Herperts de Jager, of New Amsterdam, ran away to Manhattan. One of them soon returned, and in accordance with the regulation made in 1630 by the West India Com-

[1] Boston Gazette, Oct. 2, 1750; G. W. Williams, History of the Negro Race in America, I. 330.
[2] Liberator, March 16, 1860.
[3] W. C. Nell's Address at the Nineteenth Anniversary of Boston Massacre.
[4] Moore, Slavery in Massachusetts, 117.
[5] Appendix A, No 3; Appendix D, No. 10.

pany,[1] requiring the return of fugitives in their various settlements, one of the officers of the colony sent to Manhattan an order to arrest and bring back the remaining three in chains.[2]

§ 8. **Intercolonial regulations.** — It will be seen that most of the colonies considered some provision against runaways necessary to the welfare of the settlements. To secure such legislation in a single colony was a comparatively easy matter; but the unorganized and sparsely settled condition of the country rendered any intercolonial regulations difficult.

The first formal agreement of this kind was arranged by the New England Confederation of Plymouth, Massachusetts, Connecticut, and New Haven, in 1643. In their Articles of Confederation was a clause which promised: "If any servant runn away from his master into any other of these confederated Jurisdiccons, That in such Case vpon the Certyficate of one Majistrate in the Jurisdiccon out of which the said servant fled, or upon other due proofe, the said servant shall be deliuered either to his Master or any other that pursues and brings such Certificate or proofe."[3] This clause contains the earliest statement of the principles regarding the treatment of fugitive slave cases, afterward carried out in the United States statutes of 1787, 1793, and 1850. There was no trial by jury, but the certificate of a magistrate was sufficient evidence to convict the runaway.

It is probable, also, that the rendition of fugitives was considered a duty incumbent upon all colonies, whatever their relation to each other, since about this time we find an agreement made for the mutual surrender of fugitives between the Dutch at New Netherlands and the English at New Haven.[4]

Not only did the slaves of the Dutch escape to the English colonies, but they often fled to the forests, where recovery must have been almost impossible unless the Indians could be induced to hunt them out. Curious rewards were sometimes offered. Maryland, in 1669, ordered that any Indian who shall apprehend a fugitive may have a "match coate," or its value.[5] Virginia would

---

[1] See *ante*, § 2.
[2] N. Y. Colonial Manuscripts, XIII. 238; Letter from Jacob Aldrich to Director Stuyvesant of New Netherlands, New Amstel, 14 May, 1659; Documentary History of N. Y. Colony, II. 556; Appendix D, No. 2.
[3] Appendix A, No. 8; Gilman, History of the American People, 605.
[4] N. Y. Colonial Manuscripts, I. 342; Doyle, English in America, I. 391.
[5] Maryland Archives, II. 523.

give "20 armes length of Roanoke," or its value,[1] while in Connecticut "two yards of cloth" was considered sufficient inducement.[2] We have record of several conferences upon this subject. Governor Burnett of New York asked his Indians to exert themselves in behalf of the Governor of Virginia, who had written to him about the escape of several of his negro servants to the mountains. The Indians promised their help in this and any other search; but as they seldom seem to have succeeded, it is probable that their sympathy was with the fugitives.[3] Again Governor Burnett demanded the restoration of a certain Indian slave whom they had kidnapped from the English. The Indians acknowledged the fact, but they said that he was then sold to others, and nothing further could be done.[4]

Canada even in these early times seems also to have been a haven for fugitives. In 1705 New York passed an act, which was renewed in 1715, to prevent slaves running away from frontier towns like Albany to Canada, because it was of great importance, they said, in time of war, "that no Intelligence be carried from the said city and county to the French in Canada."[5]

During all this time the Southern colonies, especially the Carolinas and Georgia, were also making many complaints in regard to the difficulty they had in recovering the fugitives, both Indian and negro, who were escaping in large numbers into Florida. There, among the Creek Indians and the Spanish at St. Augustine, they easily found refuge.[6] This difficulty was, however, not remedied in colonial times, but continued long after the formation of the Federal Union, and in fact until the close of the Seminole war, in 1845.

§ 9. **Intercolonial cases.** — When, as was often the case, no agreement upon the return of fugitives had been arranged between the colonies, the rendition of a slave depended wholly upon the state of feeling existing between the two peoples, and sometimes became an important question. Between the New England colonies no cases have been found recorded, although we infer

[1] Appendix A, No. 37.
[2] Acts and Laws of Connecticut, 229.
[3] N. Y. Colonial Manuscripts, V. 637; Appendix D, No. 4.
[4] N. Y. Colonial Manuscripts, V. 793.
[5] Appendix A, Nos. 50, 59.
[6] Giddings, Exiles of Florida, 281; Wilson, Rise and Fall of the Slave Power in America, I. 122.

that there must have been reason for the insertion of a fugitive slave clause in the Articles of Confederation of 1643.[1]

Of other early cases one of the most interesting is the escape from Virginia of four Englishmen belonging to the class of bound servants. They rowed in a small boat up the coast as far as Cape May, where they landed.[2] They soon found themselves objects of suspicion with the people, and, as was a common practice, took refuge among the Indians. About a year afterward their masters tracked them to their place of refuge, and captured two of them, but the others were again beyond reach. The Indians, who evidently did not always befriend runaways, had just sold one of them, William Browne, to a Swede, and Browne, learning of his former master's appearance, had found opportunity to escape. The fourth of the fugitives was still among the Mantas, and could not be secured. Of the two recaptured, one was returned without trouble, but the other, Turc, who had just entered the service of a certain Pieter Aldrich, resisted his captors. A struggle took place upon the boat in which they were carrying him away. After wounding three of his guards, he succeeded in making his escape, only to be recaptured almost immediately. When tried for the deed at New Amsterdam, he received a death sentence.[3] In this case, one of the most complete in detail left to us, may be found, in the incidents of escape, pursuit, resistance, and final rendition, all the features of the later fugitive slave cases. It is also an example wherein the laws of the period, which required the rendition of a bound white man in the same manner as a negro slave, were strictly carried out: and in the diverse fates of the four men we find instances probably typical of the fortunes of most fugitives of the time.

§ 10. **International relations.** — The proximity of the French, Spanish, and Dutch settlements led to escapes from the colonies of one power into those of another. All were slaveholding communities, and there was no disposition to shield a slave because his lot was a hard one; but the distrust and enmity between neighboring colonies owing allegiance to different sovereigns caused such escapes to lead to petty quarrels. There was no system of extradition treaties; in fact, there was as yet little international

---

[1] *Ante*, § 8.
[2] Letter from William Beekman to Director Stuyvesant, in N. Y. Colonial Manuscripts, XIII. 346; Appendix D, No. 3.
[3] N. Y. Colonial Manuscripts, XIII. 346.

law. Fugitives were demanded as an act of comity, and sometimes their delivery was refused. It was hardly a subject on which the home governments bestirred themselves. The colonies were left to make their own agreements, or to settle their own disagreements.

§ 11. **International cases.** — Thus far only those cases have been noticed which arose within and between colonies of the same nation. Let us now consider a very early case of disagreement between colonies of different nations, which occurred in 1646. The commissioners of the United Colonies made complaint to the Governor of New Netherlands that his Dutch agent at Hartford was harboring one of their Indian slaves. Soon after, Governor Stuyvesant was refused the return of some of his runaway servants from New Haven. Thereupon the angry Lords of the West India Company issued a proclamation commanding that there should be no rendition of fugitive slaves to New Haven. This provision continued in effect until Governor Elton sent back some of the fugitives to New Netherlands. It was then annulled, and a mutual agreement to return the runaways was entered into by the United Colonies and the Dutch.[1] Governor John Winthrop, in his History of New England, refers to the case, and says that Massachusetts Bay endeavored to bring about a reconciliation, and wrote to the Governor of New Netherlands intimating to him that "at their request he might send back the fugitives without prejudice to their right or reputation."[2]

Maryland also found difficulty, from the readiness with which her servants could flee north to New Netherlands. In the State Archives may be found a letter sent by the authorities to the Governor of New Netherlands, as follows: —

"Sir, — Some servants being lately fledd out of this colony, into yours, as is supposed, we could not promise o'selves from you that justice & faire correspondence betweene the two governments so neerly bordering & wch are shortly like to be nearer neighbors in delaware bay, as to hope that vpon the receiving of these O'tres & the demand of the p'ties interessted you will remand to us all such apprentice servants as are or shall run out of this government into yours; and will compell such other p'sons, as shall flie to you without a passe, being indebted or otherwise obnoxious to the

---

[1] Moore, Notes on the History of Slavery in Massachusetts, 28; Doyle, English in America, I. 391; compare Appendix A, No. 14.

[2] John Winthrop, History of New England from 1630 to 1649, p. 383; Appendix D, No. 1.

justice of this place, to make such satisfaction to the parties endamaged by their unlawful departure, upon their complaints and proofe thereof, as you shall find justice to require. And you may promise yourself the like helpe and concurrence from this governm't in that or any other thing as shalbe in the power of it: And so we bid you heartilly farewell & rest.
"To the ho'le the Governor of the New Netherlands."[1]

In 1659 the Dutch had occasion to ask the same favor of Maryland. Whether there had been trouble between the colonies since the earlier letter we do not know, but the spirit of the communication was quite different. Instead of assurances of good will, and expressions of a belief in the certainty of peaceful return, the Dutch threatened, if their servants were not secured to them, "to publish free liberty, access and recess to all planters, servants, negroes, fugitives, and runaways which may go into New Netherland."[2]

Trouble was also constantly arising between the French and English, or French and Dutch, in regard to the many runaways who fled from the Eastern colonies northward to Canada. In 1750 there was a dispute about a certain negro belonging to the English, but at that time in possession of the Sieur de la Corne St. Luc; and, in a letter to a friend, one of the officers of the colony makes the following explanation concerning them: "In regard to the negro in possession of Sieur de la Corne St. Luc I thought proper not to send him back every negro being a slave wherever he be. Besides, I am only doing what the English did in 1747. Ensign de Malbronne on board Le Screux had a negro servant who was at first taken from him; I took pains to reclaim him, but the English refused to surrender him on ground as above."[3]

§ 12. **Relations with the mother country.** — With only one country across the sea was any question of fugitives likely to arise. In England white slavery had long since died out, except as a punishment for crime; villeinage ceased about the time the colonies were settled. But the status of black slaves who were taken from the colonies to England was in practice unchanged.

The principle thus apparently established by custom was overthrown by a succession of legal decisions, culminating in the

[1] Archives of Maryland, Proceedings of Council, 1636–1667, pp. 134, 135.
[2] Archives of Maryland, Proceedings of Council, III. 472.
[3] Letter from M. de la Jonquière to M. de Rouillé, in N. Y. Colonial Manuscripts, X. 209; Appendix D, No. 5.

famous Somersett Case. It was first decided by Thomas Grahame, judge in the Admiralty Court, Glasgow, that a certain negro who had been brought into Great Britain must be liberated, on the ground that a guiltless human being taken into that country must be free.[1] In 1762 occurred another similar case. A bill had been filed in equity by an administrator to recover money given by his intestate to a negro brought to England as a slave. The suit was dismissed by Lord Northington, who said that as soon as a man set foot on English ground he was free.[2]

The Somersett case came ten years later. The circumstances were as follows. A Mr. Stewart, accompanied by his slave Somersett, left Boston on the 1st of October, 1769, and went to London, where he kept his slave until October 1, 1771. Then Somersett ran away, but his owner soon secured him and had him placed on board a vessel bound for Jamaica, probably with the intention of selling him as a slave. A writ of habeas corpus was then served upon the captain of the ship, and on the hearing Lord Mansfield decided that Somersett must be discharged. In England, he said, slavery could exist only by positive law; and in default of such law there was no legal machinery for depriving a man of his liberty on the ground that he was a slave. The importance of the case for the colonies lay not in the assertion of the principle that slavery depended on positive law, for the American statute-books were full of positive law on slavery; the precedent thus established determined the future course of England against the delivery of fugitives, whether from her colonies or from other countries.[3]

§ 13. **International regulations under the Articles of Confederation (1781-1788).** — When, on March 1, 1781, the Articles of Confederation went into effect, the only action taken by the United States on the subject of fugitives had been the negotiation of a treaty with the Delaware Indians, August 7, 1778, by which the parties bound themselves not "to protect in their respective States criminal fugitives, servants, or slaves, but the same to apprehend,

---

[1] Massachusetts Historical Society Collections, Third Series, IX. 2; Appendix D, No. 7.

[2] J. Quincy, Reports of Cases, 96; Appendix D, No. 8.

[3] Moore, Slavery in Massachusetts, 117; T. R. Cobb, Historical Sketch of Slavery, 2, Law of Negro Slavery, 164; Massachusetts Historical Society Collections, Third Series, IX. 2; Josiah Quincy, Reports of Cases, 96; Hurd, Law of Freedom and Bondage, II.

secure, and deliver."[1] In seven of the eight other treaties negotiated with Indian tribes from 1784 to 1786, clauses were introduced for the return of black prisoners, or of "negroes and other property."[2] The States affected were chiefly Southern; but the article on the same subject in the Treaty of Peace in 1782 and 1783, was intended as much to protect the slaveholders of New York as those of Virginia. It was distinctly agreed that the British should not carry away "any negroes or other property."[3] The failure to abide by this agreement led to reclamation by the American government, but no indemnity was ever secured.[4]

§ 14. **Ordinance for the Northwest Territory.** — Since all the thirteen colonies recognized slavery, the Revolution made no difference in any previous intercolonial practice as to the delivery of slaves; in framing the Articles of Confederation no clause on the subject was thought necessary. The precedent of the New England Confederation was forgotten or ignored. But the action of the States of Vermont, Pennsylvania, Massachusetts, Connecticut, and Rhode Island, in taking steps toward immediate or gradual emancipation, from 1777 to 1784, brought up a new question,— the status of fugitives in free regions. Before the change of conditions in the States was completely understood, the same question had arisen in the Western territories. Jefferson, in 1784, proposed to draw a north and south line through the mouth of the Kanawha, west of which there should be no slavery after 1800.[5] The next year a Northern man proposed a similar limitation in the territory north of the Ohio, and added a clause for the return of fugitive slaves to the original slave States.[6] Neither of these two propositions was carried, but the principles both of exclusion of slavery and of the return of fugitives appear in the Northwest Ordinance of 1787, the first legislation by Congress looking toward the surrender of fugitives by any Territory or State. In providing a government for the new Territory, it was enacted, July 13, 1787, that "any person escaping into the same from whom labor or service is lawfully claimed in any one of the original States, such fugitive may be lawfully reclaimed, and conveyed to the

[1] Appendix B, No. 1.   [2] Appendix B, Nos. 3, 5.
[3] Appendix B, No. 2.   [4] *Post*, § 22.
[5] Randall, Jefferson, I. 397-400; Winsor, VII. 528; Journals of Congress, IX. 153-156.
[6] Appendix B, No. 4; Journals of Congress, X. 79; Bancroft, History of the U. S. (last rev.), VI. 132-134; Bancroft, Constitution, I. 178-180; Hildreth, III. 458.

person claiming his or her labor or service as aforesaid."[1] The fugitive clause seems to have provoked no discussion, but to have been accepted as a reasonable condition of the limitation of slavery.

§ 15. **The Fugitive question in the Constitutional Conventions.** — While the Northwest Ordinance was passing through Congress, the Philadelphia Convention was framing a new Constitution, and the return of fugitives was again eagerly insisted upon by the slave States. The necessity of some positive stipulation that fugitives should be returned was felt to be even more necessary in a Constitution meant permanently to bind together a free and a slaveholding section. The only debate of which we have a record occurred August 28, 1787. Mr. Butler of North Carolina pressed the point in behalf of the Southern States. To his first proposition, "that fugitive slaves and servants be delivered up like criminals,"[2] Mr. Wilson objected; he saw no reason for obliging the state to arrest fugitives at public expense, while Mr. Sherman saw no more propriety in the public seizing and surrendering a slave or servant than a horse.[3] Mr. Butler therefore withdrew the proposition. He soon introduced a more particular provision, which was accepted and inserted in the Constitution, as follows: —

"NO PERSON HELD TO SERVICE OR LABOUR IN ONE STATE, UNDER THE LAWS THEREOF, ESCAPING INTO ANOTHER, SHALL, IN CONSEQUENCE OF ANY LAW OR REGULATION THEREIN, BE DISCHARGED FROM SUCH SERVICE OR LABOUR, BUT SHALL BE DELIVERED UP ON CLAIM OF THE PARTY TO WHOM SUCH SERVICE OR LABOUR MAY BE DUE."[4]

In the various Constitutional Conventions, there was little discussion upon the matter. The Southern States in general considered the clause sufficient to protect their property. General Charles C. Pinckney, in South Carolina, said: "We have obtained the right to recover our slaves in whatever part of America they may take refuge, which is a right we have not had before. In short, considering all circumstances, we have made the best terms for the security of this species of property it was in our power to make. We would have made better if we could, but on

[1] Appendix B, No. 6. On the Northwest Ordinance in general, see Winsor, VII. 538; J. H. Merriam, Legislative History of the Ordinance of 1787 (Worcester, 1888); Lalor's Cyclopædia, III. 30–34.
[2] Elliot's Debates, V. 487.   [3] Ibid., V. 487.
[4] Appendix B, No. 7.

the whole I do not think them bad."[1] In North Carolina, Mr. Iredell explained to the Convention that the Northern delegates, owing to their peculiar scruples on the subject of slavery, did not choose the word "slave" to be mentioned; but since the present laws were so prejudicial to the inhabitants of the Southern States, some such clause was necessary.[2] In Virginia, Mr. Grayson discussed the provision giving Congress exclusive legislation over ten square miles surrounding the capital. It seemed to him that, unless the ten miles square be considered a State, " persons bound to labor who shall escape thereto will not be given up. For they are only to be delivered up after they shall have escaped into a State."[3] This objection, though perfectly good at the time, was later overcome by the adoption by Congress of the laws of Maryland for the regulation of the District of Columbia, whereby it was made slave territory. Mr. Mason did not think the clause provided sufficiently for the protection of their slaves,[4] but Mr. Madison urged its adoption, as a better security than anything they then had.[5]

In the North, there was apparently no discussion upon this article. Everywhere, however, it was thought that without such a clause the Southern States would not consent to the Union, and, in a spirit of compromise, the provision was accepted.

[1] Elliot's Debates, III. 277.   [2] Ibid., III. 182.   [3] Ibid., III. 401.
[4] Ibid., III. 428.   [5] Ibid., III. 335.

CHAPTER II.

LEGISLATION FROM 1789 TO 1850.

§ 16. Effect of the fugitive slave clause in the Constitution.
§ 17. The first Fugitive Slave Act (1793).
    § 18. Discussion of the first act.
§ 19. Propositions of 1797 and 1802.
§ 20. Propositions from 1817 to 1822.
§ 21. Period of the Missouri Compromise (1819-1822).
§ 22. Status of the question from 1823 to 1847.
    § 23. Canada and Mexico places of refuge.
    § 24. Status of fugitives on the high seas.
§ 25. Kidnapping from 1793 to 1850 : Prigg case.
§ 26. Necessity of more stringent fugitive slave provisions.
    § 27. Action of Congress from 1847 to 1850.
    § 28. Slavery in the District of Columbia.
§ 29. The second Fugitive Slave Act (1850).
    § 30.. Provisions of the second Fugitive Slave Act.
    § 31. Arguments for the bill.
    § 32. Arguments against the bill.

§ 16. **Effect of the fugitive slave clause in the Constitution.** — By obtaining in the Constitution the insertion of a clause requiring the return of fugitives, a great step for the advancement of the interests of slavery had been taken. For this embodiment in the Constitution ever afterward formed a basis for the slaveholder's argument that the Constitution recognized and defended slavery, and was a justification to Northern men in their support of the later fugitive slave laws.

Although the clause did not in terms apply to the Territories, the Ordinance of 1787 was, on August 7, 1789, confirmed in terms which by implication continued the sixth article, including the rendition of slaves;[1] and in the earliest treaties made by the United States with Indian tribes, under the new Constitution, the return of negroes was expressly required.[2]

§ 17. **The first Fugitive Slave Act (1793).** — For some time, however, the provision of the Constitution remained unexecuted; and

---

[1] Statutes at Large, I. 50.   [2] Appendix B, No. 8.

it is a striking fact that the call for legislation came not from the South, but from a free State; and that it was provoked, not by fugitive slaves, but by kidnappers. The case seemed to suggest that an act of Congress was necessary, more definite in conditions and detail than the provision of the Constitution.

A free negro named John was seized at Washington, Pennsylvania, in 1791, and taken to Virginia. The Governor of Pennsylvania, at the instigation of the Society for the Abolition of Slavery, asked the return of the three kidnappers; but the Governor of Virginia replied that, since there was no national law touching such a case, he could not carry out the request.[1]

On the matter being brought to the notice of Congress by the Governor of Pennsylvania,[2] a committee, consisting of Mr. Sedgwick, Mr. Bourne of Massachusetts, and Mr. White, was appointed in the House of Representatives to bring in a bill or bills "providing the means by which persons charged in any State with treason, felony, or other crime, who shall flee from justice, shall, on the demand of the executive authority of the State from which they fled, be delivered up, to be removed to the State having jurisdiction of the crime; also providing the mode by which a person held to service or labor in one State under the laws thereof, escaping into another, shall be delivered up on the claim of the party to whom such service or labor may be due."[3]

A bill prepared by the House committee, of which Mr. Sedgwick was chairman, was reported, November 15, 1791;[4] but for some reason which does not appear, it was dropped, and a Senate committee, of which Calvert was chairman, was appointed, March 30, 1792, "to consider the expediency [of] a bill respecting fugitives from justice and from the service of their masters."[5] Nothing was done during this session, and, November 22, 1792, a second Senate committee was appointed, consisting of Johnston, Calvert, and Read,[6] and they submitted a bill, December 20, 1792.[7] Unfortunately, we have no details of the debate; but on December 28,

---

[1] Cong. Globe, 31 Cong. 1 Sess., Appendix, 1585. Annals of Cong., 2 Cong. 1 Sess., H. of R., 147.
[2] State Papers, Miscellaneous, I. 39–43.
[3] House Journal, 2 Cong. 1 Sess., 444; Annals of Cong., 148.
[4] House Journal, 2 Cong. 1 Sess., 454; Annals of Cong., 179.
[5] Senate Journal, 170; Annals, 115.
[6] 2 Cong. 2 Sess., Senate Journal, 460; Annals of Cong, 616.
[7] Senate Journal, 16; Annals, 622.

a third Senate committee was appointed by adding Taylor and Sherman to the committee of November 22, and to them the bill was recommitted with instructions to amend.[1] At last, January 3, 1793, the bill was reported in a form not unlike that finally agreed upon.[2] Of the amendments offered, the text of only one is preserved in the Journals; it was for the insertion of a less sum than five hundred dollars as the penalty for harboring a fugitive, or resisting his arrest.[3] It was not adopted. After two debates, of which we have no record, the bill passed the Senate, January 18.[4] In the House it seems to have elicited little discussion, and it passed, February 5, by a vote of 48 to 7.[5] The bill became law by the signature of the President, February 12, 1793.[6]

In thus uniting with the clause providing for the extradition of fugitives from justice one requiring the return of fugitive slaves, Congress was but following examples set in 1643 by the Articles of Confederation,[7] and again in 1787 by the Constitution.[8] From the scanty records, it is possible to discern only that there was serious difference of opinion in the Senate, and that the measure finally adopted was probably a compromise. In the one amendment stated, there is a faint protest against the harshness of the law.[9]

§ 18. **Discussion of the first act.** — The provisions of the act of 1793 are quoted elsewhere;[10] their purport was as follows. The act provided at the same time for the recovery of fugitives from justice and from labor; but the alleged criminal was to have a protection through the requirement of a requisition, a protection denied to the man on trial for his liberty only. The act was applicable to fugitive apprentices as well as to slaves, a provision of some importance at the time. In the Northwest Territory there

---

[1] Senate Journal, 25, 26; Annals, 623.
[2] Senate Journal, 28; Annals, 625.
[3] Senate Journal, 35; Annals, 630.
[4] Senate Journal, 34, 35; Annals, 630.
[5] House Journal, 105; Annals, 861.
[6] Appendix B, No. 9.
[7] *Ante*, § 8; Appendix A, No. 8.
[8] *Ante*, § 15.
[9] For general discussions of the act, see Von Holst, Constitutional History, I. 309–315; Hildreth, History of the U. S., IV. 406–440; Lalor's Cyclopædia, II. 315–316; Stephens, War between the States, I. 629–636, 674; Bancroft's History of the U. S. (last revision), VI. 309, 310; Goodell, Slavery and Antislavery, 227; Curtis, History of the Constitution, II. 450–467; Hurd, Law of Freedom and Bondage, II. 142; Story, Commentaries, III. 673–678; McMaster, History of the American People, I. 508, II. 356, 357; Elliott's Debates, V. 357, 487; Schouler, History of the U. S., I. 219, 220; Tucker, History of the U. S., I. 500.
[10] Appendix B, No. 9.

were so-called negro apprentices, who were virtually slaves, and to whom the law applied, since it was in terms extended to all the Territories. Proceedings began with the forcible seizure of the alleged fugitive.

The act, it will be observed, does not admit a trial by jury. It allowed the owner of the slave, his agent or attorney, to seize the fugitive and take him before any judge of a United States Circuit or District Court, or any local magistrate.[1] The only requirement for the conviction of the slave was the testimony of his master, or the affidavit of some magistrate in the State from which he came, certifying that such a person had escaped. Hindering arrest or harboring a slave was punishable by a fine of five hundred dollars. The law thus established a system allowing the greatest harshness to the slave and every favor to the master. Even at that time, when persons might still be born slaves in New York and New Jersey, and gradual emancipation had not yet taken full effect in Rhode Island and Connecticut, it was repellent to the popular sense of justice; there were two cases of resistance to the principle of the act before the close of 1793.[2]

§ 19. **Propositions of 1797 and 1802.** — Until 1850 no further law upon this subject was passed, but as the provisions of 1793 were found ineffectual, many attempts at amendment were made. In 1796 a troublesome question arose out of the seizure, under the act of 1793, of four negroes who had been manumitted in North Carolina. A retroactive act of that State had declared them slaves again, and they had fled to Philadelphia where they were arrested. January 30, 1797, they petitioned Congress for relief, and after an exciting debate the House by a vote of 50 to 33 refused to receive the petition.[3] There is nothing in the scanty records which connects this case or petition with an attempt to amend the act; but it is altogether likely that it occasioned Murray's motion of December 29, 1796, for a committee to report on alterations of the law;[4] and that it led to the almost simultaneous appointment of a House committee on January 2,[5] and a Senate committee on January 3.[6] No report is recorded.

[1] *Post*, § 27. [2] *Post*, §§ 34, 35.
[3] Annals of Congress, 1796–97, p. 2015, and 1801–2, p. 343.
[4] House Journal, 4 Cong. 2 Sess., 65; Annals of Cong., 1741, 1767.
[5] Murray, Cooper, and Kiltera. Annals of Cong., 1767.
[6] Sedgwick, Reed, and Henry. Senate Journal, 4 Cong. 2 Sess., 39; Annals of Cong., 1528.

The coming on of difficulties with France, and the Alien and Sedition Acts of 1798, absorbed the popular attention. In 1800 debates on the slave trade and on the reception of petitions from free negroes began. January 22, 1801, a House committee was appointed to report a bill increasing the stringency of the act.[1] The bill was reported, but failed to be considered.[2] In the next Congress the matter was at last brought to an issue. A committee, of which Nicholson of Maryland was chairman, was appointed, December 11, 1801,[3] and reported only seven days later. The report was made a special order for December 21.[4] On that day no debate is recorded, but a petition from a free colored soldier of the Revolution was contemptuously denied reception.[5] January 14 and 15, the bill was debated freely, and from the debate and sundry amendments the character of the bill may be inferred. Not only harboring, but employing a fugitive, was made punishable; and it was ordained that every black employed must be furnished with an official certificate, and that every person who employed a negro must publish a description of him. Southern members "considered it a great injury to the owners of that species of property, that runaways were employed in the Middle and Northern States, and even assisted in procuring a living. They stated that, when slaves ran away and were not recovered, it excited discontent among the rest. When they were caught and brought home, they informed their comrades how well they were received and assisted, which excited a disposition in others to attempt escaping, and obliged their masters to use greater severity than they otherwise would. It was, they said, even on the score of humanity, good policy in those opposed to slavery to agree to this law."[6] This appeal to the humanity of the North failed to produce the requisite effect. On the test vote, January 18, 1802, every Southern member except two voted for the bill, every Northern member except five against it; the vote was 43 to 46, and the bill was laid aside.[7]

[1] Appendix B, No. 10.
[2] House Journal, 6 Cong. 2 Sess., 220; Annals of Cong., 1053.
[3] Nicholson, Goddard, Holland, J. Smith (Va.), Lowndes. House Journal, 7 Cong. 1 Sess., 34; Annals of Cong., 317.
[4] House Journal, 7 Cong. 1 Sess., 45; Annals of Cong., 335.
[5] Annals of Cong., 343.
[6] House Journal, 7 Cong. 1 Sess., 125; Annals of Cong., 422, 423; Appendix B, No. 10.
[7] House Journal, 7 Cong. 1 Sess., 125, 128; Annals of Cong., 423, 425.

§ 20. **Propositions from 1817 to 1822.** — For many years the question of amendment of the law does not appear to have come up in Congress. The abolition of the slave trade seems to have absorbed the attention of Congress. Several treaties were negotiated including clauses on the return of fugitives.[1] The question was brought up again in 1817 by Pindall of Virginia, who for several years urged a revision of the act. A committee of which he was chairman was appointed, December 15, 1817, and reported a bill, December 29, 1817.[2] This third proposition of general amendment led to a debate, January 26 and 29, 1818, in which for the first time we have a record of discussion on the principles of the act and its relations to human freedom. The opposition was based not only on constitutional, but on humanitarian grounds.[3] A petition of the Pennsylvania Abolition Society, asking for a milder law than that of 1793, added fuel to the discussion.[4]

The principle of the bill was that the fugitives should be surrendered by a requisition on the State Executive, as in the case of fugitives from justice: the question of proof was thus left to the courts of the State of the claimant, and there was to be no habeas corpus. The strongest expression of disapproval is found in the speech of Mr. Adams of Massachusetts, who said, "that, in guaranteeing the possession of slaves, the Constitution did not authorize or require the General Government to go as far as the bill proposed to render this bill effectual; that the bill contained provisions dangerous to the liberty and safety of the free people of color in other sections of the Union."[5] Mr. Rich of Vermont desired "that it might be so amended as to guard more effectually the rights of free persons of color. This motion he enforced by urging the oppressions to which these persons were now subjected, and the necessity of some regulation on the subject, which he thought might be very properly connected with this bill."[6] Mr. Livermore also showed that it exposed the colored men of the North to the peril of being dragged South, and there convicted.[7]

All these objections, however, were considered of little value by some who, like Smith of Maryland, thought that the subject of

[1] *Post*, § 22.
[2] House Journal, 15 Cong. 1 Sess., 50, 86, 182, 186, 189, 193, 198; Annals of Cong., 446, 447, 513, 819, 829, 831, 840, 1339, 1393.
[3] Appendix B, No. 13.
[4] Annals of Cong., 829.
[5] Annals of Cong., 838.
[6] Annals of Cong., 15 Cong. 1 Sess., 829, 830.
[7] Annals of Cong., 838.

the free colored population and their protection should be treated separately, while Mr. Holmes of Massachusetts suggested that the operation of the writ of habeas corpus would render such acts of injustice improbable.[1] Mason, of the same State, objected to a trial by jury, which had been suggested, because "juries in Massachusetts would in ninety-nine cases out of one hundred decide in favor of the fugitives, and he did not wish his town [Boston] infected with the runaways of the South."[2]

Upon two constitutional points the opponents of the bill made a stand. Mr. Sergeant wished to change the bill materially, by making "the judges of the State in which . . . slaves are seized the tribunal to decide the fact of slavery, instead of the judges of the State whence the fugitives escaped," but this was negatived by a large majority.[3]

Another objection to the bill, raised by Mr. Whitman, is noteworthy, since some years later it was the point made most prominent in Judge Story's decision in the Prigg Case.[4] Mr. Whitman disapproved of the provision making it a penal offence for a State officer to refuse his assistance in executing the act. He did not believe that Congress had any right to compel State officers to perform this duty; they could do no more than authorize it.[5]

A vote was taken, January 30, 1818, in the House, and the bill passed by a vote of 84 to 69.[5] It was ordered that the title be "An Act to provide for delivering up persons held to labor or service in any of the States or Territories who shall escape into any other State or Territory."

For the first time since 1793, amendment of the act seemed within reach. The Senate showed itself in other questions more inclined than the House to consider the claims of the South; but although Dagget's amendment to strike out the elaborate provision for the return of fugitives by executive requisition was not adopted,[6] the Senate first voted to limit the bill to four years,[7] and then added other amendments. The result was a non-concurrence with the House, and the failure of the bill,[8] March

[1] Annals of Cong., 838.
[2] Annals of Cong., 838.
[3] Appendix B, No. 13.
[4] *Post*, § 25.
[5] House Journal, 15 Cong. 1 Sess., 198; Annals of Cong., 840.
[6] Appendix B, No. 14.
[7] Appendix B, No. 15.
[8] Senate Journal, 15 Cong. 1 Sess., 128, 135, 174, 202, 227, 228, 233; House Journal, 328; Annals of Cong., 165, 210, 259, 262, 1339.

13-16, 1818. A last attempt to take the bill up failed, April 10, 1818.[1]

§ 21. **Period of the Missouri Compromise (1819-1822).** — The loss of the bill of 1818 seems not to have discouraged the friends of amendment of the act of 1793. December. 17, 1818, a resolution of the Maryland legislature was laid before the House, calling for protection against the citizens of Pennsylvania who harbored or protected fugitives.[2] A committee was appointed, January 15, 1819, which promptly reported next day, but the bill was not considered.[3]

The question of fugitives came incidentally into the great debate of the next session on the admission of Missouri. The region which sought admission as a slave State was flanked on the east by free territory, and was therefore peculiarly difficult to protect. A compromise, which made Missouri a slave State, prohibited slavery in all other territory gained from France north of 36° 30'.[4] In the prohibitory clause, however, it was provided "that any persons escaping into the same from whom labor or service is lawfully claimed in any State or Territory of the United States, such fugitive may be reclaimed, and conveyed to the person claiming his or her labor or service as aforesaid."[5] During the immigration into Missouri which now began, large numbers of slaveholders took their slaves with them, and on the passage opportunities for escape were often found. In one instance, at least, recorded in Ohio, the public sympathy was so strongly with the fugitives that they were successfully protected from their masters even in court.[6]

Hardly was the ink dry on the President's signature of the Missouri Compromise (March 15, 1820) before propositions were made in both the House and Senate for new general fugitive slave acts. March 18, a House committee was appointed,[7] but no report is recorded. April 3, an inquiry was set on foot into the provisions of a Pennsylvania act hindering the operation of the act of 1793,[8] and the Secretary of State submitted a copy of

[1] Annals of Cong., 1716.
[2] Cf. Appendix B, No. 17.
[3] House Journal, 15 Cong. 1 Sess., 188, 191; Annals of Cong., 546, 551.
[4] Annals of Cong., 16 Cong. 1 Sess., 469, 1587.
[5] Appendix B, No. 16.
[6] Liberator, Jan. 24, 1840 (N. Y. Evening Post).
[7] House Journal, 16 Cong. 1 Sess., 427; Annals of Cong., 1863.
[8] Appendix B, No. 18.

the obnoxious act, April 18. On the day of the Secretary's report a proposition in the Senate to instruct the Judiciary Committee to report a bill was voted down.[1] Positive evidence cannot be obtained, but it would seem that a continued effort was made to take advantage of the agitation on the slavery question to secure a new fugitive slave act, as was done in 1850.

One more attempt was made in 1821-22. Mr. Wright presented, December 17, 1821, a resolution of the Maryland General Assembly praying for relief against the abettors of the fugitives in Pennsylvania.[2] He desired a special committee, but the question was referred to the Committee on the Judiciary, which reported a bill, January 14, 1822.[3] March 27 to April 1, it was debated, but finally tabled.[4] The character of the bill does not distinctly appear in the records.

§ 22. **Status of the question from 1823 to 1847.** — Although no amendment could be procured to the act of 1793, the government of the United States had repeatedly, by diplomatic demands and treaties, undertaken to recover fugitives, or their value, for Southern owners. The first Indian treaty negotiated under the Constitution, that of April 7, 1790, with the Creeks, required the return of negroes held as prisoners of war.[5] A similar clause appeared in the treaty made in 1814, at the end of the war with the Creeks, a war which had been provoked in part by their ready reception of fugitives.[6] In 1832 the government went so far as to promise to expend seven thousand dollars in paying for "slaves and other property alleged to have been stolen" by the Seminoles.[7]

With Great Britain, also, the encouragement of fugitives became a subject for negotiation. Much bitterness had been felt at the carrying away by the British, in 1783, of slaves who had taken refuge with them.[8] In the treaty of Ghent, therefore, a strict clause forbade the carrying away by the British of "any slaves or other private property."[9] A large number of slaves had, during the war, been received on board British vessels, and the humane but specious plea was set up by the British government that

---

[1] Senate Journal, 16 Cong. 1 Sess., 319, 326; Annals of Cong., p. 618.
[2] Appendix B, No. 18.
[3] House Journal, 17 Cong. 1 Sess., 143; Annals of Cong., 553, 558, 710.
[4] Annals of Cong., 17 Cong. 1 Sess., 1379, 1415, 1444.
[5] Appendix B, No. 8.   [6] Appendix B, No. 11.
[7] Appendix B, No. 19.   [8] *Ante*, § 13; Appendix B, No. 2.
[9] Appendix B, No. 12.

the clause applied only to slaves received after the date of the peace. A convention of 1818 submitted the question to the Emperor of Russia, who in 1822 made a decision not wholly favorable to either party; and in 1826,[1] by a second convention, Great Britain agreed to pay $1,204,960. This last award was obtained by a Pennsylvanian, Gallatin, acting under the direction of President John Quincy Adams, a citizen of Massachusetts.

§ 23. **Canada and Mexico places of refuge.** — The existence on the northern and southwestern frontiers of regions in which slavery was practically, if not yet legally, extinct, brought about another set of complications. January 24, 1821, a resolution was presented in Congress from the General Assembly of Kentucky, protesting against the kindly reception of fugitives in Canada, and asking for negotiation with Great Britain on the subject.[2] In 1826, Mr. Clay, Secretary of State, instructed Mr. Gallatin, United States Minister at the Court of St. James, to propose the "mutual surrender of all persons held to service or labor under the laws of either country who escape into the territory of the other." The British government replied that any such agreement was impossible, and, though a second attempt was made by the United States, it was without success.[3]

In 1841 Mr. Woodbridge submitted a resolution to the Senate requesting the Committee on Foreign Relations to consider the expediency of entering into an arrangement with Great Britain for the arrest of fugitive slaves charged with crime who might escape over the northern boundary of the United States.[4] No action was taken upon the resolution.

The North, however, was not the only region to which slaves were fleeing at this time. Complaint was heard after 1830, that the "freedom and equality granted blacks by the Mexican Constitution and law of 1829, was attracting large numbers of slaves from Louisiana,"[5] while in Florida the Seminole trouble was not yet ended.

The last case of this kind occurred just at the outbreak of the Civil War. A slave by the name of Anderson was found one

---

[1] Am. State Papers, Foreign, IV. 106–126, VI. 346–354.
[2] Annals of Cong., 16 Cong. 2 Sess., 94.
[3] S. G. Howe, Refugees from Slavery in Canada, 12–14; Niles's Register, XXIII. 26, LV. 289.
[4] Appendix B, No. 21 ; cf. No. 24.
[5] Niles's Register, XXIII. 26.

day by Mr. Seneca T. P. Diggs, wandering about his plantation in Howard County, Missouri, without a pass. Mr. Diggs thereupon arrested him as a fugitive slave. In the struggle which followed, the desperate runaway plunged a knife into Mr. Diggs's heart. His captor dead, Anderson hastened on to Canada.[1] There he lived a quiet and industrious life until 1860, when the American government called upon Canada, under the extradition treaty, to give up Anderson for punishment. He was arrested, but applied to the Toronto court for a writ of habeas corpus, which was refused. An appeal was immediately made to the Queen's Bench, England, which granted the writ.[2] In the trial Anderson was defended by Mr. Gerrit Smith in an eloquent speech, which made a great impression, and was circulated all over the United States.[3] The prisoner was discharged on a technical point.[4]

§ 24. **Status of fugitives on the high seas.** — When in 1830 gradual emancipation began in the British colonies, and in 1837 slavery ceased to exist there, a new set of complications arose. American vessels carrying slaves from one part of the United States to another were repeatedly driven or conveyed into British ports, and the slaves were there treated as ordinary fugitives, that is, as free men. Thus the Comet in 1830,[5] and the Encomium in 1834,[6] were cast away on the Bahamas, and the slaves on board could not be recovered. In 1835 the Enterprise was forced by stress of weather to enter a port of the Bermudas,[7] and the officers were not permitted by the British authorities to restrain the persons on board.

In none of these three cases were the negroes restored; but in 1840 the British government paid an indemnity for the first two cargoes, on the ground that at the time of the wrecks slavery had not yet been completely extinguished in the colonies.[8] No indemnity was allowed in the Enterprise case, and the British government declared that it could assume no responsibility in cases arising since the abolition of slavery.[9] Elaborate resolutions intro-

[1] Liberator, Dec. 31, 1860.
[2] Pamphlets on Anderson case, Boston Public Library; Appendix D, No. 65.
[3] Life of Gerrit Smith, 115.   [4] Liberator, Jan. 22, 1861.
[5] Von Holst, II. 312; Calhoun, III. 9, 464, 486; Senate Docs., 25 Cong. 3 Sess., No. 216.
[6] Wilson, Slave Power, I. 439–442; Congressional Globe, XIV. 50.
[7] Goodell, Slavery and Antislavery, 252, 253; Von Holst, Calhoun, 204–209.
[8] House Docs., 27 Cong. 2 Sess., V., No. 242; Congressional Globe, XIV. 50.
[9] Senate Docs., 26 Cong. 1 Sess., III., No. 11.

duced by Calhoun, March 4, 1840, and passed, April 15, by a unanimous vote of the Senate, condemned the British principle.[1] But when, in the next year, the slaves on board the American ship Creole rose and by force carried her into Nassau,[2] the British government refused to return them either as slaves or as murderers.[3] Webster, as Secretary of State, strenuously urged the surrender. In 1853, an arbitrator decided that an indemnity must be paid to the American government.[4] On the other hand, when, in 1839, a Spanish vessel, L'Amistad, in which the slaves on board had revolted and killed their master, was brought into an American port, the Supreme Court refused to permit their surrender, on the ground that they were free by Spanish law, and therefore could not be tried for murder.[5]

§ 25. **Kidnapping from 1793 to 1850: Prigg case.** — Since slavery was now extinct in the more northern States, their population contained many free negroes. Upon them the eyes of the slave trader were often turned, as easy prey under the law of 1793, and many cases of kidnapping occurred. It was such instances, involving as they did the most manifest injustice and cruelty, that first aroused the sympathies of the people.[6] The border States like Pennsylvania were often the scene of these acts. The neighboring white families first began to try to protect the negroes settled near them, and a little later to give a helping hand to those escaping from slavery, and at last, in the underground railroad,[7] to complete a systematic organization for the assistance of fugitives. Cases of kidnapping are recorded as early as 1808.[8] In 1832 the carrying away of a black woman without process of law not only roused the people of Pennsylvania, but led to a decision which took away much of the force of the act of 1793.

A slave woman, Margaret Morgan, had fled from Maryland to Pennsylvania. Five years later, in 1837, Edward Prigg, an attorney, caused her to be arrested and sent back to her mistress without recourse either to the national or State act on the subject. In the act he disregarded a law of Pennsylvania, brought about in

---

[1] Congressional Globe, XIV. 80, 113-118; Calhoun, III. 462; Appendix B, No. 20.
[2] Senate Docs., 27 Cong. 1 Sess., II., No. 51.
[3] Cobbett's Case, 47; Dana's Wheaton, note 62; cf. Appendix B, No. 23.
[4] Lawrence's Wheaton, 207, *n.*
[5] Von Holst, I. 321, 322; Opinions of the Attorney Generals, III. 484; 15 Peters, 518.
[6] R. Smedley, Underground Railroad, 26.
[7] See *post*, §§ 71-76.   [8] See *post*, § 38.

1826 through the efforts of the Society for the Abolition of Slavery, which forbade the carrying out of the State of any negro with the intention of enslaving him. Accordingly, Mr. Prigg was arrested and convicted in the county court. The Supreme Court of Pennsylvania sustained the decision. Thence the case was taken to the Supreme Court of the United States. There the counsel for Mr. Prigg argued that the statute of Pennsylvania on which the indictment was founded was unconstitutional, since it conflicted with the law of 1793. Justice Story delivered the opinion of the court, and upon this decision all future judgments were based. He announced that the law must be carried out through national authorities alone; the States or State magistrates could not be forced into action.[1] After this, many States, seeing the advantage thus given them, passed laws which forbade the officers to aid in a fugitive slave case, and also denied the use of their jails for imprisonment.[2] Plainly the Prigg case showed a growing indisposition on the part of the States to carry out the law, however severe its provisions might be; and this disposition to evade its obligations is still further evidenced by the cases given in the next chapter.

§ 26. **Necessity of more stringent fugitive slave provisions.** — The increasing number of rescues,[3] and the occurrence of several cases of resistance, proved conclusively the inadequacy of the law of 1793. After the Prigg decision the provisions made for its execution through national powers were entirely insufficient. Underlying all these acts, the South also could but perceive a sentiment the growth of which, unless checked in some way, would at last permanently injure, if not destroy, their peculiar institution.

§ 27. **Action of Congress from 1847 to 1850.** — From 1822 until 1848 apparently no effort was made to secure a new law. Then a petition received in 1847 from the Legislature of Kentucky, urging the importance of passing such laws as would enable the citizens of slaveholding States to recover their slaves when they escaped into non-slaveholding States,[4] gave rise to a bill from the Committee on the Judiciary.[5] The bill provided " for the more effectual exe-

[1] Appendix B, No. 22; 16 Peters, 957; Report of Case of Edward Prigg, Supreme Court of Pennsylvania, 202; Bledsoe, Liberty and Slavery, 355; J. F. Clarke, Antislavery Days, 69.
[2] *Post*, §§ 78, 79. [3] *Post*, §§ 34, 41, 42.
[4] Senate Journal, 30 Cong., 1 Sess., 59; Congressional Globe, 51.
[5] Senate Journal, 30 Cong., 1 Sess., 313; Congressional Globe, 722.

cution of the third clause of the second section of the Fourth Article of the Constitution."[1] It passed only to the second reading. In 1849, Mr. Meade proposed in the House to instruct the Committee on the Judiciary to report a fugitive slave bill.[2] No report apparently was ever made, but this was the last ineffectual proposition. In 1850, a new law was successfully carried in both Houses.

§ 28. **Slavery in the District of Columbia.** — During this period, from 1840 to 1850, the subject of slavery and fugitives in the District of Columbia began to occasion debate, which was never long silenced. It was notorious that almost under the windows of the Capitol negroes were confined in public jails on the ground that they were fugitives; and that a free negro so confined might be sold for his jail fees. Resolutions for an investigation of the condition of the jails were offered in 1848 by Mr. Giddings;[3] and Mr. Hall also introduced more sweeping propositions to repeal all laws of Congress and of Maryland which authorized or required courts, officers, or magistrates to issue process for arrest or commitment to the jail of the District of any fugitive slave.[4] Congress, however, was in a mood too conciliatory toward the South to consider these propositions; and no action was taken.

§ 29. **The second Fugitive Slave Act (1850).** — In the early part of the first session of the Thirty-first Congress, Mr. Mason of Virginia introduced a bill to make the provisions of the fugitive slave act more severe,[5] and the bill was reported from the Committee on the Judiciary, January 16, 1850. Two additional amendments were soon offered by Mr. Mason. The first imposed a fine of one thousand dollars and imprisonment for twelve months upon any one who should obstruct the execution of the law. The second provided that the testimony of a fugitive should not be admitted. Mr. Seward, in opposition, proposed on the 28th to allow a fugitive the right of trial by jury, with a fine of five thousand dollars

---

[1] Senate Journal, 30 Cong. 1 Sess., 313; Congressional Globe, 722.
[2] Appendix B, No. 29.
[3] Appendix B, Nos. 25, 27, 28.
[4] Appendix B, No. 26.
[5] Appendix B, No. 30. In this number of the Appendix is a summary of the legislative history of the measure, from the introduction of Mason's bill, Jan. 4, 1850, to the signature of the act by President Fillmore, Sept. 18, 1850, with references to the records of Congress.

and the forfeiture of office should the right be disallowed by any judge or marshal.[1]

Mr. Clay's "Omnibus Bill," by which he intended to settle the territorial question then before Congress, and at the same time to check the antislavery movement, contained a fugitive slave clause, though not so severe in its provisions as Mr. Mason's.[2] This bill, however, was not debated as a whole, but each proposition considered separately, and thus Mr. Mason's bill became the basis of the fugitive slave provision in the Compromise of 1850.

The measure was considered, and various amendments were offered, until August 26, 1850, when it was passed by the Senate, and a few days later by the House;[3] the signature of President Fillmore was readily appended, and it became law, September 18, 1850.[4]

§ 30. **Provisions of the second Fugitive Slave Act.** — Every provision of the act was arranged for the protection and benefit of the slaveholders. It was based upon the law of 1793, but a number of new regulations were added.[5] Commissioners were to be chosen by the Circuit Courts of the United States and the Superior Courts of the Territories, to act with the judges of those courts in fugitive slave cases. Such commissioners could be fined one thousand dollars for refusing to issue a writ, and were liable for the value of any slave escaping from them. The testimony re-

[1] Congressional Globe, 31 Cong. 1 Sess., 236.
[2] Senate Journal, 31 Cong. 1 Sess., 118.
[3] Congressional Globe, 31 Cong. 1 Sess., 248; Appendix B, No. 68. The test vote in the House stood as follows: —

States.	For.	Against.	Not voting.	Total.
New England States . . .	7	15	10	32
Middle States	9	33	21	63
Interior and Pacific States	16	27	8	51
Total, Free States . .	32	75	39	146
Border Slave States . . .	32	0	6	38
Planter States	45	0	9	54
Total, Slave States .	77	0	15	92
Total	109	75	54	238

[4] Appendix B, Nos. 83, 84. For general discussions of the act, see Von Holst, III. 548-557, IV. 9-12, 20-29; Wilson, Slave Power, II. 302-329; Greeley, American Conflict, I. 210-221; Cooley's Story, § 1921; Lalor's Cyclopædia, II. 315-317; Bryant and Gay, U. S., IV. 397-401.
[5] For the text of the act, see Appendix B, No. 31.

quired for rendition was the official declaration of the fact of the escape of a slave by two witnesses, and the establishment of his identity by oath. The testimony of the accused could not be admitted. The right of trial by jury was not affirmed, and was therefore practically denied. A sheriff might call upon any bystander for help in executing the law, and the penalty for harboring or aiding in a rescue was increased from five hundred dollars, as in 1793, to one thousand dollars, and imprisonment for not more than six months. Should the slave escape, damages to the same amount were to be paid to the claimant. If a mob were feared, military force might be employed; and by a discrimination little likely to win respect for the act, the fee of the commissioner was to be increased from five to ten dollars whenever the case was decided in favor of the claimant.

§ 31. **Arguments for the bill.** — The debate on the Fugitive Slave Bill more than any other part of the Compromise illustrates the character of the slavery conflict. Most of the Southern members urged the immediate necessity of a new law, but some of the more ardent considered the evil to be one which could be reached only through a change in public sentiment, and they thought all legislation valueless.[1] Mr. Mason thus presented the evils with which the law must cope. He stated that the border States had found it an impossibility to reclaim a fugitive when he once got within the boundaries of a non-slaveholding State; "and this bill, or rather the amendments, . . . have been framed with a great deal of consideration, to reach, if practicable, the evils which this experience has demonstrated to exist, and to furnish the appropriate remedy in enabling the owner of a fugitive to reclaim him." Under the existing laws, "you may as well go down into the sea and endeavor to recover from his native element a fish which has escaped from you, as expect to recover such a fugitive. Every difficulty is thrown in your way by the population. . . . There are armed mobs, rescues. This is the real state of things."[2]

Not only were the laws thus set aside by individuals, but also through the Underground Railroad an organized system of depredation was carried on, whereby thousands of dollars were every year lost to the slaveholder.[3] As an illustration of the extent to

---

[1] Congressional Globe, 31 Cong. 1 Sess., Appendix, 1610.
[2] Congressional Globe, 31 Cong. 1 Sess., 1583.
[3] Congressional Globe, 31 Cong. 2 Sess., Appendix, 1051.

which this disregard of law was carried, Mr. Yulee, one of the most extreme of the Southern men, instanced a convention which was then in session in New York "for the very purpose, openly avowed, of congratulation upon their successful violation of the Constitution in respect to fugitives, and to devise ways and means to encourage the escape of slaves."[1]

Such, according to the Southern Congressmen, was the condition of affairs. They then proceeded to contrast it with the situation as contemplated by the Constitution, and supported by the decision of the Supreme Court in the Prigg case. Mr. Butler insisted that this bill required "nothing more than is enjoined by the Constitution, and which contains the bond of union and the security of harmony; and in the name of Washington, I would invoke all parties to observe, maintain, and defend it." He said it was the handiwork of sages and patriots, and resulted from intelligent concessions, for the benefit of all.[2] Many speeches were filled with prophecies, more or less openly expressed, of the dissolution of the Union. Mr. Soulé said the South must fight for its rights, since it is the weaker of the two sections.[3] It had come down to the question, How could the Union be preserved?[4] Some concessions must be made. Mr. Badger urged the bill, because it "will give assurance, it will satisfy the public mind that the Government is disposed, is truly anxious, to accomplish the restitution of fugitive slaves; sincerely wished and is resolved to do right to the uttermost of its power. The proof of this will be complete, because we furnish the best means for the recovery of the slave himself, and if these fail we can secure prompt and adequate indemnity for the loss."[5]

§ 32. **Arguments against the bill.** — On the Northern side, there seems to have been an admission that some bill of the kind was necessary for the interests of the Union. The opposition dwelt chiefly, therefore, upon the details of the measure. Many considered them unjust, as recognizing only one class of rights, those of the masters. Mr. Chase, from the antislavery wing, demanded that a claim of this kind be put on the same footing as any other statutory right. "Claims of right in the services of individuals

---

[1] Congressional Globe, 31 Cong. 2 Sess., Appendix, 1622.
[2] Congressional Globe, 31 Cong. 1 Sess., 79.
[3] Congressional Globe, 31 Cong. 1 Sess., 78.
[4] Von Holst, III. 493.
[5] Congressional Globe, 31 Cong. 1 Sess., Appendix, 1597.

found under the protection of the laws of a free State must be investigated in the same manner as other claims of right. If the most ordinary controversy involving a contested claim of twenty dollars must be decided by jury, surely a controversy which involves the right of a man to his liberty should have a similar trial. ... It will not do for a man to go into a State where every legal presumption is in favor of freedom, and seize a person whom he claims as a fugitive slave, and say, 'This man is my slave, and by my authority under the Constitution of the United States I carry him off, and whoever interferes does so at his peril.' He is asked, 'Where is your warrant?' and he produces none; 'Where is your evidence of claim?' and he offers none. The language of his action is, 'My word stands for law.'"

CHAPTER III.

PRINCIPAL CASES FROM 1789 TO 1860.

§ 33. Change in character of cases.
  § 34. The first case of rescue (1793).
  § 35. President Washington's demand for a fugitive (1796).
§ 36. Kidnapping cases.
  § 37. Jones case (1836).
  § 38. Solomon Northrup case (about 1830).
  § 39. Washington case (between 1840 and 1850).
  § 40. Oberlin case (1841).
§ 41. Interference and rescues.
  § 42. Chickasaw rescue (1836).
  § 43. Philadelphia case (1838).
  § 44. Latimer case (1842).
  § 45. Ottoman case (1846).
§ 46. Interstate relations.
  § 47. Boston and Isaac cases (1837, 1839).
  § 48. Ohio and Kentucky cases (1848).
§ 49. Prosecutions.
  § 50. Van Zandt, Pearl, and Walker cases (1840, 1844).
§ 51. Unpopularity of the Fugitive Slave Act of 1850.
§ 52. Principle of the selection of cases.
  § 53. Hamlet case (1850).
  § 54. Sims case (1851).
  § 55. Burns case (1854).
  § 56. Garner case (1856).
  § 57. Shadrach case (1851).
  § 58. Jerry McHenry case (1851).
  § 59. Oberlin-Wellington case (1858).
  § 60. Christiana case (1851).
  § 61. Miller case (1851).
  § 62. John Brown in Kansas (1858).

§ 33. **Change in character of cases.** — The cases of escape which occur in the period beginning with the formation of the Constitution, and ending with the passage of the Fugitive Slave Law in 1850, will be found, in comparison with those of colonial times, much more frequent, more complex in action, and more varied in detail. Instead of many colonies under governments independent one of another, there was now one government and one country;

nevertheless, the extinction of the system of bondage and the rise of the antislavery sentiment in the Northern States brought into the cases new and difficult elements. No attempt will be made to mention the cases in their chronological order, or to describe them all. They will be classified into cases of simple escape, of kidnapping, of rescue, and of State interference; and typical examples will be described in each category.

§ 34. **The first case of rescue.** — The first attempt to enforce the act of 1793, of which any record has been discovered, immediately revealed its unfairness, and the indisposition of the North to carry it out.

Mr. Josiah Quincy, then a young lawyer, afterwards known as a public man and the President of Harvard College, has left an interesting account of his connection with the case. "He states that the process was issued by a justice of the peace, that he was retained as counsel for the alleged slave, that he prepared his brief, and went down loaded with all the necessary authorities. He found a great crowd of people assembled; but while he was in the midst of the argument, he heard a noise, and, turning around, he saw the constables lying sprawling on the floor, and a passage opening through the crowd, through which the fugitive was taking his departure without stopping to hear the opinion of the court, and that was the last of that case, and that was the last of the law of 1793 in Massachusetts."[1]

§ 35. **President Washington's demand for a fugitive.** — As has been noticed in a previous chapter, George Washington's boyhood was connected with white slavery. Now, at the zenith of his public life, we find one of his chattels the occasion of the first recorded refusal on moral grounds to return a slave. In 1796, President Washing-

---

[1] Mr. Quincy also states, that "about a fortnight elapsed, when I was called upon by Rufus Green Amory, a lawyer of eminence at the Boston bar in that day, who showed me a letter from a Southern slaveholder, directing him to prosecute Josiah Quincy for the penalty under the law of 1793, for obstructing the agent of the claimant in obtaining his slave under the process established by that law. Mr. Amory felt, no less than myself, the folly of such a pretence; and I never heard from him, or from any one, anything more upon the subject of prosecution. This fact, and the universal gratification which the fact appeared to give to the public, satisfied my mind, that, unless by accident, or stealth, or in some very thin settled part of the country, the law of 1793 would be forever inoperative, as the event has proved in Massachusetts." — Meeting at Faneuil Hall to protest against the Fugitive Slave Law, letter read from Josiah Quincy, Boston Atlas, Oct. 15, 1850; Goodell, Slavery and Antislavery, 232; Appendix D, No. 12.

ton wrote to Mr. Whipple, Collector of Portsmouth, N. H., to send back to him one of his slaves who had escaped to that place, if it could be done without exciting a mob. This letter has been preserved, and the following extract gives us an insight into President Washington's opinions upon the rendition of fugitives: —

"However well disposed I might be to gradual abolition, or even to an entire emancipation of that description of people, (if the latter was in itself practicable,) at this moment it would neither be politic nor just to reward unfaithfulness with a premature preference, and thereby discontent beforehand the minds of all her fellow serv'ts, who, by their steady attachment, are far more deserving than herself of favor."[1]

Mr. Whipple answered, that any return would be impossible; public sentiment was too strong against it.

§ 36. **Kidnapping cases.** — The great number of cases of kidnapping throughout the period from 1793 to 1850 show what cruel and unjust deeds were possible under the existing system, and served as nothing else could to rouse people to the defence of negroes. Various were the methods by which, in spite of law, kidnappers were enabled to secure their prey. Perhaps the most common practice, in places where the courts were known to be friendly to slavery, was to arrest a man on some false pretence, and then, when he appeared in court without opportunity to secure papers or witnesses, to claim him as a fugitive slave. Most of these cases occurred in communities bordering upon or near the Southern States. The risk and trouble of transporting slaves across free States were so great, that up to 1850 we seldom hear of kidnapping cases, and rarely of the capture of a genuine fugitive in the New England States.

The natural consequence of such acts of outrageous violence was to rouse people to the forcible rescue of the captured negroes. In the earliest cases, colored people seem to take the leadership; later on, the whites joined, and became most active in the work.

§ 37. **Jones case.** — The following instance well exemplifies this form of oppression. George Jones, a respectable colored man, was arrested on Broadway, New York, in 1836, on the pretext that he had committed assault and battery. As he knew that no such charge could be sustained against him, he at first refused to go with his captors; but finally he yielded, on the assurance of his

[1] Appendix D, No. 13.

employer that everything possible should be done for him. He was then placed in Bridewell, and his friends were told that when they were wanted they "would be sent for"; but, soon after one o'clock that same day, he was taken before the Hon. Richard Riker, Recorder of New York, and to the satisfaction of that magistrate was proved to be a slave. Thus, in less than two hours after his arrest he was hurried away as the property of the kidnappers: their word had been accepted as sufficient evidence, and he had not been allowed to secure the presence of a single friendly witness.[1]

§ 38. **Solomon Northup case.** — Sometimes, if they feared to enter their case in court, slave hunters could find opportunity, by watching a negro for a while, to carry out their plans through some small deception. One of the most striking of these cases is that of Solomon Northup, who has written an account of his experiences as freeman and as slave. He was born in 1808 in New York State. His father had been made a free man by the provisions of his master's will. Thus Solomon was brought up under the influences of freedom, and knew little of slavery. After his marriage, he lived for some years in Saratoga. Here he earned a comfortable livelihood. During the day he worked about the hotels, and in the evenings he was often engaged to play the violin at parties. One day, two men, apparently managers of a travelling circus company, met him and offered him good pay if he would go with them as a violinist to Washington. He consented. Their behavior seemed to him peculiar, but he remained in their service, only to find himself one morning in a slave pen in Washington. How he got there remained always a mystery, but it is evident that he must have been drugged. Resistance was useless. He was carried South and sold to Mr. Epps, a hard master, with whom he remained for twelve years.

After he had long given up all hopes of escape, a friend was found in a Northern man who was working on the same plantation. Mr. Bass consented, though at a great risk to himself, to write some letters, telling Solomon's story to his Northern friends. The letters reached their destination, and, under the law of 1840 against kidnapping, a memorial was prepared to the Governor of New York. He became interested, and immediately sent a man South to find Northrup. After a long search, the agent was directed to Mr.

[1] Appendix D, No. 19.

Epps's plantation. Much to the disappointment of the master, who used every means to prevent his return, Solomon was identified at last, and went back to New York again a free man. Efforts were made to prosecute the kidnappers; but as sufficient evidence could not be obtained, no case was made out.[1]

§ 39. **Washington case.** — So bold did these stealers of men become, that they sometimes resorted to simple force, without the slightest attempt at concealment. A case of this kind occurred in Washington, D. C., between 1840 and 1850. Three or four men seized a negro who was employed in a hotel near the Capitol, and dragged him away. Mr. Hall, proprietor of the house, after trying in vain to prevent the arrest, succeeded at last in compelling them to take the man before a magistrate. The justice declined to assume jurisdiction in such a case, and before any other protection could be provided, the man was hurried by the kidnappers into a hack, and taken across the Potomac into bondage.[2]

§ 40. **Oberlin case.** — Occasionally the result was less fortunate for the captors. In Oberlin, three slave hunters seized by force a negro man and his wife, and carried them to an inn for the night. In the mean time the people of the town decided that the negroes must have a trial. They therefore employed a lawyer, who discovered that the writ for the capture was illegal, and secured a hearing. The captives were placed in jail, but, aided by some undivulged agency, they managed to break the grates of their prison windows, and escaped to Canada before the day set for trial.[3]

§ 41. **Interference and rescues.** — After a kidnapping case had occurred in a Northern village or town, measures were frequently taken by the indignant citizens to prevent the recurrence of such acts. They organized vigilance committees, or the antislavery societies took it up as a part of their work. In a free community, public sentiment would not allow negro towns-people to stand entirely unprotected. Thus many of the cases of interference and rescue were the result of some organized movements on the part of the white people, though occasionally they came about through the unpremeditated action of a mob.

§ 42. **Chickasaw rescue.** — The first case which has been found occurred in 1836. A writ of habeas corpus was served against

---

[1] Appendix D, No. 16.   [2] Appendix D, No. 42.
[3] Appendix D, No. 26.

Captain Eldridge of the brig Chickasaw, for holding two colored women in his ship with the intention of carrying them South. As both presented free papers at the hearing, the judge ordered them discharged; but the agent of John B. Morris of Baltimore, who demanded their return, declared that he would soon have sufficient evidence to prove them fugitives. Thereupon the colored people rushed in, took the women to a carriage, and carried them away to safety.[1]

§ 43. **Philadelphia and Kennedy cases.** — A similar but unsuccessful attempt was made in Philadelphia in 1838. A slave had been delivered to the man claiming to be his master. As the captors were about to take him away, a crowd of colored people gathered and attempted to rescue him. It was not so simple a matter in a large city as in a country town. A body of police soon appeared, protected the slaveholders, and finally arrested some of the leaders among the free blacks.[2]

A few years later, in Carlisle, Pennsylvania, three negroes were arrested and their identity established as the slaves of Messrs. Kennedy and Hollingsworth of Maryland. The colored people of the neighborhood had caused a writ of habeas corpus to be issued and a second hearing was held. Judge Hepburne decided that the magistrate first employed had no right to commit the alleged fugitives, but he himself remanded them. A riot ensued, and some thirty-six persons were tried for participating in it.[3]

§ 44. **Latimer case.** — In the Latimer case, the first of that series of famous fugitive slave trials which took place in Boston, was strongly developed the feeling against kidnapping, or in fact against the rendition of a slave under any circumstances.

In 1842, George Latimer was seized in Boston without a warrant, at the request of James B. Grey of Norfolk, Virginia. Latimer's counsel, Samuel E. Sewall and Amos B. Merrill, sued out a writ of habeas corpus, but after argument Chief Justice Shaw denied it. Mr. Grey asked for time to procure evidence against Latimer from Virginia. The judge ruled that the request should be granted, and that Latimer should for the time being be kept in the custody of the city jailer, Nathaniel Cooledge. A writ of personal replevin, under the act of 1837 securing trial by jury,[4] was then sworn out,

---

[1] Appendix D, No. 20.
[3] Appendix D, No. 35.
[2] Appendix D, No. 22.
[4] See *post*, § 81.

but Justice Shaw decided that, according to the decision by the Supreme Court in the Prigg case, the law was illegal.[1]

The proceedings aroused great indignation throughout the city and State. Meetings to devise means of aiding Latimer were held in Faneuil Hall and Belknap Street church. Stirring speeches were made by Wendell Phillips and others, and resolutions condemning the proceedings of the· authorities, and remonstrating against the return of Latimer, were adopted. Bands of ruffians strove to break up the meetings, and succeeded in greatly disturbing them. To rouse the people, to give expression to public sentiment, and to spread the news from day to day, Dr. H. I. Bowditch and Dr. W. F. Channing edited a paper called "The Latimer Journal and North Star." This was published for a number of weeks by the friends of the fugitive. Petitions were sent to the sheriff to remove the jailer, and to the Governor asking the removal of the sheriff if he did not accede to their demand. Thereupon Latimer's custodian agreed to give him up for a sufficient payment. The sum of four hundred dollars was accordingly raised, the proceedings came to an abrupt termination, and Latimer was released.

The excitement produced, however, did not die out immediately, and some of the results were far-reaching. So intense was the public excitement, that, soon after, a petition was prepared and sent to Congress, asking an amendment to the Constitution. This was signed by fifty thousand people in Massachusetts, and presented in the House by Mr. Adams. Another, signed by sixty-five thousand people, was sent to the legislature. The effect was the act of 1843, forbidding all officers to aid in the recapture of a fugitive slave, or to permit the use of State jails for their imprisonment. The petition to Congress was not received. A resolution from the Latimer committee, which proposed an amendment to the Constitution so as to base representation on "free persons," brought about much discussion, and was not received in the House. In the Senate it excited even more violent opposition, and the resolutions were laid on the table and not ·printed.[2]

§ 45. **Ottoman case.** — Similar indignation was felt in Boston over the case of Captain Hannum of the brig Ottoman. He had found a runaway concealed on board, but had set sail to return, evidently with the intention of taking the man back into captivity. A

---

[1] *Ante*, § 25.   [2] Appendix D, No. 28; see *post*, § 81.

steamer was sent out to rescue the slave, but the Ottoman managed to elude it, and the man was lost. At a meeting held September 24, 1846, a committee was appointed for the purpose of preventing similar outrages.[1]

§ 46. **Interstate relations.**—The spirit of opposition to the execution of the Fugitive Slave Law made itself felt, not only in popular demonstrations and in legislation, but in interstate relations. We have already noticed the Prigg case,[2] and its effect in relieving the States from any responsibility in the enforcement of the law. Other States took advantage of this decision, and of the general principle of international law, that one nation or state is not bound to enforce the municipal law of another.

§ 47. **Boston and Isaac cases (1837-1839).**—In 1837 a runaway was found on the ship Boston, then on her homeward voyage from Georgia to Maine. After landing, the slave succeeded in getting to Canada. The Governor of Georgia charged the captain with slave-stealing, and demanded his return as a fugitive from justice. The Governor of Maine would not comply with the request, because, as he said, the laws of that State recognized slaves not as property, but as persons. The indignant legislature of Georgia adopted resolutions calling upon Congress so to amend the laws that the Governor of Maine should be compelled to give up slave stealers as fugitives from justice. Resolutions were presented in the United States Senate, but no action was taken.[3]

The refusal to use State machinery against fugitives extended to the process of extradition against persons connected with the rescue of slaves. Thus in the Isaac case, in 1839, Virginia asked New York for the arrest of three colored men who were accused of abetting a slave's escape. The Governor of New York returned answer, that no State could demand the surrender of a fugitive from justice for an act which was made criminal only by its own legislation.[4]

§ 48. **Ohio and Kentucky case.**—Kentucky, in 1848, demanded from the Governor of Ohio the extradition of fifteen persons on the charge of aiding the escape of a fugitive. Governor Bell refused, on the ground that Ohio laws did not recognize property in man.[5]

[1] Appendix D, No. 34.   [2] *Ante*, § 25.
[3] Appendix D, No. 21.   [4] Appendix D, No. 24.
[5] Appendix D, No. 37.

§ 49. **Prosecutions.** — The effects of the aid and protection thus given fugitives by Northern people or governments awakened among the slaveholders a feeling of wrong and indignation. The Fugitive Slave Law was clear, and they determined to carry it out to the letter. They began, therefore, energetically to prosecute people for aiding and harboring escaping slaves. The case just mentioned shows how difficult it was to secure prosecutions beyond the State boundaries. When the offence occurred within the bounds of a slave State, the judgments were most severe, and the heaviest possible fines and longest terms of imprisonment were inflicted for simple acts of charity.

§ 50. **Van Zandt, Pearl, and Walker cases.** — Mr. Van Zandt, returning into the country from Cincinnati one day in 1840, took nine fugitive slaves from Kentucky into his farm wagon. He was stopped by three persons, and all but two of the slaves were recaptured. Mr. Van Zandt was arrested, taken into court, and fined twelve thousand dollars, which exhausted his entire property.[1]

A still more severe penalty was that imposed upon Captain Drayton, of the schooner Pearl, in 1848. He took on board seventy-five fugitive slaves, and sailed up the Potomac. An armed steamer, sent in pursuit, overtook them and brought them back. Captain Drayton and another officer of the schooner were placed in prison, where they remained for twenty years, and at last were relieved only through the efforts of Charles Sumner.[2]

Another instance of the same sort is the case of Mr. Jonathan Walker, in 1844. With seven fugitives he embarked from Pensacola in an open boat for the Bahama Islands, but he received a sun-stroke and was obliged to leave the management of the craft in the hands of the negroes. On account of the accident, they were overtaken by two sloops, and both fugitives and their protector captured. Mr. Walker was twice tried, imprisoned, sentenced to stand in the pillory, and branded on the hand with the letters S. S., slave stealer.[3] The crime and the punishment have alike been glorified in Whittier's verses: —

> "Then lift that manly right hand, bold ploughman of the wave !
> Its branded hand shall prophesy ' Salvation to the Slave !'
> Hold up its fire-wrought language that whoso reads may feel
> His heart swell strong within him, his sinews change to steel."[4]

[1] Appendix D, No. 25.   [2] Appendix D, No. 40.
[3] Appendix D, No. 31.
[4] Liberator, Aug. 15, 1845, "The Branded Hand."

§ 51. **Unpopularity of the Fugitive Slave Act of 1850.** — The passage of the new law probably increased the number of antislavery people more than anything else which had occurred during the whole agitation. Many of those formerly indifferent were roused to active opposition by a sense of the injustice of the Fugitive Slave Act as they saw it executed in Boston and elsewhere. Hence, in the cases of the period from 1850 to the outbreak of the Civil War, we shall find a new element. The antislavery party, grown strong, resisted the regulations, and instead of the unquestioned return of a fugitive, as in colonial times, or of prosecutions carried on under the simple conditions of the act of 1793, the struggle became, long and complex. In fact during this time hardly an important case can be cited in which there was not some opposition to the natural course of the law. These exasperating effects were not at first apparent to the South, since before the famous rescues began several cases of rendition showed the power of the Executive. As the escapes grew more and more frequent yearly, increasing all the time in boldness, the slave-holders put forth greater efforts to punish the offenders, and prosecutions were numerous. But the "new law had no moral foundation," and against such an act public sentiment must sooner or later revolt, no matter how severe may be its provisions.[1] As Mr. James Freeman Clarke has said, "It was impossible to convince the people that it was right to send back to slavery men who were so desirous of freedom as to run such risks. All education from boyhood up to manhood had taught us to believe that it was the duty of all men to struggle for freedom."[2]

§ 52. **Principle of the selection of cases.** — The large number of cases occurring between 1850 and 1860 renders it impossible to present a detailed account of them all in a brief monograph. The selection, therefore, includes only such as are typical of the various phases of the agitation.

§ 53. **Hamlet case (1850).** — The first recorded action under the provisions of the law of 1850 took place on the 26th of September of that year, just eight days after the passage of the act. James Hamlet, a free negro, who with his family had been living for several years in New York, was on that day arrested by a deputy United States Marshal as the fugitive slave of Mary Brown of Baltimore. After a hasty examination by Commissioner Gardi-

[1] Von Holst, IV. 10, 11.   [2] J. F. Clarke, Antislavery Days, 92.

ner, he was surrendered in accordance with the new law. These proceedings were not sufficiently well known at the time to excite a mob, but when discovered they roused so strong a feeling that the money necessary to redeem Hamlet was almost immediately raised, and on the 5th of October he was brought back from slavery.[1]

§ 54. **Sims case (1851).**— Another instance in Boston, often mentioned as the first under the law of 1850, but really six months later than the Hamlet case, is that of Thomas M. Sims. A common method of seizure was followed. Marshal Tukey arrested Sims on a false charge of theft. Mr. Potter of Virginia then claimed him as his slave. Court Square was filled with people. The Marshal feared a popular outbreak while the matter was pending, and, to the indignation of the city, caused the court-house in which Sims was confined to be surrounded with chains. As these were but four feet from the ground, the judges as they went in and out from the sessions were forced, morning and night, to bow beneath them. The building was also strongly guarded by a company of armed men, ever afterward known as the "Sims Brigade." Robert Rantoul, Jr. and Samuel E. Sewall conducted Sims's case. Commissioner Curtis overruled the constitutional objections to the Fugitive Slave Law, and to the judicial functions of the Commissioners of the United States courts. Then, despite all efforts of the antislavery people in his behalf, the certificate which sent Sims back to Virginia was made out and signed by Commissioner Curtis.[2] The Liberator says of the popular sentiment: "One feeling was visible on almost every countenance, commiseration, humiliation,— commiseration for the victim, humiliation at the degradation of Massachusetts. No man talked, no man thought, of violence. Why? Because it is acquiesced in? No! no! Because it is approved? A thousand times, no! but because government is pleased to enforce the law, and resistance is hopeless."[3] Sims was taken from his cell in the early morning, observed only by a few faithful vigilants, and, amid platoons of armed men, conducted to the United States ship Acorn, which was detailed to carry him back to the South.[4]

The indignation of the antislavery people remained to be expressed, and a mass meeting was held on the Common and in

[1] Appendix D, No. 43.
[2] Appendix D, No. 48.
[3] Liberator, April 17, 1851.
[4] Daily Morning Chronicle, April 26, 1851.

Tremont Temple. Wendell Phillips and Theodore Parker addressed the assemblage, and Phillips noticed the fact that hostile troops had not been seen in the streets of Boston since the redcoats marched up from Long Wharf.[1]

§ 55. **Burns case** (1854). — The rendition of Anthony Burns in 1854 was the last great fugitive slave case which occurred in Boston. Burns was the property of Charles F. Suttle of Virginia. He escaped in 1854, and came to Boston. One of the first things he did was to write a letter to his brother, still a slave in the South. Unfortunately, though this was mailed in Canada, by some oversight it was dated in Boston. Since a letter to a slave was always opened by the master, Burns's hiding place was discovered.[2] He was arrested upon the usual charge of theft. Then, upon a warrant issued by Judge Loring, he was claimed as a fugitive slave by Suttle.

When the knowledge of the arrest began to circulate, the most intense excitement prevailed. Handbills asking all antislavery people to go to Boston were sent throughout the country. Public meetings held in Faneuil and Meionaon Halls were crowded with representatives from all the towns about.[3] One of the people who took part in the attempted rescue which followed one of these meetings thus describes it: —

"On the evening of the 26th of May, we went down to Faneuil Hall to hear Wendell Phillips. He counselled waiting until morning before any attempt to rescue Burns should be made, but the excited audience silenced him with shouts of 'No, no! to-night! to-night!'

"Mr. Phillips saw that it was useless to try to go on, so he sat down and Mr. Theodore Parker began speaking. At first he advocated the same plan, but at last, as he found the crowd growing more and more eager and uproarious, he said, 'Well, if you will, let us go!' and led the way out of the hall. The people followed, and my friend and I were among the first to reach the court-house. There we found prepared for us long beams and boxes of axes. Five or six men seized one of these beams, and before its pressure the large door of the court-house crushed like glass. Mr. Higginson first stepped in, but just then a pistol shot was heard, and the mob fell back. Mr. Higginson looked around,

---

[1] Liberator, April 17, 1851. [2] Appendix D, No. 57.
[3] Boston Journal, May 29, 1854.

and entreated them not to desert him, but the favorable moment was gone. The people should have lost no time in filling the house, for the marines had been ordered from the Navy Yard, and when they appeared nothing further could be done."[1] In this riot James Batchelder, one of the Marshal's guards, was killed.

At the trial, though Burns was ably defended by Mr. R. H. Dana and others, it was of no avail. His identity was unfortunately established from the first. He had recognized and addressed his master, and also a Mr. Brant, who had once hired him. The order for his rendition was therefore at once given.[2]

Guarded by a large military force he was conducted through the streets, filled with an indignant multitude, to the United States cutter Morris, which had been ordered by the President to take him back.[3] Many buildings on the route were hung with black, and so great was the popular excitement, that Rev. J. F. Clarke, an eyewitness of the affair, has said: "It was evident that a very trifling incident might have brought on a collision, and flooded the streets with blood."

The difficulty of enforcing the act was shown in the precautionary measures immediately adopted by the government. The city police, the militia, the marines, and some regular troops, were ordered out to the task of guarding one poor fugitive. It cost the country one hundred thousand dollars to send this single slave back to his master.[4]

Not long after Burns's return, a sum of money, to which Charles Devens, United States Marshal at his trial, contributed largely, was raised in Boston and the vicinity for his purchase; but it was found impossible to effect it.[5]

Mr. Higginson, Wendell Phillips, and Theodore Parker, with others, were indicted for riot, but the indictment was quashed by Judge Curtis on technical grounds, and they were discharged.[6]

§ 56. **Garner case (1856).** — Of all the cases of rendition, the saddest, and next to the Burns case probably the best known at the

[1] Personal statement of Mr. Elbridge Sprague, made to the writer. Col. T. W. Higginson suggests a few minor corrections in Mr. Sprague's narrative. The first person to step in was an unknown negro: the beam used was found in Court Square; none were prepared beforehand; there was but one box of axes.

[2] Boston Daily Advertiser, 1854, Worcester Spy, May 31, 1854, Argument of Mr. R. H. Dana.

[3] Liberator, Aug. 22, 1854.   [4] Von Holst, V. 64.
[5] Appendix D, No. 57.   [6] Commonwealth, June 26, 1854.

time, was that of Margaret Garner. In accounts of the Underground Railroad we are told that winter was the favorite season for flight in the section of the country south of the Ohio, since ice then covered the river, and the difficulty of crossing by boat did not arise. It was at this season that Simeon Garner, his son Robert, and their families, fled from Kentucky and crossed the frozen stream to the house of a colored man in Cincinnati. They were soon traced thither, and after a desperate hand to hand struggle the house was entered. There the pursuers found that Margaret Garner, preferring for her children death to slavery, had striven to take their lives, and one lay dead. The case was immediately brought into court, where, despite the efforts made to save them, rendition was decided upon. On the way back, Margaret, in despair, attempted to drown herself and her child in the river; but even the deliverance of death was denied her, for she was recovered and sold, to be carried yet farther south.[1]

§ 57. **Shadrach case (1851).** — In the three typical cases just described, neither the law's delay, violent interference, nor the desperation of the slave, availed to prevent the return of the fugitive to the oppressor. Let us turn from this group, and take up those more important cases wherein the law was not allowed to complete its course, but rescues were accomplished, either by free negroes or antislavery people. First in time and importance comes the case of Shadrach, which occurred in Boston in February, 1851.

In May, 1850, a slave named Frederic Wilkins had run away from Virginia and come to Boston, where he found employment as a waiter in the Cornhill Coffee House under the alias of Shadrach. He had been there not quite a year, however, when John De Bere, his master in Norfolk, sent some one in pursuit of him. A warrant was served and he was arrested while at work. United States Commissioner Riley then took him to the court-house, where Mr. List, a young lawyer of antislavery sympathies, offered his aid as counsel, and Messrs. Charles G. Davis, Samuel E. Sewall, and Ellis Gray Loring also came to his assistance. Mr. List obtained some delay in the proceedings; but since, by the act of 1843,[2] the use of State jails had been denied for fugitives, the officers were obliged to keep the prisoner in the court-room until another place of confinement could be found. By this time a large number of people had gathered about the building, and were trying

[1] Appendix D, No. 58.   [2] See *post*, § 81.

to force an entrance. For a long time they were unable to enter, but at last opportunity was given as Mr. Davis opened the door to leave the court-room. In spite of all efforts on the part of the officers to close the door, a body of colored people under the lead of Lewis Hayden rushed in and seized the prisoner. They carried him triumphantly out of the court-room on their shoulders, and soon saw him safely started for Canada. Mr. Davis and others were prosecuted for aiding in the rescue, but nothing was proved against them. Intense excitement prevailed in the city, and finally throughout the country, since Congress took up this infringement of the law.[1]

Mr. Clay, February 17, 1851, introduced a resolution which requested the President to send to Congress "any information he may possess in regard to the alleged recent case of a forcible resistance to the execution of the laws of the United States in the city of Boston," and communicate to Congress "what means he has adopted to meet the occurrence," and "whether, in his opinion, any additional legislation is necessary to meet the exigencies of the case."[2] President Pierce then issued a proclamation announcing the facts to the country, and calling on all people to assist in quelling this and other disturbances. The Senate's request was also answered in an Executive message to Congress, which announced to them that the President would use all his constitutional powers to insure the execution of the laws. Such unusual national interference gave the case wide celebrity, and, as Von Holst says, "The pretensions and assumptions of the South were encouraged in a very unwise way, by the fact that, by such a manner of treating the matter, people seemed to recognize that it was entitled to hold the whole North responsible for every violation of the compromise, which could properly be laid at the door of only a few individuals. The proclamation and the message placed the compromise in a far more glaring light than the liberation of Shadrach."[3]

§ 58. **Jerry McHenry rescue (1851).** — Later, a case occurred at Syracuse, New York, which was a significant illustration of the successful action of a vigilance committee. Jerry McHenry, a respectable colored man who had lived for several years in that

---

[1] Appendix D, No. 47.
[2] 31 Cong. 2 Sess., Senate Journal, 187; Congressional Globe, 580.
[3] Von Holst, III. 25.

city, was arrested in October, 1851, as a fugitive slave. At the examination, which took place at two o'clock in the afternoon, he found opportunity to break away from the officers and escape through the crowd, which opened to allow him to pass. He was, however, immediately pursued and recaptured. It so happened that an Agricultural Fair and a convention of the Liberty Party were going on at that time in Syracuse, and the city was unusually full of people. When the alarm bell gave notice to the vigilance committee that a negro had been seized, Mr. Gerrit Smith, who was attending the meetings, and Rev. Samuel J. May, with others, hastened to the scene. The Commissioner, after the capture, had again taken up the trial, but such a disturbance was made by the crowd which gathered outside that he was forced to adjourn. Meanwhile, Mr. Smith with the committee had planned a rescue, and at about half-past eight fully two thousand people had assembled, and an assault was begun upon the court-house. They broke doors and windows, overpowered the officers, and at last bore Jerry away in triumph.

He remained in the home of a friend until he could be sent to Canada. Prosecutions were immediately instituted, and eighteen persons indicted for taking part in the rescue, but nothing came of the case. On the other side, Henry W. Allen, Marshal in the case, was tried for kidnapping. The judge declared the Fugitive Slave Act unconstitutional, but a verdict of not guilty was rendered.[1]

§ 59. **Oberlin-Wellington rescue (1858).** — Sometimes, however, general sentiment was so strong that the rescue became, not an action instigated and carried through by three or four determined men, but the indignant uprising of a whole town. Such was the Oberlin-Wellington case, celebrated for the great number of prosecutions and the high character of those engaged in it. Two kidnappers from Kentucky induced an Oberlin boy, by a bribe of twenty dollars, to entice away a negro named John Rice on pretence of giving him work. Having taken him to a lonely spot, he was seized and carried about eight miles across country to Wellington, there to await the south bound train.

On the way the party was overtaken by an Oberlin College student, who at once gave the alarm. A crowd gathered and followed the kidnappers to the railway station. There, by placing

---

[1] Appendix D, No. 51.

a ladder upon the balcony they succeeded in rescuing John from the upper story of the house in which he was confined. For this violation of the law thirty-seven citizens of Oberlin and Wellington were indicted. This produced the greatest excitement all over the country, and the case grew more and more complicated, until the proceedings had lasted several months. Public meetings to express sympathy with the prosecuted were held in many places. Some of them were imprisoned to await the trial, but no severe sentences were imposed.[1]

§ 60. **Christiana case** (1851). — Occasionally the rescue of fugitives was not accomplished by a sudden unorganized movement, but by a deliberate armed defence on the part of the slaves and their friends. In the Christiana case the affair was marked by violence and bloodshed, while the fact that the Quakers Castner Hanway and Elijah Lewis were afterward prosecuted made it notorious; and the further fact that the charge was not, as usual, that of aiding a fugitive, but of treason, gave it still greater interest.

In and about Christiana, Pennsylvania, there were many negroes who had formerly been slaves, descriptions of whom were frequently furnished to kidnappers by a band of men known throughout the country as the "Gap Gang." A league for mutual protection had therefore been formed by the colored people, and prominent among them for intelligence and boldness was William Parker. Soon after the passage of the law of 1850, Edward Gorsuch and a party came from Maryland to Christiana for a fugitive slave. With United States officers from Philadelphia they went immediately to the house of William Parker, where the man they were seeking was sheltered. When their demand was refused, they fired two shots at the house. This roused the people, and a riot ensued in which the fugitive escaped. Mr. Gorsuch was killed, his son desperately wounded, and the rest put to flight. Castner Hanway at the beginning of the struggle was notified of the kidnappers' presence, and, though feeble in health, hastened to the scene. When ordered by Marshal Kline to aid him in accordance with the law, he refused; yet, far from leading in the affair, he tried in every way to prevent bloodshed and bring about peace.

After it was over, Parker, with two other colored men, knowing that arrest must follow, secreted themselves under piles of shav-

[1] Appendix D, No. 62.

ings in an old carpenter's shop. At night they sent four wagons in different directions as decoys for the detectives, and were carried safely away by a fifth. Many negroes hid that night in the corn shocks, and under the floors of houses, until escape could be made in safety.[1]

Castner Hanway was arrested, and arraigned before the United States court on the charge of treason; but no proof of a conspiracy to make a general and public resistance to the law could be found, and he was acquitted. Afterward it was desired to try Hanway and Lewis for "riot and murder," but the grand jury ignored the bill, and all prisoners were released. With these prosecutions the end of the affair was apparently reached, though perhaps its influence may be traced in a succeeding case.

§ 61. **Miller case (1851).** — A noted kidnapper from Maryland, in 1851, seized a free negro girl living at the house of Mr. Miller, in Nottingham, Pennsylvania, and took her to Baltimore. Mr. Miller followed them, and succeeded in getting her freed. He then started back, but never reached home. Search was made, and his body found upon the way. It was thought that the murder was committed in revenge for the part he had taken in the Christiana riot.[2]

§ 62. **John Brown in Kansas (1858).** — It was during this period also that John Brown was endeavoring to put into execution his famous plan for freeing the slaves. This is interesting, not only as typical of organized efforts to free the slaves on the plantations, but also because of its connection with other phases of the slavery question, into which we shall not attempt to enter here. His idea was first to gather as large a force as possible, then, when his men were properly drilled, to run off the slaves in large numbers; to retain the brave and strong in the mountains, and to send the weak and timid to the North by the "Underground Railroad."[3]

In December, 1858, Brown divided his forces into two divisions, and went into Missouri. Here he succeeded in freeing eleven slaves, and, though pursued by a far superior number of Missourians, took them safely into Kansas. The affair, by its boldness, created great excitement throughout the South. The Governor of Missouri offered three thousand dollars reward, and the Presi-

---

[1] Appendix D, No. 49.   [2] Appendix D, No. 50.
[3] Sanborn, Life and Letters of John Brown, 420; Douglass, Life and Times of John Brown, 279, 282.

dent of the United States two hundred and fifty dollars, for Brown's capture; within a very short time he had succeeded in conveying himself and his eleven fugitives safely into Canada, and the horses which he had appropriated from the slaveholders in order to carry his protegés out of Kansas were afterward publicly sold by him in Ohio.[1]

[1] Von Holst, John Brown, 104.

CHAPTER IV.

FUGITIVES AND THEIR FRIENDS.

§ 63. Methods of escape.
    § 64. Reasons for escape.
    § 65. Conditions of slave life.
    § 66. Escapes to the woods.
    § 67. Escapes to the North.
    § 68. Use of protection papers.
    § 69. Fugitives disguised as whites: Craft case.
§ 70. Underground Railroad.
    § 71. Rise and growth of the system.
    § 72. Methods pursued.
    § 73. Colored agents of the Underground Railroad.
    § 74. Prosecutions of agents.
    § 75. Formal organization.
    § 76. General effect of escapes.

§ 63. **Methods of escape.** — The great increase in the number of fugitives after 1850 was in part due to the uneasiness felt by Northern people under a law which made them co-workers with the South in a system of slave hunting, and in part to the greater ease of communication now afforded between the two sections. The knowledge that there was in the North a body of "abolitionists" eager to aid them from bondage to freedom was also spreading more widely each day among the slaves.

Public interest in the subject was more and more aroused, not only by the cases of cruelty and injustice which were forcibly brought to the attention of Northern communities, but also by the romantic and thrilling episodes of the escapes. To understand the attitude of the North toward fugitives, it is necessary to examine some of the different methods used by the fugitives in their flight. Perhaps a better point of view than that of the outside observer will be gained by placing ourselves in the position of the slave, and examining his motives for flight, the difficulties which he encountered at home, the manner in which he overcame them, and, finally, the various paths of escape then open to him, and the agencies which befriended him and forwarded him on his way.

§ 64. **Reasons for escape.** — First, why did the slave seek to escape? However unlike the attending circumstances, we find upon investigation that the negro's desire to run away may be traced to one of but three or four motives. Among the more intelligent slaves, who could comprehend the nature and injustice of their position, it often rose solely from the upspringing in their hearts of that love of freedom natural to all men. It is probable that in the greater number of cases this was the motive at the root of the matter. A fugitive, on being questioned at an Underground Railroad station as to his reasons for escape, replied that he had had a kind master, plenty to eat and to wear, but that notwithstanding this for many years he had been dissatisfied. He was thirsting for freedom.[1] Another said that his owner had always been considerate, and even indulgent to him. He left for no other reason than simply to gain his liberty.[2]

A second reason, and that which perhaps most frequently led them to take the decisive step in this often long premeditated act, was the cruel treatment received from their masters. An owner upon one of the Southern plantations said his slaves usually ran away after they had been whipped, or something had occurred to make them angry.[3]

A third and very effective cause was the fear of being sold South, where slave life, spent in toil under the merciless masters of the rice swamps and cotton fields, was seen on its darkest side. Such was the horror with which the slave regarded this change, that the threat of it was constantly used by owners as one of the surest means of reducing their rebellious slaves to submission. In the Virginia Slave Mother's Farewell to her Daughters who have been sold into Southern bondage, Whittier has well expressed their feelings.[4]

[1] Still, Underground Railroad, 410. [2] Ibid., 444.
[3] F. L. Olmsted, Journey in the Back Country, 49.

[4] "Gone, gone, — sold and gone
To the rice swamp dank and lone, —
Where the slave-whip ceaseless swings,
Where the noisome insect stings,
Where the fever demon strews
Poison with the falling dews,
Where the sickly sunbeams glare
Through the hot and misty air, —
Gone, gone, — sold and gone
To the rice swamp dank and lone

Many cases of this kind came to light through the examinations at the Underground Railroad stations. Three brothers once learned that the next day they were to be sent South with a slave trader then in the vicinity. Filled with terror at the prospect, they preferred the danger of death in the swamps to the certainty of life in the unknown country. That night they made their escape, but it was only after weeks of wandering in swamps and morasses that they reached a haven.[1]

So long as a black family remained together upon one plantation, their love for one another operated as the strongest bond to prevent their departure; but when, as constantly happened, the sale and separation of the members scattered families far and wide, with no hope of reunion, the firmest and often the sole tie which bound them to the South was broken. There was no longer anything to hold them back.[2]

§ 65. **Conditions of slave life.** — These are some of the motives which led the slave to plan an escape. It will now be well to glance at those surrounding conditions, incident to the time and country, which made successful flight particularly difficult. First, the slave was a negro; and in the South, where the presumption was that every black man must be a slave, the color of his skin gave not only a means of tracing him, but also made him liable at any moment to questioning and arrest.

In both city and country patrols were appointed, whose duty it was to keep strict watch over the negroes; and any slave found away from his plantation, unless in livery or provided with a pass,

> From Virginia's hills and waters, —
> Woe is me, my stolen daughters!
>
> "There no mother's eye is near them,
> There no mother's ear can hear them;
> Never, when the torturing lash
> Seams their back with many a gash,
> Shall a mother's kindness bless them,
> Or a mother's arms caress them. . . .
>
> "Oh, when weary, sad, and slow
> From the fields at night they go,
> Faint with toil, and racked with pain,
> To their cheerless homes again, —
> There no brother's voice shall greet them
> There no father's welcome meet them."

[1] Still, Underground Railroad, 443.   [2] Ibid., 448.

could be whipped and sent back to his master.[1] It was also lawful for any white man to seize and carry a stray slave to the nearest jail.[2] The next morning, if not claimed, he was advertised in a manner of which the following is an example: —

"Was taken up and committed to the jail of Halifax Co., on the 26th day of May, a dark colored boy who says his name is Jordan Artis; said boy says he was born free, and bound out to Mr. Beale, near Murfreesboro, Hartford Co., N. C., and is now twenty-one years of age. Owner is requested to come forward, prove property, pay charges, and take said boy away within time prescribed by law, otherwise he will be dealt with as the law directs.

"O. P. SHELL, *Jailer*.

"Halifax Co., N. C., June 8, 1855."[3]

If not claimed within one year, such a prisoner could be sold by the jailer. Thus Olmsted remarks that "the security of the whites is not so much dependent upon patrols, as on the constant, habitual, and instinctive surveillance and authority of all white people over the blacks."[4]

§ 66. **Escapes to the woods.** — If an opportunity for escape should present itself, the first question for the slave was, "In what direction shall I turn?" Many slaves knew nothing of the Northern people, or had heard of Canada only as a cold, barren, uninviting country, where the negro must perish. To those who had neither the courage nor the knowledge requisite for a long journey, the woods and swamps near by offered the only refuge. There they built cabins, or lived in caves, and got food by hunting and fishing, and by raids upon the neighboring plantations.

In one of the papers of the day an underground den is noticed, the opening of which, though in sight of two or three houses, and near roads and fields, where passing was constant, had been so concealed by a pile of straw, that for many months it had remained unnoticed. When discovered, on opening a trap-door, steps were seen leading down into a room about six feet square, comfortably ceiled with boards, and containing a fire-place. The den was well stocked with food by the occupants, who had been missing about a year.[5]

[1] Williams, History of the Negro Race in America, 293.
[2] Still, Underground Railroad, 27.
[3] F. L. Olmsted, The Cotton Kingdom, 157.
[4] F. L. Olmsted, Journey in the Back Country, 444.
[5] W. I. Bowditch, Slavery and the Constitution; Macon (Ga.) Telegram, Nov. 27, 1838.

In most cases slaves were not so bold, and preferred concealment on an uninhabited island, or a bit of land surrounded by morasses. We often find advertisements of the time, mentioning such places as the probable refuge of runaways. The Savannah Georgian of 1839 offers a reward for two men who have been out for eighteen months, and are supposed to be encamped in a swamp near Pine Grove Plantation.

In the Great Dismal Swamp, which extends from near Norfolk, Virginia, into North Carolina, a large colony of these fugitive negroes was established, and so long was the custom continued that children were born, grew up, and lived their whole lives in its dark recesses. . Besides their hunting and fishing, they sometimes obtained food and money, in return for work, from the poor whites and the negroes who had homes on the borders of the swamp. It was this practice of remaining out near home which, under easy masters, brought about the habitual runaways, — men who were constantly escaping, and after a little time returning, often of their own accord.[1] One of his masters said of William Browne, afterward a well known speaker upon slavery, that he hesitated some time before he invested seven hundred dollars in William, for he was "a noted runaway."[2] Again, in a Southern paper advertising a sale of slaves, one description is thus given: "Number 47, Daniel, a runaway, but has not run away during the last two years, aged 28 years."[3]

§ 67. **Escapes to the North.** — Of those who, with heroic hearts and firm courage, determined to reach even Canada, many had seldom left the plantation on which they were born, and were so completely ignorant of geography and relative distances, that the best and quickest way northward could seldom be chosen. They knew nothing of the facilities for communication possessed by their masters through newspapers and telegraph, and would often fancy themselves safe when they had travelled but a short distance from home. In reality, the white people about were often fully informed against them, and arrests were almost sure to follow.[4]

The journeys of the fugitives were necessarily long, since un-

---

[1] Ball, Mammoth Pictorial Tour of United States, 54; F. L. Olmsted, Journey in the Back Country, 155.

[2] W. I. Bowditch, Slavery and the Constitution; Macon (Ga.) Telegram, Nov. 27, 1838.

[3] Liberator, April 12, 1839.

[4] Wm. Parker, Freedman's Story, in Atlantic Monthly, February and March, 1866; Letter from Gerrit Smith, in Liberator, Dec. 28, 1838.

frequented ways were generally chosen, and but part of the day could be used. There is a record of a man who had "taken a whole year in coming from Alabama to Cincinnati. He had travelled only in the night, hiding in the woods during the day. He had nothing to eat but what he could get from the fields, sometimes finding a chicken, green corn, or perhaps a small pig."[1]

Although the methods pursued were innumerable, and varied from those of the man whose only guide was the north star, to those of the party aided onward by the most elaborate arrangements of the Underground Railroad, the fugitive was obliged to follow one of two great routes, by water or by land. From the earliest times the ship had been a favorite refuge. Once on board a craft bound to a Northern port, the fugitive was almost certain of reaching that destination, and, once arrived, could hope for protection from the Northern friends of whom vague rumors had penetrated the South. New laws, therefore, bore more and more heavily upon captains who should be found guilty of harboring a slave, and many cases were made public of cruel treatment experienced by slaves at the hands of captains who sent them directly back. Nevertheless, escapes on shipboard still occurred frequently through the years of slavery. A method commonly used by women in getting on board was to disarm suspicion by appearing to be carrying some freshly laundered clothes to the sailors.

§ 68. **Use of protection papers.** — Another method called for less physical effort on the part of the fugitive, but for greater coolness. It was simply to procure from some freeman his protection papers, and to show them whenever necessary to disarm suspicion. As the descriptions could seldom be made to agree, both giver and receiver were placed in situations of the greatest risk. It was thus, however, that Frederick Douglass travelled in the most open manner from Baltimore to New York, and escaped from a bondage to which he never afterward returned.[2]

§ 69. **Fugitives disguised as whites: Craft case.** — Sometimes the boldest plans succeeded best if supported by sufficient firmness and presence of mind. Three negroes possessed of a considerable sum of money once determined upon a plan, startling in its simplicity and success. They hired a good travelling coach and horses. They then bribed a white beggar to dress as a Virginian

[1] J. F. Clarke, Antislavery Days, 93.
[2] Life and Times of Frederick Douglass, 196.

gentleman, while they mounted the coach as his driver and footmen; and in this guise they successfully made their way into Canada.[1]

Another example of unconcealed flight is found in the often told story of the escape of William and Ellen Craft, in 1848. They lived in Macon, Georgia, and were generally well treated. But Ellen had been compelled to go North with her mistress, and leave her little child at home; during this absence, the child died uncared for. From that time she determined to escape.[2]

William at last arranged a plan which was successfully carried out. Ellen was nearly white. She personated a young Southern planter, while William accompanied her as her servant. She carried her right arm in a sling so that she might not be expected to write, bandaged her smooth face, and put on a pair of green goggles. Thus disguised, she succeeded in buying tickets for herself and servant without discovery. In the train she was terrified to see a gentleman who had known her from childhood. He even sat down by her, and spoke, but to her great relief, he saw in her only a young invalid going North for his health. From Savannah they took a steamer to Charleston. There they had some difficulty in passing inspection, but their most dangerous stopping place was Baltimore, where every white man with a slave was required to prove his right of property before he could be allowed to go on to Philadelphia. After some conversation Ellen told the officer that she knew no one in Baltimore, and had no proofs that William was her slave; but that he was necessary to her on account of her illness, and she must take him on. The officer finally relented, as the train was about to start, and Baltimore was safely passed.

At Philadelphia shelter was found among the Quakers, and thence they pushed on to Boston. Here they engaged the attention of Theodore Parker, and he protected them during their stay. William took up his trade of cabinet-making, while Ellen added to their income by sewing. They lived thus quietly until the passage of the Fugitive Slave Law in 1850. From that time, to remain even in Boston was hazardous. Soon after, there appeared one day in William's shop a man who had worked with him in the South. He immediately suspected the presence of others, and took refuge among friends. For two weeks Ellen was with Mr. Parker,

---

[1] Appendix D, No. 41; Antislavery Almanac, 74.
[2] J. F. Clarke, Antislavery Days, 83.

who wrote his sermons during her stay with her sword in a drawer under his inkstand, and a pistol in his desk.

They were then taken to Mr. Ellis Gray Loring's home. Here William showed a most honorable spirit. When he found Mr. Loring was not at home he would not remain, saying, " I am subjecting him to a heavy fine and imprisonment, and I must go at once to look for some other shelter."

His pursuers, who had come from Georgia, were staying at the United States Hotel. The knowledge of their object was soon spread abroad, and they dared not go into the streets for fear of a mob. Handbills, calling attention to them, were placed everywhere, and cries of " Slave hunters! there go the slave hunters! " were heard on all sides. At last, they were absolutely compelled to leave the city. William and Ellen no longer felt safe, and therefore went to England, where the remainder of their life was spent in peace.[1]

§ 70. **Underground Railroad.**—From the preceding sketch of the conditions of escape, it is plain that no such numbers as are known to have fled could possibly have escaped from their masters' power had they depended solely upon their own exertions. From the beginning of the antislavery agitation, about 1830, and especially near 1850, a mysterious organization made it a business to receive, forward, conceal, and protect fugitives. To that organization the name of " Underground Railroad " was given, and the many methods used by those connected with it can best be given under a more elaborate description of the system.

§ 71. **Rise and growth of the system.**—The first efforts toward any systematic organization for the aid and protection of fugitive slaves are found among the Quakers in Pennsylvania. The great number of cases of kidnapping which occurred in this State after the passage of the law of 1793, by their injustice roused people to action in behalf of the free blacks; and, their sympathies once enlisted for the colored race, it was but a step to the aid of the fugitive negroes.[2] From this time, as the number of runaways increased, new agencies were constantly being established, until from the slave States to Canada a perfect chain of stations was arranged, not more than one day's journey apart.[3] The system is

[1] Appendix D, No. 41.
[2] Smedley, The Underground Railroad, 26.
[3] Lalor's Cyclopædia, I. 5; Williams, History of the Negro Race in America, II. 58, 59.

said to have extended from Kentucky and Virginia across Ohio, and from Maryland, through Pennsylvania and New York, to New England and Canada.[1]

As negroes began to disappear, and their masters found themselves unable to trace them farther than certain towns in Pennsylvania, they said, in bewilderment, "There must be an Underground Railroad somewhere," and this expression, suiting the popular fancy, became the general name by which the whole system was known.[2]

§ 72. **Methods pursued.**— Although often varied by circumstances, the general method of work was always the same. In the South, money was usually the motive, and for its sake the managers of the Railroad could usually get some one to aid a slave in escaping and crossing the line. In the North it was an unselfish, and sometimes dangerous, work of charity.

Fugitives arrived at the first station, ignorant, half-clothed, and hungry. There they were fed, and, in order to elude the advertisements sent through the States, disguises were provided. For women, the large veiled bonnet and plain attire of the Quakeress proved one of the best costumes. The men received a slip of paper, with a word or two which would be recognized at the next place, and, unless special caution was needed, were sent forward on foot. Women and children were often taken in close carriages, sometimes constructed for this special purpose.[3]

Stations, that is, the houses of persons known to be interested, were reached between sunset and ten o'clock in the evening. A tap at the door would rouse some member of the family, and the fugitive would be taken to the barn, or some place of concealment.[4] Often, too, these houses were not merely places for a night's tarrying, but homes where the ill and fatigued might remain and be cared for until strong enough for the onward journey.[5]

To conduct people over this long line, and to baffle all pursuers, required quick wit, as well as great courage and greatness.[6] So successful were the conductors in this respect that a discouraged slave hunter, after a fruitless search, said "as easy to find a needle in a haymow as a Quakers."[7]

[1] Clarke, Antislavery Days, 81.
[2] Smedley, The Underground Railroad, 35.
[3] ...cedom, 6.
[4] Ibid., 568-570. [5] Ibid., 172. [6] Ibid., 355.
[7] Ibid., 146.

When fugitives were concealed, and persons desiring to search the house appeared, it was the custom to receive the searchers courteously. One of the family immediately engaged them in conversation, and offered them refreshments. The hunt was thus delayed as long as possible, so that the fugitive might be helped away. In one case, while the slave's master was thus entertained upon the front piazza, the mistress of the house quietly conveyed the hunted negro out at the back door, and placed him under an inverted hogshead standing by. Then, with the most unconcerned manner, she allowed the man to search until he was satisfied that there could be no fugitive in that house.[1]

§ 73. **Colored agents of the Underground Railroad.** — An example of the most courageous and successful action may be found in the life of Harriet Tubman,[2] who when a young girl made her escape from slavery alone and unassisted. After several years of work in the North, she determined to go back for her family. This trip was safely accomplished, and followed by others, until during her life she had made nineteen journeys, never losing a person. The Rev. James Freeman Clarke gives the following account of her methods : —

"She said she first obtained enough money, then went to Maryland, where she privately collected a party of slaves and got them ready to start. She satisfied herself that they had enough courage and firmness to run the risks. For if once a negro entered her party, there was no falling back. Fully determined herself, she would allow no one to return.

"She next made arrangements so that they should set out Saturday night, as there would be no opportunity on Sunday for advertising them, so that they had that day's start on their way north. Then she had places prepared where she could be sure the ; they could be protected and taken care of, if she had the action to pay for that protection. When she was at the North, enlisted to raise funds until she got a certain amount, and then fugitive ne₁ to carry out this plan. She always paid some colored increased, ne; after the person who put up the posters advertising from the slav₍nd pull them down as fast as they were put up."[3]

arranged, not m ᵈ the party were closely pursued, she would take a train southward bound, as no one seeing a

[1] Appendix D, No. 41.
[2] Smedley, The Undergrou ailroad, 58.   [2] Harriet, the Moses of her People.
[3] Lalor's Cyclopædia, I. 5 ;
II. 58, 59.

company of negroes going in this direction would for an instant suppose them to be fugitives. As their leader out of bondage, her people gave her the name of "Moses," and thus she is generally known.

§ 74. **Prosecutions of agents.** — Such acts as those daily performed by the conductors on the Underground Railroad could not be carried on under the existing laws without leading to prosecutions. Large rewards were many times offered for Harriet's capture, but she eluded all efforts to stop her work. At one time the Maryland legislature offered a reward to any person who should secure Thomas Garrett in any public jail in the State. He was a Delaware Quaker, who, it is said, helped twenty-nine hundred slaves in escaping. The Governor was required to employ the best legal skill to prosecute him on the charge of aiding runaways.[1] He was afterward tried and fined a sum which consumed his entire property. As this was paid, the officer who received it said that he hoped the remembrance of this punishment would prevent any further trouble. Mr. Garrett, undaunted, replied that they had taken all that he possessed, but added, "If thee knows any poor fugitive who wants a breakfast, send him to me."[2] In fact, he seemed absolutely fearless. Angry slaveholders often called upon him, and demanded their property. He never denied knowledge of their slaves, or of having helped them on their way, but, in the most quiet manner, positively refused to give information concerning them.[3]

§ 75. **Formal organization.** — In 1838 the first formal organization of the Underground Railroad was made, with Robert Purvis as President. It was said that two marketwomen in Baltimore were their best helpers. They had come into possession of a number of passports, or "freedoms," which were used by slaves for part of the distance, and then were returned to serve the same purpose again.[4]

In all transactions connected with this organization the greatest secrecy was necessarily observed, seldom more than two or three persons at a station being allowed any knowledge of it. In the Liberator of 1843, a notice is found cautioning people against exposing in any way the methods used by fugitives in escaping, as

[1] Liberator, March 2, 1860.
[2] Pamphlet proposing a Defensive League of Freedom, 6.
[3] Smedley, Underground Railroad, 241.   [4] Ibid., 355.

it only helped the pursuers in the next case. The fugitives themselves were usually careful in this respect. Frederick Douglass absolutely refused until after the abolition of slavery to reveal the method of his escape.[1]

Mrs. G. S. Hillard, of Boston, was in the habit of putting fugitives in an upper room of her house. A colored man was placed there, and when Mrs. Hillard went up to see him, she found he had carefully pulled down all the shades at the windows. She told him that there was no danger of his being seen from the street. "Perhaps not, Missis," he replied, "but I do not want to spoil the place." He was afraid lest some one might see a colored face there, and so excite suspicions injurious to the next man.[2]

§ 76. **General effect of escapes.** — Although many fugitives were aided previous to 1850, it was after the new law went into effect that the great efforts of the Abolitionists were centred on this form of assistance. Of such importance did it become, that at the beginning of the Civil War one of the chief complaints of the Southern States was the injury received through the aid given their escaping slaves by the North.[3]

It was, however, really the "safety valve to the institution of slavery. As soon as leaders arose among the slaves who refused to endure the yoke, they would go North. Had they remained, there must have been enacted at the South the direful scenes of San Domingo."[4]

[1] Douglass, My Bondage and Freedom, 323.
[2] J. F. Clarke, Antislavery Days, 83.
[3] Lalor's Cyclopædia, I. 5; Congressional Globe, 36 Cong. 1 Sess., Appendix, 250.
[4] Williams, History of the Negro Race in America, II. 58, 59.

CHAPTER V.

PERSONAL LIBERTY LAWS.

§ 77. Character of the personal liberty laws.
§ 78. Acts passed before the Prigg decision (1793-1842).
§ 79. Acts passed between the Prigg decision and the second Fugitive Slave Law (1842-1850).
§ 80. Acts occasioned by the law of 1850 (1850-1860).
§ 81. Massachusetts acts.
§ 82. Review of the acts by States.
§ 83. Effect of the personal liberty laws.

§ 77. **Character of the personal liberty laws.** — The personal liberty laws were statutes passed in the Northern States whose object was to defeat in some measure the national Fugitive Slave Law. Often their ostensible purpose was to protect the free negroes from kidnappers, and to this end they secured for the alleged fugitive the privilege of the writ of habeas corpus, and the trial by jury. Sometimes, however, they frankly avowed their aim as a deliberate attempt to interfere with the execution of the United States statutes. In the following examination of these laws, they will be considered first chronologically, and afterward more minutely according to their subject matter. In previous chapters we have noticed many instances wherein fugitives have been befriended by individuals, or by organizations like the Antislavery Societies or the Underground Railroad. But the action of the State governments in the personal liberty bills, from the time the Fugitive Slave Act of 1793 began to be executed to the outbreak of the Civil War, showed that the dissatisfaction of the North was fundamental, and was not confined merely to the few in the van of the Antislavery movement.

§ 78. **Acts passed before the Prigg decision (1793-1842).** — Although the so-called personal liberty laws were not passed until about 1840, Indiana[1] and Connecticut[2] had before that time provided that on appeal fugitives might have a trial by jury. The Connecticut law, in contrast to the hostile spirit of later legislation, was

[1] Revised Laws of Indiana, 1824, p. 221.   [2] Laws of Connecticut, 1838, p. 32.

entitled, "An Act for the fulfilment of the obligation of this State imposed by the Constitution of the United States in regard to persons held to service or labor in one State escaping into another, and to secure the right of trial by jury in the cases herein mentioned." Notwithstanding this preamble, the law provided for fining State officials who might take part in fugitive slave cases.

The first definite personal liberty laws were passed by Vermont[1] and New York,[2] in 1840, and were entitled Acts "to extend the right of trial by jury." They not only insured jury trial, but also provided attorneys to defend fugitives. This was the only law of the kind New York ever passed, and proved of little value, since it soon fell into disuse, and was almost forgotten.

§ 79. **Acts passed between the Prigg decision and the second Fugitive Slave Law (1842–1850).** — After the Prigg decision in 1842, wherein it was declared that the law must be executed through national powers only, and that State authorities could not be forced into action,[3] a new class of statutes sprang up. The State legislatures seized the opportunity afforded them by Judge Story's opinion, to forbid State officers from performing the duties required of them by the law of 1793, and prohibited the use of State jails in fugitive slave cases. Such laws were passed in Massachusetts,[4] Vermont,[5] Pennsylvania,[6] and Rhode Island.[7] In 1844, Connecticut repealed her act of 1838, as being then unconstitutional, but retained the portion forbidding State officers to participate in the execution of the law.

§ 80. **Acts occasioned by the law of 1850 (1850–1860).** — The provisions of the law of 1850 roused yet more opposition in the North, and before 1856 many of the States had passed personal liberty bills. The new national law avoided the employment of State officers. This change in the statute brought about a corresponding alteration in the State legislation, and we therefore find the acts of this period differing somewhat from those of earlier years. They almost invariably prohibited the use of State jails, they often forbade State judges and officers to issue writs or to give assistance to the claimant, and punished severely the seizure of a free person with the intent to reduce him to slavery.

[1] Acts and Resolves of Vermont, 1840, p. 13.
[2] Laws of New York, 1840, p. 174.
[3] See *ante*, § 27.
[4] Laws of Massachusetts, 1843, p. 33.
[5] Acts and Resolves of Vermont, 1843, p. 11.
[6] Laws of Pennsylvania, 1847, p. 206.
[7] Acts and Resolves of Rhode Island, 1848, p. 12.

Should an alleged fugitive be arrested, the personal liberty acts were intended to secure him a trial surrounded by the usual legal safeguards. The identity of the person claimed was to be proved by two witnesses; or they gave him the right to a writ of habeas corpus; or they enjoined upon the court to which the writ was returnable a trial by jury. At the trial the prisoner must be defended by an attorney, frequently the State or county attorney, and a penalty was provided for false testimony. Any violation of these clauses by State officers was punished by penalties varying from five hundred dollars and six months in jail, as in Pennsylvania, to the maximum punishment in Vermont, of two thousand dollars' fine and ten years in prison.

Such acts were passed in Vermont,[1] Connecticut,[2] and Rhode Island,[3] in Massachusetts,[4] Michigan,[5] and Maine.[6] Later, laws were also enacted in Wisconsin,[7] Kansas,[7] Ohio,[8] and Pennsylvania.[7] Of the other Northern States, two only, New Jersey and California, gave any official sanction to the rendition of fugitives. In New Hampshire, New York, Indiana, Illinois, Iowa, and Minnesota, however, no full personal liberty laws were passed.[9]

§ 81. **Massachusetts acts.** — Let us now examine the purport of these acts in the various States. The general tenor and effect are best seen in Massachusetts, which may be selected as a typical

---

[1] Laws of Vermont, 1850, p. 9.
[2] Public Acts of Connecticut, 1854, p. 80.
[3] Laws of Rhode Island, 1854, p. 22.
[4] Laws of Massachusetts, 1855, p. 924; 1858, p. 151.
[5] Laws of Michigan, 1855, p. 415.
[6] Laws of Maine, 1857, p. 38.   [7] Lalor, III. 162.
[8] Laws of Ohio, 1857, p. 170; 1858, p. 10.
[9] The following tabulation shows the provisions of the personal liberty laws as distributed among the States: —

Judges and justices forbidden to take cognizance. Massachusetts, 1843, Vermont, 1843; Connecticut, 1838; Rhode Island, 1854; Maine, 1855; Pennsylvania, 1847.

Writ of habeas corpus. Massachusetts, 1855; Michigan, 1855; Maine, 1857, Connecticut, 1838 and 1844.

Jury trial. Indiana, 1824; New York, 1840; Vermont, 1840, 1850, and 1858; Connecticut, 1838; Michigan, 1855; Massachusetts, 1855.

Use of jails forbidden. Massachusetts, 1843 and 1855; Vermont, 1843 and 1858; Pennsylvania, 1847; Rhode Island, 1848; Maine, 1855; Michigan, 1855; Ohio, 1857.

Attorneys employed to defend fugitives. New York, 1840; Vermont, 1840, Massachusetts, 1855; Maine, 1857.

False testimony punished. Connecticut, 1838 and 1844; Michigan, 1855.

Admission of national officers. Connecticut, 1838 and 1844, Vermont, 1844; Maine, 1855; New Hampshire, 1857.

State. In 1837, Massachusetts passed a law "to restore the trial by jury, on questions of personal freedom." This secured to the prisoner a writ of personal replevin, which was to be issued from and returnable to the Court of Common Pleas for the county in which the plaintiff was confined, and was to be issued fourteen days at least before the return day. If the prisoner were secreted, the court might send out a capias to take the body of the defendant. This act allowed an appeal to the Supreme Judicial Court.

In 1842, the Latimer case [1] occurred. This so aroused public sentiment that a great petition, signed by sixty-five thousand people, was sent to the legislature, asking for a new personal liberty law. On the basis of the Prigg decision, a law was enacted which forbade State magistrates to issue certificates or take cognizance of the law of 1793, and withheld the use of State jails for the imprisonment of fugitives.[2]

In 1851, in the Shadrach case,[3] there was opportunity for testing the value of this law. The fugitive was not indeed confined in any jail, but there was little difficulty in providing a place of detention, and the court-house was secured. In this year, acting upon a clause in the Governor's message, which treated of the new Fugitive Slave Law of 1850, a committee in the legislature made a report, accompanied by resolutions and a bill further to protect personal liberty; but no law was passed, and there the matter rested until 1855.[4]

After the Sims[5] and Burns[6] cases, in which the court-houses were again used in the place of jails, the heat of public indignation led to petitions to the legislature asking for a more stringent personal liberty law. A joint committee prepared a bill, which was passed, but was vetoed by Governor Gardner, who had been advised by the Attorney General that some of the clauses were unconstitutional. But so strong was the influence in its favor that it was passed over the veto by a two-thirds vote.[7] The feeling that it was probably unconstitutional, however, must have strengthened in the next three years: for in 1858[8] we find another

[1] See *ante*, § 44.
[2] Laws of Massachusetts, 1843, p. 33.
[3] See *ante*, § 57.
[4] Parker, Personal Liberty Laws, 27.
[5] See *ante*, § 54.
[6] See *ante*, § 55.
[7] Parker, Personal Liberty Laws, 27; Laws of Massachusetts, 1855, p. 924; Appendix D, No. 60, case of William Johnson.
[8] Laws of Massachusetts, 1858, p. 151.

act which amended the act of 1855. This limited some provisions, and repealed the following sections: the tenth, which required that any person who should give a certificate that a person claimed as a fugitive was a slave should forfeit any State office he might hold; the eleventh, which forbade any person acting as attorney for a claimant to appear as counsel or attorney in the State courts; the twelfth, which made a violation of the preceding section sufficient ground for the impeachment of any officer of the Commonwealth; the thirteenth, which forbade any United States officer empowered to give certificate or issue warrants from holding a State office; and the fourteenth, which made liable to removal any person holding a State judicial office who should also hold the office of Commissioner.

§ 82. **Review of the acts by States.** — Of the other New England States, Maine had no personal liberty law until 1855.[1] Two years after, however, in 1857,[2] a portion of an act declaring free all slaves brought by their masters into that State was devoted to a provision "to punish any attempt to exercise authority over them."

In New Hampshire, one of the laws of 1857[3] enacted that every person holding any person as a slave for any length of time, under any pretence, should be deemed guilty of felony; but provided that this should not apply to United States officers executing any legal process.

Vermont, by an act in 1840,[4] extended to fugitives the right of trial by jury, but after three years this was repealed,[5] only to be renewed in 1850.[6]

Connecticut, as has been noticed, had no personal liberty law. Rhode Island first passed such an act in 1848.[7] This forbade State officers to take cognizance of fugitive slave cases, and the use of State jails. Another statute, in 1854,[8] extended these provisions so as to apply to the national law of 1850.

The act of 1840 was the only Personal Liberty Law of New York.[9] Pennsylvania, some seven years later, forbade the use of jails, and punished State officers for participating in fugitive slave

---

[1] Acts and Resolves of Maine, 1855, p. 207.
[2] Ibid., 1857, p. 38.
[3] Acts and Resolves of New Hampshire, 1857, p. 1876.
[4] Acts and Resolves of Vermont, 1840, p. 13.
[5] Laws of Vermont, 1843, p. 11.
[6] Ibid., 1850, p. 9.
[7] Acts and Resolves of Rhode Island, 1848, p. 12.
[8] Laws of Rhode Island, 1854, p. 22.
[9] Laws of New York, 1840, p. 174.

cases.[1] It also enacted a regulation of the same character as late as 1860.

Ohio made but one provision on the subject, and that lasted but a year. Her jails were closed to suspected slaves in 1857,[2] but in 1858 this law was repealed.[3]

Michigan passed such an act in 1855,[4] with the usual clauses on the use of jails and jury trial, and imposed a fine on false testimony against the defendant.

In 1858 Wisconsin and Kansas also passed similar acts.[5]

§ 83. **Effect of the personal liberty laws.** — Since the avowed purpose of these laws was to obstruct the execution of one of the United States statutes, national and State legislation were thus brought into direct conflict; but the Fugitive Slave Law was held constitutional by the Supreme Court, and any attempt to prevent its enforcement by positive means, however righteous from an ethical standpoint, must be considered an infraction of the Constitution, and of the common understanding between the States, on which the Union was founded.[6] The provisions denying the use of State institutions and officers, though distinctly unfriendly, were not unconstitutional. Many of the Abolitionists, however, held the national law to be unconstitutional, and at the same time morally so repugnant that it ought never to be executed.[7] The State laws were brought up by South Carolina, in her declaration of the causes of secession, as one of the chief grievances against the North; and President Buchanan, in his Message of 1860,[8] said they were "the most palpable violations of constitutional duty which had yet been committed." They must certainly be classed in principle with the Nullification Ordinance of 1832. Indeed, the legislature of Wisconsin, after the Supreme Court had overridden the decision of the State courts in the case of Ableman *v.* Booth that the national law was contrary to the national Constitution, passed some resolutions in which a "positive defiance is urged as the 'rightful remedy'" against such legislation.[9]

[1] Laws of Pennsylvania, 1847, p. 206.   [2] Laws of Ohio, 1857, p. 170.
[3] Laws of Ohio, 1858, p. 10.   [4] Laws of Michigan, 1855, p. 415.
[5] Lalor, III. 162.
[6] Hurd, Law of Freedom and Bondage, II. 763; Von Holst, IV. 551; Parker, Personal Liberty Laws.
[7] Phillips, No Slave Hunting in the Old Bay State; Phillips, Argument against repeal of Personal Liberty Law; Pierce, Personal Liberty Law, 4; Johnson, Speech on Personal Liberty Law, New York, 1861.
[8] 36 Cong. 2 Sess., Congressional Globe, Appendix, 2.   [9] Lalor, III. 162.

CHAPTER VI.

THE END OF THE FUGITIVE SLAVE QUESTION (1860-1865).

§ 85. The Fugitive Slave Law in the crisis of 1860-61.
§ 86. Propositions to enforce the Fugitive Slave Law.
§ 87. Propositions to repeal or amend the law.
§ 88. The question of slaves of rebels.
  § 89. Slavery attacked in Congress.
  § 90. Confiscation bills.
  § 91. Confiscation provisions extended.
  § 92. Effect of the Emancipation Proclamation (1863).
§ 93. Fugitives in loyal slave States.
  § 94. Typical cases.
  § 95. Question discussed in Congress.
  § 96. Arrests by civil officers.
§ 97. Denial of the use of jails in the District of Columbia.
  § 98. Abolition of slavery in the District of Columbia.
  § 99. Regulations against kidnapping.
§ 100. Repeal of the Fugitive Slave Acts.
  § 101. Early propositions to repeal the acts.
  § 102. Discussion of the repeal bill in the House.
  § 103. Repeal bills in the Senate.
  § 104. The repeal act and the thirteenth amendment.
§ 105. Educating effect of the controversy.

§ 85. **The Fugitive Slave Law in the crisis of 1860-61.**— If the number of interesting fugitive slave cases falls off in the latter part of the decade from 1850 to 1860, it is not because the law was better enforced, but because it was little enforced. The continued interference of the friends of the slave had proved that a fugitive could not safely be recovered in Massachusetts, and that no punishment could be secured for those who helped him to his freedom. The personal liberty bills added serious·legal obstacles. The Supreme Court of Wisconsin even went so far as to declare the national act of 1850 unconstitutional.[1] In 1859 John Brown, in his Harper's Ferry raid, attempted to establish a centre to which

[1] Ableman v. Booth, 3 Wis., 1.

fugitives might flock; and although he was defeated, he had the sympathy of a large number of persons in the North, including some public men.

In the violent debates of 1860-61, one of the frequent charges brought by the southern members against the North was its persistent refusal to execute the Fugitive Slave Act, or to permit it to be executed.[1] Even Republican members disclaimed responsibility for their party, and urged that the personal liberty bills should be repealed.[2] Other bolder spirits seized the opportunity to urge a repeal of the act, and in the various compromise propositions introduced were several attempts to modify the existing constitutional provision on the subject.

§ 86. **Propositions to enforce the Fugitive Slave Law.** — In the crisis of 1860 the South seemed to expect a general settlement of the slavery question like that of 1850, and therefore demanded a more effective act for the return of fugitives. President Buchanan, in his message of December 4, 1860, recommended "explanatory" constitutional amendments which should recognize the master's right to the recovery of his fugitive slaves, and the validity of the Fugitive Slave Law. He recommended also a declaration against State laws impairing the right of the master, as being violations of the Constitution, and consequently null and void.[3] This recommendation was followed, December 12, 1860, by no less than eleven resolutions upon the subject in the House.[4] Of these five were constitutional amendments. Several provided, as a pacific measure, that the town, county, or State, guilty of neglect to return a fugitive, might be sued by the owner of the slave for the amount thus lost to him.[5] The most arbitrary proposition was that of Mr. Hindman. It denied representation in Congress to any State which should hold in force laws hindering the delivery of fugitives.[6]

Another resolution inquired into the expediency of declaring it

[1] Globe, 1860-61, p. 356, App. 197.
[2] Globe, 1860-61, (Baker) 228, (Burnham) 970.
[3] Senate Journal, 36 Cong. 2 Sess., p. 18. Appendix C, No. 1.
[4] House Journal, 36 Cong. 2 Sess., p. 60; Congr. Globe, 36 Cong. 2 Sess., 77. Appendix C, Nos. 2-12. For a list of proposed constitutional amendments bearing on fugitive slaves, I am indebted to Mr. H. V. Ames, of the Harvard Graduate School, who has kindly furnished me transcripts from his material for a forthcoming monograph on proposed amendments to the Constitution.
[5] Cong. Globe, 3 Cong. 2 Sess., 114. Appendix C, Nos. 2-12.
[6] House Journal, 36 Cong. 2 Sess., 70; Cong. Globe, 36 Cong. 2 Sess., 79. Appendix C, No. 10.

felony to resist an officer of the United States in the execution of the law, or to attempt to rescue a runaway.[1]

§ 87. **Propositions to repeal or amend the law.** — On the other hand, antislavery members insisted that the provision for the return of fugitives was already too severe; but only one of the resolutions proposed any amendment in favor of the slave. Mr. Kilgore proposed to give a trial by jury before a fugitive should be returned.[2]

As early as 1860 Mr. Blake had introduced into the House a bill to repeal the law of 1850. It was read twice, and referred to the Committee on the Judiciary, from whom it was never reported.[3] At that time Congress, in alarm at the state of the country, was vainly striving to mend matters by making the Fugitive Slave Law even more effective. March 1, 1861, the select committee of thirty-three brought in a bill for the amendment of the law of 1850; it allowed an appeal to the Circuit Court of the United States where jury trial was to be given. The bill passed the House the same day; but in the Senate it never got beyond the first reading.[4]

§ 88. **The question of slaves of rebels.** — With the beginning of the Civil War in 1861 the last period in the study of fugitive slaves opens, to close only with the repeal of the Fugitive Slave Law and the abolition of slavery.

New conditions now surrounded the slaves. Their masters were away in the army; many homes were broken up, and confusion reigned instead of law; the strict discipline and oversight necessary for the maintenance of the slave system was impossible. Opportunities for escape occurred everywhere and at all times. Since war had brought the Northern people down into their own land, the slave no longer needed to travel hundreds of miles to find friends; the Northern camps were perhaps but a few miles from his own plantation. In this way negroes began to gather around the Federal camps in such numbers that the question of disposing of them became serious. If the Fugitive Slave Law of 1850 were considered as still binding, their apprehension and return were necessary; but many of the masters were in arms against the government; should they still be protected in their property? The

---

[1] House Journal, 36 Cong. 2 Sess., 67; Cong. Globe, 36 Cong. 2 Sess., 77. Appendix C, No. 3.

[2] House Journal, 36 Cong. 2 Sess., 70; Cong. Globe, 36 Cong. 2 Sess., 78. Appendix C, No. 11.

[3] Cong. Globe, 36 Cong. 2 Sess., 1328.   [4] Appendix C, No. 25.

belligerent position of the South seemed to preclude any right on the part of disloyal owners to ask for the benefit of the law.

To meet the changed conditions no policy had as yet been developed by the government. The first solution of the problem was made at Fortress Monroe by General Butler. He drew an analogy from international law, which makes material of war imported into the country of a belligerent lawful prize to the army or navy of the other belligerent. Regarded as property, the slaves of rebels could be of great service to them, and of equal help to the government in suppressing rebellion. Regarded as persons, they had escaped from communities where rebellion was in progress, and they asked protection from the government to which they were still loyal. In May, 1861, General Butler therefore replied to all demands for fugitives that he should retain them as "contraband of war." The answer was widely spread, and "contraband" became the name by which such negroes were known.[1]

§ 89. **Slavery attacked in Congress.** — A series of attacks upon slavery now began in Congress. To many persons the fact that the institution was recognized in the Constitution seemed sufficient ground for protecting it. No doubt was entertained of the power of Congress to confiscate the ordinary property of rebels; but such persons deprecated all interference with slaves, who were supposed to possess a kind of constitutional immunity, wholly unknown to and above all other property.[2] In the minds of antislavery men, "no greater fallacy was ever asserted than this attempt thus to link 'the institution' and the Constitution indissolubly together, to engraft the former upon the latter, to make slavery the corner stone of the nation, to be guarded and protected by the government."[3] Nevertheless, the existence of slavery in the Border States which had remained loyal made Congress very cautious as to general enactments. On the other hand, no form of property held by rebels was so vulnerable; slaves could not only be seized as the lines of the Northern troops extended, they could, by actual law or by kindly reception, be invited across the lines. Both the passions aroused by civil war and a humane pity for the slave urged the government to deprive the master engaged in secession of the services of his slave.

[1] Liberator, Nov. 1, 1861; Edw. L. Pierce, in Atlantic Monthly, November, 1861.
[2] Cong. Globe, 36 Cong. 2 Sess., 1076.
[3] Cong. Globe, 36 Cong. 2 Sess., 1077.

§ 90. **Confiscation bills.** — July 18, 1861, Mr. Chandler and Mr. Trumbull introduced general confiscation bills in the Senate; they were both referred to the Committee on the Judiciary. In the discussion Mr. Trumbull offered as an amendment " that whenever any person claiming to be entitled to the service or labor of any other person, under the laws of any State, shall employ such person in aiding or promoting any insurrection, or in resisting the laws of the United States, or shall permit or suffer him to be so employed, he shall forfeit all right to such service or labor, and the person whose service or labor is thus claimed shall be thenceforth discharged therefrom, any law to the contrary notwithstanding."[1]

The proposition aroused considerable opposition, since it was a step far in advance of anything which had yet been done against the interests of slavery, and any proposition which advocated "an act of emancipation," however limited and qualified, was the signal for hot discussion. The opposing party announced that "nothing will come of it but more irritation,"[2] and in each crisis statesmen should "observe all possible toleration, all conciliation, all liberality."[3] Mr. Wilson upheld the opposite opinion, and thought that the time had come when this government, and the men who are in arms under the government, should cease to return their fugitive slaves to traitors.

The bill passed the Senate July 22, 1861. In the House it was amended so as to limit the negroes to be freed more strictly to those employed in military service.[4] The bill went back to the Senate, which concurred in the amendment,[5] and it received the signature of the President, August 6, 1861.[6]

§ 91. **Confiscation provisions extended.** — Propositions more far reaching were introduced into the Senate in the session of 1861-62.[7] January 15, 1862, Mr. Trumbull, from the Committee on the Judiciary, to whom the various propositions had been referred, reported an original bill, and asked that the committee be discharged from the consideration of others.[8] March 14, 1862, Mr.

---

[1] Cong. Globe, 37 Cong. 1 Sess., 218. Appendix C, Nos. 30, 31.
[2] Cong. Globe, 37 Cong. 1 Sess., 219.
[3] Cong. Globe, 37 Cong. 1 Sess., 412.
[4] House Journal, 37 Cong. 1 Sess., 197; Cong. Globe, 409, 410. Appendix C, No. 31.
[5] Senate Journal, 37 Cong. 1 Sess., 178; Cong. Globe, 434. Appendix C, No. 31.
[6] Cong. Globe, 37 Cong. 1 Sess., 454. Appendix C, No. 31.
[7] Appendix C, Nos. 37, 40, 44.   [8] Appendix C, No. 52.

Harris introduced into the Senate a bill to confiscate the property of rebels and for other purposes.[1] These propositions were considered at length, but never came to a vote. It is not necessary to enter here into the discussion of confiscations and of the constitutional right of Congress to free the slaves; in most of the bills there was a provision against the return of slaves to disloyal masters.

The Harris bill declared that, before any order for the surrender of fugitives should be given, the claimant must establish not only his title to the slave, as was then provided by law, but also that he is and has been loyal to the United States during the Rebellion. Mr. Pomeroy objected to this because it would make it "obligatory on the government of the United States to surrender a person claimed to be indebted to another for service or labor, if the claimant proves that he is loyal to the government. Would not this re-enact the Fugitive Slave Law of 1850?"[2] An amendment was therefore adopted which so changed the law that any reference to the act of 1850 was avoided.[3] After several debates the proposition was recommitted, May 6.[4] Mr. Clark reported a bill, May 14, which retained the provision in regard to fugitives as at first offered.[5]

In the House, resolutions on confiscation and emancipation were offered on the first day of the session, but the final action was based upon one of several bills introduced by Mr. Eliot, May 14, 1862.[6] His first bill, upon the confiscation of the property of the rebels, need not be followed out here; but the second bill provided for the emancipation of the slaves of disloyal masters, and forbade their return as fugitives. After various recommitments[7] a bill was brought in, according to which, in any suit brought by a claimant to recover the possession of slaves to enforce such service or labor, it was to be a sufficient bar to allege and prove that the master was disloyal to the government.[8] The bill then passed the House by a vote of 82 to 54.[8]

---

[1] Appendix C, No. 59. Referred to the Committee on the Judiciary, and reported by them, April 16, 1862. Appendix C, No. 67.
[2] Cong. Globe, 37 Cong. 2 Sess., 944.
[3] Cong. Globe, 37 Cong. 2 Sess., 946.
[4] Appendix C, No. 71.   [5] Appendix C, No. 72.
[6] Appendix C, No. 73. Previous bills introduced by Mr. Eliot had been unfavorably reported on by the Judiciary Committee. Appendix C, No. 69.
[7] Appendix C, No. 75.   [8] Appendix C, No. 78.

When it came up in the Senate, June 23, 1862, Mr. Clark moved to strike out all after the enacting clause, and to insert a substitute which would again unite the confiscation and emancipation bills. This amendment was rejected by the House, and a conference committee was appointed which reported July 11 and 12. The fugitive from a disloyal master was by this compromise to be deemed a captive of war, and forever freed from servitude.[1] The report was adopted by both houses, and approved by the President, July 17, 1862.[1] From that date any slave of a disloyal master who could make his way into the territory occupied by the Northern troops was *ipso facto* free. The fugitive was to become a freeman.

§ 92. **Effect of the Emancipation Proclamation (1863).** — The complete emancipation of the negroes within the Confederate lines was the next logical step, and was demanded as a war measure. It deprived the Confederacy of the aid of these slaves, and at the same time made it possible to arm and employ the former slaves against their masters. September 22, 1862, President Lincoln issued his preliminary proclamation, by which he warned the South that, unless it should return to its allegiance, all persons held as slaves in the States in rebellion on the 1st of January, 1863, should be "thenceforth and forever free."

At the end of one hundred days the final and absolute Proclamation was put forth, January 1, 1863. It declared also that negroes might be received into the armed service of the United States ; and henceforth throughout the war, the former slaves were enrolled as soldiers and did good service for the government.

The effect of this proclamation was to end slavery, and with it the return of fugitives, within the Confederate lines. But here the legal machinery of the government had no effect; the State laws relating to slavery might be considered suspended, but practically the laws and practices of the Confederacy prevailed. On the other hand, the Fugitive Slave Law yet existed upon the statute-book where the Union had power; the arrest and imprisonment of fugitives was yet legal, and many desired to see the law repealed as another step toward the final crushing out of the system.

§ 93. **Fugitives in loyal slave States.** — From the beginning of the war one of the most embarrassing questions which had come before Congress was, How shall the slaves of loyal owners be treated? The necessity of holding the Border States firm for the Union disposed

[1] Appendix C, No. 79.

many to support only the most conciliatory measures; but these States were a part of the theatre of war. Northern armies now occupied parts of the Confederacy as well, and among the great numbers of blacks who flocked to the Union camp it was impossible to separate the slaves of the loyal from the disloyal. Moreover, it was necessary that there should be some uniformity of method. Without specific law, the reception given to fugitives from loyal masters must vary with the views of each commanding officer with whom they sought refuge.

§ 94. **Typical cases.** — Cases began to occur very early in the struggle. In 1861 a slave called Wisdom ran away from Georgetown, and was taken in by some wagoners belonging to the Northern army. He soon found work, but his master succeeded in tracing him, and came to camp to claim him. He demanded the slave of Captain Swan, officer of the day. Captain Swan hoped the man might be smuggled away, and so delayed the search as long as possible. The master then went to Colonel Cowden, who immediately ordered the slave to be surrendered, without the form of proceedings prescribed by the act of 1850, and in disregard of the fact that the master was not provided with the necessary certificate. When the facts became known in Massachusetts and elsewhere, there was great indignation. The Colonel was hung in effigy in Boston, with the following inscription: "Colonel Cowden, of Burns rendition notoriety, is now practising his tricks at kidnapping in Washington." [1]

Major Sherwood of the 11th West Virginia Regiment had, in 1861, employed a colored refugee as his servant. The owner sent a United States marshal to Brigadier General Boyle, who gave an order for his rendition. Major Sherwood sent a message that he would give up his sword, but, while he was in command, no fugitive should be returned. He was placed under arrest for disobedience, to await court-martial; but General Staunton ordered General Boyle's order revoked, and Major Sherwood was never tried. In the mean time the boy had been sent away concealed under the seat of an ambulance, and reached Canada in safety.[2]

§ 95. **Question discussed in Congress.** — As early in the war as 1861, a number of resolutions were brought into Congress, designed to meet this difficulty,[3] and Mr. Lovejoy introduced a bill making it a

[1] Liberator, July 19, 1861; Appendix D, No. 68.
[2] Williams, History of Negro Race in America, 245; Appendix D, No. 69.
[3] Appendix C, Nos. 36, 43, 44, 46, 47, 48.

penal offence "for any officer or private of the army or navy to capture or return, or aid in the capture or return" of fugitive slaves.[1] The bill was referred to the Committee on the Judiciary, which reported adversely upon it, April 16, 1862.[2] December 16, 1861, Mr. Hale had offered a resolution, which was adopted, looking toward a uniform method of dealing with the slaves of rebels.[3] Mr. Sumner brought in another on December 17, which forbade the employment of the armies in the surrender of fugitives.[4] "I ask, sir," said the writer of a letter read by Mr. Sumner, " shall our sons, who are offering their lives for the preservation of our institutions, be degraded to slave catchers for any persons loyal or disloyal? If such is the policy of the government, I shall urge my son to shed no more blood for its preservation."[5] Another protest came from two German companies in one of the Massachusetts regiments, who, when they enlisted, entered the service with the understanding that they should not be put to any such discreditable service. They complained, and with them the German population generally throughout the country."[6]

Some proof that the owner of the slave was at least loyal to the government seemed necessary, if rendition were to be made at all; though antislavery men were determined to admit no return of fugitives under any circumstances. December 20, 1861, a resolution of Mr. Wilson's was adopted, for an additional article of war forbidding officers from returning fugitives under any consideration.[7] A bill was introduced, discussed, and somewhat amended, but never passed.[8]

Mr. Blair's bill, of February 25, 1862, from the Committee on Military Affairs in the House, was to the same purpose.[9] This, however, was successfully carried in both houses, and signed by the President, May 14, 1862. In the discussion, Mr. Mallory opposed the bill, because it seemed to him that it would prevent the President of the United States from sending a military force into a State to aid the authorities in enforcing a national law which stands upon the statute-book.[10] Mr. Bingham answered this objection by saying that it simply determined that for the future, as in the past, the

[1] Appendix C, No. 35.
[2] Appendix C, No. 66.
[3] Appendix C, No. 41.
[4] Cong. Globe, 37 Cong. 2 Sess., 110; Appendix C, No. 42.
[5] Cong. Globe, 37 Cong. 1 Sess., 130.
[6] Cong. Globe, 37 Cong. 1 Sess., 130.
[7] Appendix C, No. 47.
[8] Appendix C, No. 48.
[9] Appendix C, No. 58.
[10] Cong. Globe, 37 Cong. 2 Sess., 955.

army and navy should not exercise functions which belong solely to the civil magistrates.¹

§ 96. **Arrests by civil officers.** — The act of May 14, 1862, applied only to army officers. Notwithstanding the opportunities then offered for escape, wandering negroes were still liable to be seized by civil authorities and placed in jail. In this way numbers of negroes, many of them really free, were arrested, on the supposition of being runaways, and were imprisoned without trial for an indefinite length of time. An advertisement in 1863 shows the method then in use.

" There was committed to the jail of Warren County, Kentucky, as a runaway slave, on the 29th September, 1862, a negro man calling himself Jo Miner. He says he is free, but has nothing to show to establish the fact. He is about thirty-five years of age, very dark copper color, about five feet eight inches high, and will weigh about one hundred and fifty pounds. The owner can come forward, prove property, and pay charges, or he will be dealt with as the law requires.

"R. J. POTTER, J. W. C.

" March 16, 1863. 1 m."²

§ 97. **Denial of the use of the jails in the District of Columbia.** — Several efforts were made to remedy this state of things, at least in the territory over which Congress had exclusive control. December 4, 1861, Mr. Wilson, who had been investigating the condition of the District of Columbia jail in Washington, offered a joint resolution for the release of all fugitives from service or labor therein held.³ It appeared that some sixty persons were imprisoned solely because they were suspected of being runaways, and had been allowed no opportunity to prove the contrary. A free boy from Pennsylvania came to Washington with the 5th Pennsylvania Regiment. He was found in the streets and sent to jail. Another boy, who was working for the soldiers on the railroad, was also taken up and placed there.⁴

Mr. Wilson struck at the root of the matter by a resolution, which was agreed to, looking to the revision of all the laws in the District of Columbia providing for the arrest of persons as fugitives from service or labor, and to consider the expediency of abolishing slavery in the District.⁵

---

¹ Cong. Globe, 37 Cong. 2 Sess., 956.
² Liberator, May 1, 1863 Extract from Frankfort Commonwealth.
³ Appendix C, No. 33.
⁴ Cong. Globe, 37 Cong. 2 Sess., 10.   ⁵ Appendix C, No. 33.

On December 9, 1861, Mr. Bingham introduced a resolution for the repeal of all acts in force in the District of Columbia which authorized the commitment of runaways and suspected runaways to the jail; it was referred to the Committee on the Judiciary.[1] Mr. Fessenden asked that the Committee on the District of Columbia investigate and report upon the condition of the jail; this was agreed to.[2]

A few weeks later, December 30, 1861, Mr. Grimes presented a bill in the Senate in regard to the administration of criminal justice in the District. This was read and referred to the committee, which reported it, January 6, 1862.[3] Efforts were immediately made to prevent fugitive slaves from being included in the general jail delivery contemplated by the bill. Mr. Powell, in the debate upon his amendment to that purpose, urged that so long as the institution of slavery existed in the South, no such measure ought to prevail.[4] Mr. Grimes supported his measure by giving some examples of exceedingly unjust cases which had occurred. " A young colored fellow, who came as a servant of an officer from the vicinity of Pittsburg, was thrown into this jail in August last. The regiment to which he was attached went forward toward the face of the enemy. There was nobody here to look after him. There is no doubt as to his being a free boy, yet he was there on the first day of this month." To such cases he desired to have the law apply. " They have here in this District and in Maryland what they call an apprehension fee. They have a law which declares that if any slave wanders a certain distance from the residence of his master, he may be taken up as a fugitive. There are persons in this vicinity, I am credibly informed, who are lying in wait all around your city and the surrounding country, in hope that they can find some poor colored man or woman who is out picking berries and visiting a friend, and who will wander a little further than the distance established by law from the residence of the master."[5] The opinion that such injustice ought to be corrected prevailed, and the amendment was rejected. After much discussion the bill passed the Senate, January 14, 1862,[6] and it was approved by the President on the same day. Thenceforward the Fugitive Slave Law was practically a dead letter at the seat of government, since the necessary

[1] Appendix C, No. 39.
[2] Appendix C, No. 38.
[3] Cong. Globe, 37 Cong. 2 Sess., 182 ; Appendix C, No. 51.
[4] Cong. Globe, 37 Cong. 2 Sess., 313.
[5] Cong. Globe, 37 Cong. 2 Sess., 264.
[6] Appendix C, No 51.

machinery was lacking, and the spirit of the administration was opposed to it. The new act was in effect a national personal liberty bill.

§ 98. **Abolition of slavery in the District of Columbia.** — The work contemplated by all the propositions was finally accomplished in one act. On December 16, 1861, Mr. Wilson had offered a bill in the Senate for the total abolition of slavery in the District of Columbia. It was reported with amendments a few weeks after the passage of the act denying the use of jails, and on February 24, 1862, Mr. Wilson presented a supplementary bill.[1]

The debates upon this proposition were long and interesting. The South regarded it as "an entering wedge of something more comprehensive and radical,"[2] as preparatory to the abolition of slavery in the whole country by Congress. The antislavery party rejoiced that at last an opportunity had come for freeing the national capital from the disgrace of slavery. The bill passed both houses, and was approved April 16, 1862.[3] By the final section of the act the black code of Maryland was wiped out, and the severe local provisions against fugitives, which had not been repealed by the previous act, were at last taken away. It remained only to attack the last stronghold of the system, — the two acts of 1793 and 1850.

§ 99. **Regulations against kidnapping.** In the act of April 16, 1862, were included regulations against kidnapping, — a practice made easy by the unsettled state of the country. It seems to have been largely carried on not only by Southerners, but also by unprincipled soldiers connected with the Union army. The Liberator of March 27, 1863, notices such a case. Some men from the 99th Regiment of New York Volunteers kidnapped a free colored man at Norfolk, Virginia. They took his horse, cart, and the provisions which he had just bought, and offered him for sale to be sent South. During the absence of his captors for a few moments, the man was able to work off his bonds and to escape in the darkness. He immediately went before a provost marshal, told his story, and recognized one of his captors who was just entering the door. What the consequences of this meeting were the "Liberator" does not tell us; but the impression is given that the negro was saved from his pursuers.[4]

---

[1] Appendix C, Nos. 42, 54, 56.
[2] Wilson, Rise and Fall of the Slave Power in America, iii. 273.
[3] Appendix C, Nos. 62, 65.   [4] Appendix D, No. 68.

§ 100. **Repeal of the Fugitive Slave Acts.** — By the successive acts of Congress and the President, the legal effect of the Fugitive Slave Laws was now confined practically to the limited area of the Border States. No officer, civil or military, could return a fugitive into the Confederate lines. Slavery was forbidden in the District of Columbia, and there could be no escapes thence; and Congress forbade the use of the jails of the District for the confinement of fugitives from slaveholding regions. In the free States the rendition of slaves, though still legally required, had long since ceased. The final step was delayed till 1864.

§ 101. **Early propositions to repeal the acts.** — Repeal, however, was preceded by many earlier propositions. The Committee on the Judiciary, to which was referred Mr. Howe's bill, presented December 26, 1861,[1] did not report until 1863, and then with the opinion that it ought not to pass. In introducing his repeal measure, Mr. Howe spoke of the bill of 1850 as one "which has probably done as much mischief as any other one act that was ever passed by the national legislature. It has embittered against each other two great sections of the country."[2] To take away the law of 1850 would leave in force the act of 1793, which was "good enough."

June 9, 1862, soon after the passage of the acts on the District of Columbia, Mr. Julian presented in the House another repeal bill, which was referred to the Committee on the Judiciary.[3] As the war progressed, and the antislavery sentiment began to outweigh all others, it became evident that the old law could not much longer obtain. Nevertheless the question was set aside during the session of 1862–63, but in 1863–64 five bills were introduced looking to the repeal of the acts.[4]

Mr. Morris, from the committee to whom all bills for repeal had been referred, reported a substitute for them, June 6, 1864, and this was the basis of the final action of Congress.[5]

---

[1] Appendix C, No. 49. [2] Cong. Globe, 37 Cong. 1 Sess., 1356.
[3] Appendix C, No. 76.
[4] Three bills were introduced in the House on the same day, December 14, 1863, by Messrs. Stevens, Julian, and Ashley. They were read twice and referred. Appendix C, Nos. 104, 106. Before the final consideration of the subject, on February 8, 1864, two more bills were introduced in Congress, Mr. Sumner's in the Senate, and Mr. Spalding's in the House. The former went to the Committee on the Judiciary, the latter to the Select Committee on Slavery and Freedom. Appendix C, No. 80.
[5] Appendix C, No. 80.

§ 102. **Discussion of the repeal bill in the House.** — Had the country been divided simply into two parts, the slaveholding Southern Confederacy and the free loyal North, little discussion could have arisen. The third element, the slaveholding States which remained firm for the Union, rendered the question far more complex. The bill therefore aroused much indignation. Mr. Mallory demanded, as an act of justice to his State, that "the Fugitive Slave Act be permitted to remain on the statute-book. If you say it will be a dead letter, so much less excuse have you for repealing it, and so much more certainly is the insult and wrong to Kentucky gratuitous. This act, by which you declare your intention *not* to obey the injunction of the Constitution is wanton and useless, except for the purpose of bravely exhibiting your contempt for that instrument." "The framers of the Constitution gave us the right to reclaim fugitive slaves. It was conceded not as a favor, but as a right." "Kentucky has remained true to her faith pledged to the government, and I warn you not to persevere in inflicting on her insult and outrage."[1]

Again, one of the reasons for the departure of the Southern States, was the "bad faith of the Northern States, — the fatal infringement of this part of the Constitution. It was because of Personal Liberty bills, John Brown raids, and general denunciation and intermeddling with slavery."[2] Many members urged that there could be no more reckless action than to show to the Border States an apparent disregard of the Constitution. Mr. Cox considered the law the only refuge left to a certain class of citizens to protect their "rights." It would be like saying to them, We place the penalty of the treason of the revolted slaveholders on your innocent heads. "We add to your calamities the ingratitude and treachery of the government to which you have adhered."[3]

The final discussion, June 13, opened with a long speech by Mr. King. The old arguments from the Constitution, the farseeing wisdom of the fathers, the opinion of the Supreme Court in the Prigg case, and the harm done the Border States, were again rehearsed.[4]

In answer to Mr. King, Mr. Hubbard denied that the Constitution provided for the enactment of a law by Congress, and in any

[1] Cong. Globe, 38 Cong. 1 Sess., 2774, 2775.
[2] Cong. Globe, 38 Cong. 1 Sess., 2914.
[3] Cong. Globe, 38 Cong. 1 Sess., 2914.
[4] Cong. Globe, 38 Cong. 1 Sess., 2911.

case, the treason of slavery had already absolved the people from any such obligation. It surely must be competent for this Congress to repeal any act which a previous Congress had enacted. For yet another reason the law should be repealed. Negro soldiers must be enlisted: "You cannot draft black men into the field, while your marshals are chasing women and children in the woods of Ohio with a view to render them back into bondage. The moral sense of the nation, ay, of the world, would revolt at it."[1] Again, this would make a conflict in our laws, said Mr. Morris. A colored man might enlist in our army, then, under the Fugitive Slave Law, "he might be seized and remanded to slavery; and as a further consequence, dealt with as a deserter from his post of duty."[2] It was also urged that unless slavery was to survive the war, the two acts were useless and obsolete statutes, which ought to be wiped out of existence. No one who believes that slavery is dead would desire to keep such a guaranty of the institution.[3] Mr. Hubbard then demanded the yeas and nays on the passage of the bill. It was declared in the affirmative, yeas 82, nays 57, and thus the repeal was successfully carried in the House.[4]

§ 103. **Repeal bills in the Senate.** — Mr. Sumner had already reported a repeal bill from the Committee on Slavery and Freedom in the Senate, February 29, 1864.[5] The progress of the bill was so delayed by the opposition, that Mr. Sumner at last gave notice that he should take every proper occasion to call up the bill, and press its consideration.[6]

In the debate several speeches were made against the measure, while Mr. Sumner defended it. To the antislavery party the act was constitutionally[7] and morally wrong, so against public sentiment that it could seldom be enforced, and the question of its repeal was as plain as a "diagram," "the multiplication table," or "the ten commandments."[8] They desired to strike slavery wherever they could hit it, and to " purify the statute-book, so that there should be nothing in it out of which this wrong can derive any support." It should be repealed for the sake of our cause in foreign lands.[9] " Since the outbreak of the Rebellion this statute has been

---

[1] Cong. Globe, 38 Cong. 1 Sess., 2913.   [2] Cong. Globe, 38 Cong. 1 Sess., 2919.
[3] Cong. Globe, 38 Cong. 1 Sess., 2917.   [4] Cong. Globe, 38 Cong. 1 Sess., 2920.
[5] Senate Journal, 38 Cong. 1 Sess., 196; Cong. Globe, 38 Cong. 1 Sess., 869; Appendix C, No. 80.
[6] Cong. Globe, 38 Cong. 1 Sess., 1175.   [7] Cong. Globe, 38 Cong. 1 Sess., 1710.
[8] Cong. Globe, 38 Cong. 1 Sess., 1709.   [9] Cong. Globe, 38 Cong. 1 Sess., 1713.

constantly adduced by our enemies abroad as showing that we are little better than Jefferson Davis and his slave-monger crew; for slavery never shows itself worse than in the slave-hunter. It is a burden for our cause which it ought not to be obliged to bear."

To retain the law of 1793, framed by the founders of the Republic, and repeal the act of 1850 with its manifest injustice, was suggested as a desirable compromise. Mr. Sherman, therefore, offered an amendment to this effect, and it was accepted.[1] The friends of the measure then felt that the bill as it stood was of little value to the antislavery cause. Mr. Brown maintained that it was really a proposition to reinstate slavery in its fastness in the Constitution. "The civilized world, when it beholds the spectacle of the American Senate going back for three quarters of a century to resurrect a statute of slave-catching, and pass it anew with their indorsement, will credit very little all your talk about freedom. The act will give the lie to all argument."[2]

Before further action was taken on Mr. Sherman's bill, the repeal bill from the House came before the Senate, and was reported from the committee, June 15, 1864. It was discussed for several days, but no new arguments were offered, and, June 23, 1864, the bill passed the Senate by a vote of 27 to 12.[3] On the 25th of June it received President Lincoln's signature, and the Fugitive Slave Laws were swept from the statute-book of the United States.[4]

§ 104. **The repeal act and the thirteenth amendment.** — The act was a simple one; it runs as follows: —

"Chap. CLXVI. An Act to repeal the Fugitive Slave Act of eighteen hundred and fifty, and all Acts and parts of Acts for the rendition of Fugitive Slaves.

"*Be it enacted by the Senate and House of Representatives of the United States of America in Congress assembled*, That sections three and four of an act entitled ' An act respecting fugitives from justice, and persons escaping from the service of their masters,' passed February twelve, seventeen hundred and ninety-three, and an act entitled ' An act to amend, and supplementary to, the act entitled An act respecting fugitives from justice, and persons escaping from the service of their masters, passed February twelve, seven-

---

[1] Senate Journal, 38 Cong. 1 Sess., 348; Cong. Globe, 38 Cong. 1 Sess., 1710, 1714.
[2] Cong. Globe, 38 Cong. 1 Sess., 1752.
[3] Cong. Globe, 38 Cong. 1 Sess., 3191; Appendix C, No. 83.
[4] Appendix C, No. 116.

teen hundred and ninety-three,' passed September, eighteen hundred and fifty, be and the same are hereby repealed.

"Approved, June 28, 1864."

The whole structure of statutes, decisions, and judicial machinery which had been erected to compel by national authority the people of free States to share in the responsibility for slavery, was at last overthrown. But the constitutional obligation remained; so long as a slave anywhere existed, the neighboring States were bound to pursue him, if he ran away, and might by statute provide for his return. The final step was therefore to complete the work of legal emancipation by the thirteenth amendment to the Constitution. On January 31, 1865, Congress voted to submit the following article to the States for their approval and ratification: " Art. XIII. Neither slavery nor involuntary servitude, except as a punishment for crime, whereof the party shall have been duly convicted, shall exist within the United States or any place subject to their jurisdiction." On December 18, 1865, the Secretary of State proclaimed that the amendment had been approved by twenty-seven of the thirty-six States, and was consequently adopted.

§ 105. **Educating effect of the controversy.** — The first act of 1793 was imperfect. It did not provide a national machinery whereby its provisions could be executed, and many of the States by means of the personal liberty laws refused to lend their officers and jails for the work. All efforts to amend the law were unsuccessful until the great compromise of 1850 gave opportunity to pass a second act.

This new measure remedied certain defects in the first statute, and was therefore more satisfactory to the slave-owners. As soon as it began to be executed, however, its provisions were found to be so severe that the trials and rescues it occasioned served only to educate the people to the evils of slavery by bringing its effects close to them. Thus, far from compelling the North to acquiesce in the system, it greatly increased the number of Abolitionists The arraying of the North and South against each other in the Civil War intensified public sentiment upon the question, and led more and more to a loose execution of the law. It was found impracticable to return slaves to disloyal masters, and a law to prevent any such return was the next step toward the doing away of the whole system. Next came the question of the duty and power of the general government, within its exclusive jurisdiction: in 1862 all responsibility was disavowed. By this time the force of the law extended only to the loyal slave States, and the force of public opinion in 1864 withdrew the last statutory safeguard of slavery under the Constitution. A change in the text of the Constitution finally took away the force of the clause on which the return of fugitives was based.

We can see, at this distance, how clearly slavery was doomed to destruction, from the time the two sections first made it an issue in 1820; but there was no relation arising out of slavery except the territorial question which did so much as the fugitive slave controversy to hasten the downfall of the system. The contrast between the free principles of democratic government and human bondage was forced upon the attention of the North by the pursuit of fugitives in their midst. Yet without national machinery for the recapture of runaways the institution could not have long been maintained. There is no evidence that the North was profoundly stirred by the horrors of slavery before 1850; it was only when the North was called upon, in the Territories, and through the Fugitive Slave Law, to give positive aid to the system that the anti-slavery movement grew strong. Fugitive slaves and fugitive slave laws helped to destroy slavery.

APPENDIX A.

COLONIAL LAWS RELATIVE TO FUGITIVES.

THE precise text is quoted in each case. The figures in brackets [ ] refer to paragraphs in the text. The sign O indicates that the full text is to be found in the reference cited.

1. New Netherlands:— Running away from Patroons. [§ 2].

1629, June 7. Freedoms and exemptions. Granted by the West India Company to all Patroons, Masters or Private Persons who will plant Colonies in New Netherlands. — "XVIII. The Company promise the colonists of the Patroons. . . . XIX.— And any Colonist who shall leave the service of his Patroon and enter into the service of another, or shall, contrary to his contract, leave his service, we promise to do everything in our power to apprehend and deliver the same into the hands of his Patroon or attorney, that he may be proceeded against according to the customs of this country, as occasion may require." — O *Laws and Ordinances of New Netherlands*, 7.

2. Massachusetts:— Capture and protection of servants. [§ 4.]

1630–1641. "Acts respecting Masters, Servants, and Labourers." — "Sec. 3. It is also ordered, that when any servants shall run from their masters, or any other inhabitants shall privily go away with suspicion of evil intentions, it shall be lawful for the next magistrate, or the constable and two of the chief inhabitants where no magistrate is, to press men and boats or pinnaces at the publick charge, to pursue such persons by sea and land, and bring them back by force of arms. . . . Sec. 6. It is ordered, and by this court declared; that if any servant shall flee from the tyranny and cruelty of his or her master to the house of any freeman of the same town, they shall be there protected and sustained till due order be taken for their relief; provided due notice thereof be speedily given to their master from whom they fled, and to the next magistrate or constable where the party so fled is harboured." — O *Charters and General Laws of the Colony and Province of Massachusetts Bay*, 155.

3. New Netherlands:— Runaway servants. [§ 6.]

1640, Aug. 7. "Ordinance of the Director and Council of New Netherland, against Fugitives from Service, and providing for the proper drawing up of Legal Instruments." Passed 9 August, 1640. "Whereas many Servants daily run away from their masters, whereby the latter are put to great inconvenience and expense; the Corn and Tobacco rot in the field and the whole Harvest is at a stand still, which tends to the serious injury of this country, to their Masters' ruin, and to bring the magistracy into contempt. We, therefore, command all farm and house Servants faithfully to serve out their time with their Masters according to their contracts and in no manner to run away, and if they have any thing against their masters. to come to Us and make application to be heard in due form of Law, on pain of being punished and of making good all losses and damages of their Masters and serving double the time they may lose. . . .

We do, also, forbid all inhabitants of New Netherland to harbor or feed any of these Fugitive Servants under the penalty of Fifty guilders, for the benefit of the Informer; ⅓ for the new Church and ⅓ for the Fiscal." Dated as above. — O *Laws and Ordinances of New Netherlands,* 32.

4. Maryland: — Runaway apprentices felons.

1642, March 26. Act against Fugitives. — " It shall be felony in any apprentice Servant to depart away secretly from his or her Master or dame then being with intent to convey him or her Selfe away out of the Province. And on any other person that shall wittingly accompany such Servant in such unlawfull departure as aforesaid. And the offendors therein shall suffer paines of death, and after his due debts paid shall forfeit all his Lands, goods, & Chattels within the Province. Provided, that in Case his Lordship or his Leivt't-Generall shall at the request of the partie so condemned exchange such pains of death into Servitude, that then such exchange shall not exceed the term of Seaven years, and that the Master or dame of the parties so pardoned of death shall first be satisfied for the terme of such parties Service unexpired from the day of such unlawfull departure, and for double the time of his absence dureing his said departure."
— O *Archives of Maryland, Assembly Proceedings,* 124.

5. New Netherlands: — Against harboring fugitive servants. (§ 6).

1642, April 13. " We have interdicted and forbidden, as we do hereby most, expressly interdict and forbid, all our good inhabitants here, from this time henceforward, lodging any strangers in their houses, or furnishing them more than one meal and harboring them more than one night without first notifying the Director," etc. — O *Laws and Ordinances of New Netherlands,* 32.

6. Virginia: — Entertainment of fugitives. [§ 3.]

1642-3, March. Act XXI. " Whereas complaints are at every quarter court exhibited against divers persons who entertain and enter into covenants with runaway servants and freemen who have formerly hired themselves to others, to the great prejudice if not the utter undoeing of divers poor men, thereby also encouraging servants to runn from their masters and obscure themselves in some remote plantation. Upon consideration had for the future preventing of the like injurious and unjust dealings, *Be it enacted and confirmed* that what person or persons soever shall entertain any person as hireling, or sharer, or upon any other conditions for one whole yeare, without certificate from the commander or any one commissioner of the place, that he or she is free from any ingagement of service. The person so hireing without such certificate as aforesaid, shall for every night that he or she entertaineth any servant, either as hireling or otherwise, fforfeit to the master or mistris of the said servant twenty pounds of tobacco. And for evrie freeman which he or she entertaineth (formerly hired by another) for a year as aforesaid, he or she shall forfeit to the party who had first hired him twenty pound of tobacco for every night deteyned. And for every freeman which he or she entertaineth (though he hath not formerly hired himselfe to another), without certificate as aforesaid, And in all these cases the party hired shall receive such censure and punishment as shall be thought fitt by the Governor and Counsell: Allways provided that if any such runaway servants or hired freemen shall produce such a certificate, wherein it appears that they are freed from their former masters service, or from any such ingagement respectively, if afterwards it shall be proved that the said certificates are counterfeit then the retayner not to suffer according to the penalty of this act, But such punishment shall be inflicted upon the forger and procurer thereof as the Governor and Council shall think fitt." — O *Statutes at Large. Hening, Laws of Virginia,* I. 253.

7. Virginia: — Runaway servants. [§ 3.]

1642-3, March. Act XXII. " *Be it therefore enacted and confirmed* that all runaways that shall absent themselves from their said master's service shall be lyable to make satisfaction by service at the end of their tymes by indenture (vizt.) double the tyme of service soe neglected, and in some cases more if the commissioners for the place appointed shall find it requisite and convenient. And if such runaways shall be found to transgresse the second time or oftener (if it shall be duely proved against them), that then they shall be branded in the cheek with the letter R. and passe under the statute of incorrigible rogues." — O *Statutes at Large. Hening, Laws of Virginia*, I. 254.

8. New England Confederation: — Articles of Confederation. [§ 8.]

1643, Aug. 29. VIII. "It is also agreed that if any servant runn away from his master into any other of these confederated Jurisdiccons, That in such Case, vpon the Certyficate of one Magistrate in the Jurisdiccon out of which the said servant fled, or upon other due proofe, the said servant shalbe deliuered either to his Master or any other that pursues and brings such Certificate or proufe." — O *Plymouth Colony Records*, IX. 5.

9. Connecticut: — Servants and apprentices.

1644, June·3. " Whereas many stubborn, refrectary and discontented searuants and app^rntices wth drawe themselves frō their masters searuices, to improue their tyme to their owne aduantage ; for the p^reuenting whereof, It is Ordered, that whatsoeuer searuant or apprentice shall heareafter offend in that kynd, before their couenants or terme of searuice are expiered, shall searue their said Masters, as they shall be apprehended or retayned the treble terme, or threefold tyme of their absense in such kynd." — O *Connecticut Records*, I. 105.

10. New Netherlands: — Entertainment of runaways.

1648, Oct. 6. Ordinance of the Director and Council of New Netherland against Fugitives from Service. Passed 6 October, 1648. — " The Director General and Council hereby notify and warn all persons against harboring or entertaining any one bound to service either to the Company or to any private individual here or elsewhere, and against lodging or boarding them at most longer than twenty-four hours, and if any one shall be found to have acted contrary hereto, he shall forfeit a fine of fl. 150, to be paid to whomsoever will make the complaint and it may appertain." — O *Laws and Ordinances of New Netherlands*, 104.

11. Maryland : — Against fugitives.

1649. *Archives of Maryland, Assembly Proceedings*, 249.

12. Maryland : — Against fugitives.

1654, Oct. *Archives of Maryland, Assembly Proceedings*, 348.

13. Virginia : — Penalty for second offence.

1655-6, March. "Act XI. *Be it enacted by this Grand Assembly* that if any runnaway servant offend the second time against the act in March, 1642, concerning runnaway servants, that he shall not onely be branded with the letter R., and passe under the statute for an incorrigible rogue, but also double his time of service so neglected, and soe likewise double the time that any time afterward he shall neglect, and in some cases more if the Commissioners think fitt: And be it further enacted by the authority aforesaid, that he or she that shall lodge or harbour any such runnaway shall not only pay 20 lb. of tobacco per night, but also 40 lb. of tobacco per day so long as they shallbe proved to entertaine them, contrary to an act of assembly in March, 1642." — O *Statutes at Large. Hening, Laws of Virginia*, I. 401.

14. New Netherlands : — Treaty with United Colonies. [§11.]

1656. Resolution of the States General ratifying the treaty of Hartford, passed February 22, 1656. — " Respecting Fugitives. It is agreed that the same method shall be observed between the United English Colonies and the Dutch nation in this country of New Netherland, agreeably to the eighth Article of the confederation between the United English Colonies in that case provided." — O *Laws and Ordinances of New Netherlands*, 216.

15. City of Amsterdam: — Runaway colonists banished.
1656, December. Articles and Ordinances revised and enacted by the Right Honorable the Lords Burgomasters of the City of Amsterdam, according to which shall be engaged and sworn all those who shall hereafter enter the service of the Lord's Burgomasters of the City of Amsterdam, for the purpose of going with their own, or chartered ships to New Netherlands and the limits of the West India Company's Grant, etc. Passed December, 1856. — " Whoever runs off to the French, English, or any other Christian or Indian neighbors by whatsoever name they may be called, shall, in addition to the forfeiture of all his monthly pay to the City, be banished forever from New Netherland as a perjured villain, and if he afterward come to fall into the hands of the City, he shall, without any consideration, be punished by death or otherwise, according to the exigency of the case." — O *Laws and Ordinances of New Netherlands*, 273.

16. Virginia: — Entertainment of runaways.
1657-8, March. Act XV. Concerning Hireing Servants. Thirty pounds of tobacco shall be paid for every night a servant or person without a certificate is entertained. — *Statutes at Large. Hening, Laws of Virginia*, I. 439.

17. Virginia: — Punishment of runaways.
1657-8, March. Act XVI. Against Runaway Servants. Runaways shall double the time of service absent at the end of their time of indenture. For the second offence they shall be branded with the letter R. and double the time lost. — *Hening, Laws of Virginia*, I. 440.

18. Virginia: — Huie and crie after runaways.
1657-8, March. "Act CXIII. Concerning Huie and cries. Whereas huy and cries after runaway servants hath been much neglected to the greate damage and loss of the inhabitants of this colloney, *Bee it therefore enacted and confirmed by the authorite of this present Grand Assembly*, that all such huy and cries shall be signed either by the Governor or some of the Councill, or under the hand of some com'r, nameing the county where the said com'r lives, and the same shall be conveyed from house to house with all convenient speed according as the direction thereof expresseth: And every com'r of each county unto whose house by this meanes the said huy and crie shall come shall then date and subscribe the same, And the master of every house that shall make default in the speedy conveyance of any such huies and cries shall for every such default forfeit and pay unto the owners of any such runnawaie as the said hues and cries shall mention, one hundred pounds of tobacco, and where the said runnawaie servant is found he shall be apprehended and sent from constable to constable untill such runnawaie or runnawayes shall be delivered to his or theire master or mistresse, and if any neglect can be proved against the constable hee to be fined three hundred and fiftie pounds of tobacco." — O *Statutes at Large. Hening, Laws of Virginia*, I. 483.

19. New Netherlands: — Runaway servants.
1658, April 9. Ordinance of the Director General and Council of New Netherland renewing sundery Ordinances therein mentioned. Passed 9 April, 1658. — " 13thly, not to debauch or incite any person's servants, male or female, or to harbor them, as fugitives and strangers, longer than 24 hours without notifying the Fiscal, Magistrates, or Schouts, and all servant men and women remaine bound-to fulfill and complete their contracts, on pain of arbitrary correction, according to the Ordinance of the 6 October, 1648." — O *Laws of New Netherlands*, 344.

20. Virginia: — How to know a runaway servant. [§ 3.]
1658-9, March. Act III. "*It is enacted and ordained* that the master of everie such runaway shall cutt, or cause to be cutt, the hair of all such runnawayes close above their ears, whereby they may be with more ease discovered and apprehended." — O *Statutes at Large. Hening, Laws of Virginia*, I. 517.

21. Virginia: — Payment of Dutch shipmasters.
1659-60, March. Act XV. An Act for the Pay of Dutch Masters bringing in Runnaway Servants. Whenever a master shall refuse to pay the cost of returning a runnaway from the Dutch, the payment shall be made by the secretary at his office. — *Statutes at Large. Hening, Laws of Virginia*, I. 539.

22. Virginia: — Apprehension of runaways.
1660-61, March. Act X. Apprehending of Runnawayes. — "Whereas the pursuit and takeing of runnaways is hindered chiefly by the neglect of constables in making search according to their warrants, *Bee itt enacted* that every constable shall make diligent search and inquiry through his precincts, and what constable soever shall upon search apprehend such runaways shall receive from the master of the servant for his encouragement two hundred pounds of tobaccoe, and if any constable shall neglect he shall be fined three hundred and fifty pounds of tobaccoe and caske according to former act." — O *Statutes at Large. Hening, Laws of Virginia*, II. 21.

23. Virginia: — English runaway with negroes. [§ 3.]
1660-1, March. Act XIII. "*Bee itt enacted* that in case any English servant shall runaway in company with any negroes who are incapable of making satisfaction by addition of time, *Bee itt enacted* that the English so running away in company with them shall serve for the time of the said negroes absence as they are to do for their owne by a former act" — O *Hening, Laws of Virginia*, II. 26.

24. Virginia: — Glocester to have jurisdiction over runaways.
1660-1, March. It was ordered that the county of Glocester have the power to make such laws for the recovering of runaways as shall be found necessary and convenient. — *Statutes at Large. Hening, Laws of Virginia*, II. 35.

25. Virginia: — Runaway servants.
1661-2, March. Act CII. Runaways. — Penalties for running away are the same as in former acts. English servants if running away with negroes, and the negroes die or be lost, shall pay either four thousand five hundred pounds of tobacco and caske, or four years service for every negro so lost or dead. — *Hening, Laws of Virginia*, II. 117.

26. Maryland: — Against runaways.
1662. *Maryland Archives, Assembly Proceedings*, 451.

27. Virginia: — Pursuit of runaways to the Dutch.
1663, September. Act VIII. "An Act concerning the pursuit of runawayes." It is enacted that runaways are to be pursued at the public expense, and, if they have escaped to the Dutch, letters are to be written to the Governors of those Plantations to return the runaways. Expenses are to be paid according to the provisions of a former act. — *Statutes at Large. Hening, Laws of Virginia*, II. 187.

28. Maryland: — Against English servants.
1663, October. *Maryland Archives, Assembly Proceedings*, 489.

29. New Netherlands: — Quakers, etc. refused admission to colony.
1663, May 17. Ordinance of the Director General and Council of New Netherland prohibiting the bringing of Quakers and other Strollers into New Netherland. Passed 17 May 1663. — "The Director General and Council, therefore, do hereby Order and command all Skippers, Sloop captains and others, whomsoever they may be, not to convey or bring, much less to land within this government, any such Vagabonds, Quakers and other Fugitives, whether Men or Women, until they have first addressed themselves to the government, etc. . . . on the pain of the Importers forfeiting a fine of Twenty pounds Flemish for every person," etc. — O *Laws and Ordinances of New Netherlands*, 439.

30. Virginia: — Entertainment of runaways.
1666, October. Act IX. "An act against entertayners of runaways." Penalty for entertaining runaways increased to sixty pounds of tobacco for every day and night he or they shall be harbored. — *Statutes at Large. Hening, Laws of Virginia*, II. 239.

31. Maryland: — Runaways and their entertainers.

1666, May. " An Act providing ag⁺ Runaways, and all such as shall Entertayn them. Whereas there was an act providing against Runnawaies made in the year 1650, and another act made in the year 1662, both which acts being adjudged insufficient Satisfaccōn for the reparacōn of their respective Masters, mrssrse, Dame, or overseers damages sustained by their servt running from them, Be it enacted by the right honorble, the Lord Prop'y, by and with the consent of the upper and Lower House of this present general assembly, that from and after the publicacōn hereof any Servant or Servants whatsoever unlawfully absenting themselves from their said Master, Mistress, Dame, or overseer, shall serve for every day 10. And be it further enacted by the Authority aforesaid that any Master, Mistress, dame, or Overseer that shall entertain any servant unlawfully absenting himselfe as aforesaid, having been forewarned by the Master, mistress, Dame, or Overseer of the said servant, shall be fined for the first night five hundred pounds of Casked tobacco, for the second one thousand pounds of casked tobacco, for every other night fifteen hundred pounds of casked tobacco, the one half to the Lord Proprietor, the other to the informer, or them that shall sue for the same within any Court of Record within this province, to be Recovered by action of debt, plaint or Informacōn wherein no Essoyne, protection or wager of Lawe to be allowed, Provided that this Act nor anything therein conteynd shall not be adjudged to the preddice of any person or persons that shall apprehend any Runaway servants who are hereby required to use the best endeavors to Convey them to their owners or next justice of the peace to be conveyed from constable to constable until they be delivered to their said owners, if then living within this province. This act to continue for 3 years, or to the end of the next general assembly which shall first come." — O *Maryland Archives, Assembly Proceedings*, 147.

32. New Jersey: — Fugitive servants.

1668, May 30. Acts passed and assented unto by the Governor, Council, and Burgess of the General Assembly of the Province of New-Caesarea, or New Jersey, the 30th Day of May, Anno Domini 1668. " Concerning Fugitives, It is Enacted by the same Authority, that every Apprentice and Servant that shall depart and absent themselves from their Master and Dames, without leave first obtained, shall be judged by the Court to double the Time of such their Absence, by future Service over and above other Damages and costs which Master and Dame shall sustain by such unlawful Departure.

" And it is also enacted, that whosoever shall be proved to have transported, or to have contrived the Transportation of any such Apprentice or Servant shall be fined *Five Pounds*, and all such Damages as the Court shall Judge, and that the Master or Dame can make appear, and if not able, to be left to the Judgement of the Court." — O *New Jersey Laws*, 82.

33. Virginia: — Runaways.

1668, September. Act IV. About Runawayes. Moderate corporal punishment inflicted by the master or magistrate shall not deprive the master of the satisfaction allowed by the law. — *Statutes at Large. Hening, Laws of Virginia*, II. 266.

34. Virginia: — Runaways.

1669, October. Act VIII. Against Runawayes. " *Be it therefore enacted* that whosoever apprehends any runaways, whether servant by indenture, custome or covenant, not haveing a legall passe, by those in every county that shall be appointed to give passes, or a note from his master, shall have a thousand pounds of tobacco allowed him by the publique, which tobacco shall be repaid by the service of the servant to the country when free from his master, and by the hired ffreeman immediately after expiration of his covenant to the man that apprehends."

" *And be it further enacted* that he that takes up such runaway is hereby enjoyned ffirst to carry him before the next justice who is to take cognizance of his good service, and to certify it in the next assembly, and then to deliver him to the constable of the parish where that justice dwells, who is to convey him to the next constable, till he be retorned to his master, and that each constable upon receipt of such runaway give his receipt, and if escape be made from any constable, the delinquent constable to pay one thousand pounds of tobacco; and for the reimburseing the publique with the tobacco disbursed to the taker up." — O *Statutes at Large. Hening, Laws of Virginia*, II. 273.

35. Virginia: — Apprehension of Runaways.

1670, October. Act I. An Act concerning runaways. Reward for apprehending runaways is reduced to two hundred pounds of tobacco. Servants are to serve four months for every two hundred pounds of tobacco. Masters who fail to cut their servants' hair after twice running away shall be fined two hundred pounds of tobacco. Every constable through whose hands a runaway passes is to whip the servant severely. Constables allowing runaways to escape shall pay four hundred pounds of tobacco. Masters must not allow their servants to go free until the time of service has been worked out. — *Statutes at Large. Hening, Laws of Virginia*, II. 277.

36. Virginia: — Reward to the first taker up of runaways.

1670, October. Act XIII. Runawayes. Only the first taker up of a runaway shall be rewarded. — *Statutes at Large. Hening, Laws of Virginia*, II. 283.

37. Virginia: — Apprehension of Runaways. [§ 8.]

1672, October. Act VIII. An Act for the apprehension and suppression of runawayes, negroes and slaves. Runaways resisting may be killed or wounded, and if they die from the effects of a wound the publick shall pay the owner, but the person inflicting the injury is not to be questioned. Indians shall be rewarded by twenty armes length of Roanoake or the value thereof in goods for the apprehension of a runaway. Act is to continue in force only until the next assembly. — *Statutes at Large. Hening, Laws of Virginia*, II. 299.

38. Maryland: — Apprehension of runaways.

1671, April. The three acts of 1650, 1662, and 1666 have not proved sufficient encouragement to people to apprehend runaways, therefore a statute against runaways and such persons that shall give them entertainment and others that shall travel without passes is enacted. — *Maryland Archives, Assembly Proceedings*, 298.

39. New Jersey: — Fugitive servants and apprentices.

1675, November. "XXXIII. Concerning Fugitives, It is enacted by the same Authority, that every Apprentice and Servant that shall depart and absent themselves from their Masters or Dames, without leave first obtaind, shall be judged by the court to double the Time of such their Absence, by future Service, over and above other Damages and Costs which the Master and Dame shall sustain by such unlawful Departure. XXXIV. *And it is further enacted*, that whosoever shall be proved to have transported or contrived the Transportation of any such Apprentice, Servant, or Slave, shall be fined *Five Pounds*, and all such Damages as the Court shall judge, and that the Master or Dame can make appear, and if not able to be left to the Judgement of the Court. *It is further enacted*, that every Inhabitant that shall harbour or entertain any such Apprentice, Servant, or Slave, and knowing that he hath absented himself from his Service upon Proof thereof, shall forfeit to their Master or Dame *Ten Shillings* for every days Entertainment or Concealment, and if not able to satisfy, to be liable to the Judgement of the Court." — *New Jersey Laws*, 109.

40. Maryland: — Runaways.

1676, June. An Act against runaways. — *Laws of Maryland, Bacon, Index*.

41. East New Jersey: — Fugitive servants.

1682, March. Laws passed by General Assembly in East New Jersey. Chap. IX A Bill against fugitive Servants, and entertainers of them. Be it enacted by the Governor, Council, and Deputies in General Assembly met, and by the Authority of the same, that every Apprentice, or Servant, that shall depart or absent themselves from their Master or Mistress, without leave first obtained, shall be adjudged by the Court to double the Time of such their absence by future Service, besides all Costs and Damages, which the master or mistress shall have sustained by such unlawful Departure. *Be it further enacted* by the Authority aforesaid, that whosoever shall knowingly transport or contrive the Transportation of any Apprentice, Servant, or Slave, or be any aiding or assisting thereto, and be thereof lawfully convicted, shall be fined *Five Pounds*, and make full Satisfaction to the master or mistress of such Apprentice, Servant, or Slave, for all Costs or Damages which the said master or mistress can make appear to have thereby sustained. *Be it further enacted* By the Authority aforesaid, that every Inhabitant, who shall entertain, or afford any manner of Relief to such Apprentice, Servant, or Slave, knowing that he hath absented himself as aforesaid, except of real Charity, and thereof be lawfully convicted, shall pay to the master or mistress of such Servant *Ten Shillings* for every Days Entertainment and concealment, and be fined according to the Discretion of the Court." — *Acts of the Proprietary Government of New Jersey*, 238.

42. New Jersey :— Prevention of runaways.

1683. No title given. General Assembly. VI. "And for the preventing Servants running away from their Masters, and other Vagabonds, *Be it hereby enacted* by the authority aforesaid, that all Magistrates, Officers, Ordinary Keepers, and other Inhabitants within this Province, take special notice of all suspicious Travellers, and require their pass or certificates, under the Hand and Seal of the Magistrate or Magistrates, or Publick Notary of the Place of their last Abode, to satisfy the clearness of his, her, or their coming away, and for want of such Pass or Certificate, to secure such Person or Persons into the Custody of the next constable; which Person and Persons so to be secured, or their Masters, shall pay such Charge and Trouble as the Person or Persons shall be put to, in the securing them as aforesaid, before they shall be discharged, at the Discretion of two or more of the Magistrates of the said Province." — O *Acts of the Proprietary Governments of New Jersey*, 477.

43. South Carolina :— Prevention of runaways.

1683, Nov. 7. An Act to prevent Runaways. Title only preserved. Table of contents. — *Statutes at Large of South Carolina*, II.

44. Virginia :— Repeal of law of 1663, September.

1684, April. Act III. An act repealing the act concerning the persuit of runawayes. The law of September, 1663, has been found inconvenient in practice, it is therefore repealed. — *Statutes at Large. Hening, Laws of Virginia*, III. 12.

45. East New Jersey :— Runaway servants. [§ 2.]

1686, April. Chap. XI. An Act concerning Runaway Servants. Whereas the securing of Servants that Runaway, or otherwise absent themselves from their Masters lawful Occasions, is found a material encouragement to such Persons as come into this country to settle Plantations and Populate the Province ; for the better encouragement of such Persons, Be it therefore enacted by the Governor and Council and Deputies now met in General Assembly, and by the authority of the same, that if any Servant or Servants, Prentices or Covenant Servants, Run away or absent him or herself unlawfully from their Masters or Mistress' Service, being taken up or secured, so that the master or mistress hath him or her again, for the better Encouragement of such Person or Persons so securing him or them, they shall have *Twenty Shillings* paid him or them," etc. — *New Jersey Laws*, 292.

46. Virginia : Law of 1670 amended.

1686, October. Act I. Slight change in making out the certificate for apprehension of runaway. —*Statutes at Large. Hening, Laws of Virginia*, III. 29.

47. South Carolina: — Inhibition of trade with runaways.

1691. An act inhibiting the tradeing with Servants and Slaves. "*And it is alsoe enacted* by the authority aforesaid, that if any servant or servants shall at any tyme or tymes hereafter absent or withdraw him or themselves from his, her, or their master or mistresses service, such servant or servants soe offending shall for every naturall day they shall soe absent themselves serve one whole weeke, and for every weeke, if they shall att any one tyme soe long absent themselves, one whole yeare to theire master or mistresse, over and above their contracted tyme of servitude." — O *Statutes at Large of South Carolina*, II. 53.

48. Pennsylvania: — Regulation of servants.

1700. An Act for the better Regulation of Servants in this Province and Territories. "And for the Prevention of Servants quitting their masters Service, *Be it enacted* by the Authority aforesaid, that if any Servant shall absent him or herself from the Service of their Master or Owner for the Space of one Day, or more, without Leave first obtained for the same, every such Servant shall, for every such Days absence, be obliged to serve Five Days after the Expiration of his or her Time, and shall further make such Satisfaction to his or her Master or Owner for the Damages and Charges sustained by such Absence as the respective County Courts shall see meet, who shall order as well the Time to be served, as other Recompence for Damages sustained. And whosoever shall apprehend or take up any Runaway Servant, and shall bring him or her to the Sheriff of the County, such Person shall for every such Servant, if taken up within Ten miles of the Servants abode, receive *Ten Shillings*; and if Ten miles or upwards, *Twenty Shillings* Reward of the said Sheriff, who is hereby required to pay the same, and forthwith to send Notice to the master or Owner, of whom he shall receive *Five Shillings* Prison Fees upon the Delivery of the said Servant, together with all other Disbursements and reasonable Charges for and upon the same." — O *Province Laws of Pennsylvania*, I. 5.

49. New York: — Regulation of slaves.

1702. An Act for regulating Slaves. "And be it further enacted, etc., That no Person or Persons whatsoever do hereafter Employ, Harbour, Conceal or Entertain other Men's Slaves at their House, Out-house, or Plantation, without the consent of their master or mistress, either signified to them verbally, or by Certificate in writing, under the said Master or Mistress' Hand upon Forfeiture of Five Pounds for every Night or Day, to the Master or Mistress of such Slave or Slaves, so that the Penalty of such Slave do not exceed the value of the said Slave. And if any Person or Persons whatsoever shall be found guilty of Harbouring, Entertaining, or Concealing of any Slave, or assisting to the Conveying them away, if such Slave shall happen to be lost, dead, or otherwise distroyed, such Person or Persons, so Harbouring, Entertaining, Concealing, Assisting or Conveying of them away, shall be also liable to pay the Value of such Slave to the master or mistress, to be recovered by Action of Debt, in manner aforesaid." — O *Acts of Province of New York from 1691 to 1718*, p. 58.

50. New York: — Punishment of runaways to Canada. [§ 8.]

1705. An act to prevent the Running away of Negro Slaves out of the City and County of *Albany*, to the French at Canada. "Whereas the City and County of Albany are the Frontiers of this Province toward the *French* of *Canada*; and that it is of great concern to this Colony, during this time of War with the French, that no Intelligence be carried from the said City and County to the French at Canada: ... Be it enacted, and it is hereby enacted by his Excellency the Governor, Council and Assembly, etc., that all and every Negro Slave or Slaves, belonging to any of the Inhabitants of the city and county of *Albany*, who shall from and after the First Day of *August* of this present year of our Lord, One thousand seven hundred and five, be found traveling Forty miles above the City of Albany, at or above a certain place called *Sarachtoge* (unless in Company of his, her, or their Master, Mistress, or such employed by them, or either of them), and be thereof convicted by the Oaths of Two or more credible Witnesses, before the Court of Sessions of the Peace of the said City and County (which Court of Sessions are hereby Authorized and Impowered to hear and determine the same, in manner aforesaid, and thereupon to award execution), he, she, or they so Convicted, shall suffer the Pains of Death, as in cases of Felony." — *Acts of Province of New York*, 77.

51. New York: — Act of 1702 revived.

1705. An act for Reviving and continuing an Act, Intituled, An Act for Regulating Slaves, 1702 (expired in 1712). — *Acts of the Province of New York*, 79.

52. Virginia: — Runaway servants and slaves.

1705, October. Chap. XLIX. An Act concerning Servants and Slaves. XXI. Penalty for entertaining runaway servants without a certificate shall be for every day sixty pounds of tobacco. XXIII. Persons rewarded for taking up runaway according to the distance. — *Hening, Laws of Virginia*, II. 447.

53. Massachusetts Bay: — Regulation of free negroes. [§ 4.]

1707. An Act for the regulating of free negroes. "Sec. 3. And be it further enacted, that every free negro or mulatto who shall harbour or entertain any negro or mulatto servant in his or her house, without the leave or consent of their respective masters or mistresses, shall forfeit and pay the sum of five shillings to the use of the poor of the town, for each offence." — *Charters and General Laws of the Colony and Province of Massachusetts Bay*, 386.

54. South Carolina: — For the better ordering of slaves.

1712. *Statutes at Large of South Carolina*, II. 381.

55. New Jersey: — Regulation of slaves.

1713. An Act for Regulating of Slaves. Sec. 2. "Negroes, etc., not having a pass may be taken up if 5 miles from Home whipped, and Persons so taking up have 5*s.*" Sec. 3. "Negro belonging to another Province not having license, to be whipped, and the Taker of them to have 10*s.*" — *Acts of the Assembly of New Jersey*, 18.

56. New Jersey: — Regulation of white servants

1713. An Act for regulating of White Servants, and taking up Soldiers and Seamen deserting Her Majestys Service, and coming into this Colony. Sec. 2. "Servants absenting without leave to be adjudged by any one Justice to serve double the time, and pay or serve for costs." Sec. 3. "Those who counsel, aid, etc. such Servants to runaway, to forfeit 10£," etc. Sec. 4. "Those who knowingly conceal them, to pay 10*s.* per Day." Sec. 5. "Those who take up Runaways and carry them back to have 15*s.* and 6*d.* per mile for so doing." Sec. 8. "Any Boatman, etc., who shall carry them into or out of this Province, etc., not having Passes, as aforesaid, and Publick-House-keepers entertaining them to forfeit 40*s.*," etc. — *Acts of the Assembly of New Jersey*, 24.

57. Rhode Island: — Ferriage of runaways. [§ 4.]

1714, Oct. 27. "Whereas, several negroes and mulatto slaves that have run away from their masters or mistresses, under pretence of being sent or employed by their masters or mistresses upon some service, and have been carried over the ferries, out and into the colony, and suffered to pass through the several towns under the aforesaid pretence, to the considerable damage and charge of their owners, and many times to the loss of their slaves; — Be it therefore enacted by this Assembly, and by the authority thereof it is enacted, that no ferryman or boatman whatsoever, within this colony, shall carry or bring any slave as aforesaid over their ferries, without a certificate under the hands of their masters or mistresses, or some person in authority, upon the penalty of paying all costs and damages their said masters or mistresses shall sustain thereby; and to pay a fine of twenty shillings for the use of the colony, for each offence, as aforesaid. The said fine to be recovered by any two justices of the peace, upon confession or conviction of the said fact; and all persons in authority, and other His Majesty's Subjects in this colony knowing of any such slaves traveling through their township, wherein they dwell, without a certificate, as aforesaid, they are hereby required to cause such slave to be examined and secured so as the owner may be notified thereof, and have his slave again, paying the costs and charges that shall accrue thereon." —*Proceedings of General Assembly, Colony of Rhode Island and Providence Plantations, Providence*, 177 ; *Records of Colony of Rhode Island*, 177.

58. South Carolina: — Additional Act to Act of 1712.

1714. *Statutes at Large of South Carolina*, II. 620.

59. New York: — Act of 1705 revived. [§ 8.]

1715. An Act for Reviving and Continuing an Act, Intituled an act to prevent the Running away of Negro Slaves out of the city and county of Albany to the French at Albany, 1705. — *Laws Province of New York*, 218.

60. North Carolina: — Servants and slaves.

1715. An Act concerning servants and Slaves. Title only given. — *Laws of North Carolina*, 21, 27.

61. New Hampshire: — Runaway minors and servants.

1715. An Act for preventing Men's Sons or Servants absenting themselves from their Parents or Masters Service without Leave. — "That no commander of any private man of war, or master of any merchant ship or vessel coming into, tarrying or abiding in, or going forth of any port, harbour, or place within this province, shall receive, harbour, entertain, conceal or secure on board such ship or other vessel, or suffer to be there harbour'd or detain'd any man's son, being under age or apprentice or covenant servant (knowing him to be such, or after notice thereof given) without license or consent of his parent or master in writing under his hand first had and obtain'd, on pain of forfeiting the sum of *five pounds per* week, and so proportionably for a longer or shorter time, that any son, apprentice, or servant shall be held, harbour'd, conceal'd, or detain'd on board any such ship or other vessel, as aforesaid, without license and consent as aforesaid; the one moiety thereof to her Majesty, to be employed toward the support of the government of the province, and the other moiety unto the parent or master of such son, apprentice or servant that shall inform, or sue for the same, in any of her majesty's courts of record, within this province, by bill, plaint, or information, wherein no essoign, protection or wager of law shall be allowed. § 2. *And be it further enacted by the authority aforesaid,* that every apprentice or covenant servant who shall unlawfully absent himself from his master, and enter himself on board any ship or vessel, as aforesaid, with intent to leave his master's service, or incline there more than the space of twenty-four hours, and be thereof convicted before any two of her majesty's justices of the peace, or in general sessions, within this province, shall forfeit unto his master such further service, from and after the expiration of the term which his said master had in him at the time of his departure as the said court shall order, not exceeding one year." — O *Acts and Laws of His Majesty's Province of New Hampshire*, 40.

62. South Carolina: — Additional Act against runaways.

1717. *Statutes at Large of South Carolina*, III. 39.

63. Massachusetts Bay: — Transportation of apprentices and servants.

1718, October. An Act for the preventing of persons under age, apprentices or servants, being transported out of the province without the consent of their masters, parents, or guardians. "Every master of any outward bound ship or vessel that shall hereafter carry or transport out of this province any person under age, or bought or hired servant or apprentice, to any parts beyond the seas, without the consent of such master, parent or guardian, signified in writing, shall forfeit the sum of fifty pounds," etc. — *Charters and Laws of the Colony and Province of Massachusetts Bay*, 750.

64. South Carolina:—Regulation of Slaves.
1722. An Act for the better ordering and governing of slaves. — *Statutes at Large of South Carolina*, 193.

65. Pennsylvania:—Regulation of negroes.
1725. An Act for the better Regulating of negroes in this province. "And be it further enacted by the authority aforesaid, that no Person or Persons whatsoever shall imploy, or knowingly harbour, conceal, or entertain other Peoples slaves at their Houses, Out Houses, or Plantations, without the Masters or Owners consent, excepting in stress of weather or other Extraordinary Occasion, under the Penalty of *Thirty Shillings* for every Twenty four Hours he or they shall entertain or harbour him or them as aforesaid." — *Province Laws of Pennsylvania, Philadelphia*, 1725.

66. Virginia:—Earlier act amended.
1726, May. Chap. III. The clause in regard to imprisonment when slave would not give name of master has proved very inconvenient. Chap. IV. An Act for amending the Act concerning Servants and Slaves; and for the further preventing the clandestine transportation of Persons out of this colony. IV. The sheriff or under sheriff to whom the slave is committed shall cause a notice containing a full description of the runaway to be posted on the door of the court-house, and shall send a copy to each church or chapel within the county which shall be set up "in some open and convenient place" on every Lord's day for two months. Neglect on part of the sheriff shall be fined five hundred pounds of tobacco; on the part of the clerk, two hundred pounds. VI. Provisions in regard to transportation. VIII. Runaways may be let out to hire by the keeper of the gaol. IX. When demanded by the owner, the person hireing shall deliver up the servant. X. "Provided also, that where the keeper of the said public gaol shall, by the direction of such court or courts, as aforesaid, let out any such negro or runaway to hire to any person or persons whatsoever, the said keeper shall, at the time of his delivery, cause a strong iron collar to be put on the neck of such negro or runaway, with the letters (P. G.) stamped thereon; and that thereafter the said keeper shall not be answerable for any escape of the said negro or runaway." XII. Fees of the goalers given. XIII. Runaways from Maryland or Carolina shall be committed to any public gaol, and the fees shall be according to the laws of the province wherein the master dwells. XIV. The keeper of the gaol shall send descriptions of the runaway to such places of this dominion bordering on Maryland or Carolina as shall be agreed upon. XV., XVI. Fees described. XVIII. Masters of vessels shall take the following oath: "I, A. B., master of the ship (or vessel), do swear that I will make diligent enquiry and search in my said ship (or vessel), and will not knowingly or willingly carry, or suffer to be carried, in my said ship, out of this dominion, without such pass as is directed by law, any person or persons whatsoever, that I shall know to be running hence in order to deceive their creditors; nor any servant or slave that is not attending his or her master or owner, or sent by such master or owner. XX. For forging a pass persons offending shall stand two hours in the pillory, and receive thirty lashes at the whipping-post. XXI. A white servant who shall run away, change his name, or disguise himself with intent to escape, shall serve six months longer than his term for running away.— *Statutes at Large. Hening, Laws of Virginia*, IV. 168.

67. Connecticut:—Runaway servants and slaves.
1730 (probably). An Act concerning *Indian, Molatto,* and *Negro* Servants and Slaves. "That whatsoever *Negro, Molatto,* or *Indian* Servant, or Servants shall be found wandering out of the Bounds of the Town, or Place to which they belong, without a Ticket or Pass in writing, under the Hand of some Assistant or Justice of the Peace, or under the Hand of the Master, or Owner of such *negro, molatto,* or *Indian* Servants shall be deemed and Accounted to be Run-aways, and may be Treated as such; and every Person Inhabiting this colony, Finding or Meeting with any such *Negro,*

molatto, or *Indian* Servant or Servants, not having a ticket as aforesaid, is hereby impowered to Seize and Secure him, or them, and Bring him or them before the next Authority to be Examined, and Returned to his, or their master or Owner, who shall satisfy the Charge Accruing thereby. And all Ferry-Men within this colony, are hereby Required not to suffer any *Indian*, *molatto* or *negro* servant without certificate, as aforesaid, to pass over their Respective Ferries, by Assisting them therein Directly or Indirectly, on Penalty of paying a Fine of Twenty Shillings for every such Offence." — O *Acts and Laws of His Majestie's Colony of Connecticut*, 229.

68. **New York : — Slave insurrections, etc.**

1730. An Act for 'the more effectual preventing and punishing the conspiracy and Insurrection of negroes and other Slaves; for the better regulating them, and for repealing the acts therein mentioned, relating thereto. Passed the 29th of October, 1730. No fugitive slave provision. Penalty for entertaining Slaves as in 1702. Also Persons who do not discover those that entertain slaves shall pay Forty Shillings. — *Acts of Province of New York*, 193.

69. **South Carolina: — Regulation of slaves.**

1735. *Statutes at Large of South Carolina*, III. 405.

70. **Delaware : — Regulation of servants and slaves.**

1740. An Act for the better regulation of Servants and Slaves within this government (a). Sec. 5. "Be it enacted by the authority aforesaid, that from such time as any servant shall absent him or herself from his or her masters or mistress' service, without leave first obtained for the same, every such servant, for such absence, and the expenses of taking up, shall at the expiration of the time of his or her servitude, make satisfaction by servitude, according to the judgement of any court of Quarter Sessions within this government." Sec. 6. " And be it further enacted by the authority aforesaid, that if any person shall apprehend or take up any runaway servant and carry him or her before the next Justice of the Peace of the county where such servant shall be so taken up, in order to be sent to and secured in the gaol of the said county, for his or her master's or mistress' service." The sheriff or gaoler shall then send notice to the servant's owner, if known ; if not, the servant shall be advertised in some newspaper in the city of Philadelphia. The reward for taking up runaways shall be, " if ten miles distant from the place of the said servants last abode, or under, the sum of Ten Shillings, if upwards of ten miles, the sum of Twenty Shillings." " And if the master or owner of such servant so imprisoned shall, for the space of six weeks next after notice had of his or her servants imprisonment, neglect or refuse to release such servant, it shall and may be lawful for the said Sheriff, and he is hereby required and commanded, upon affidavit made of the due service of such notice, to expose every such servant to sale at public vendue, and him or her to sell to the highest bidder, for such term and sum as shall be sufficient for the defraying the 'costs and charges arising upon the apprehending and imprisoning the said servant." Sec. 7. " Suspicious persons travelling without a pass shall be deemed runaway servants and treated as such." — *Laws of Delaware*, 211, 212.

71. **Delaware : — Regulation of servants and slaves.**

1740. An Act for the better regulation of Servants and Slaves within this Government. " Sec. 14. *And be it further enacted by the authority aforesaid*, that who so ever shall take up any negro or mulatto slave at above ten miles distance from his or her masters or mistress' dwelling or habitation, and not having leave in writing from his or her master or mistress, or not being known by the taker-up to be about his or her master's or mistress' business or service, and shall convey him or her to the habitation of his or her said master or mistress, if known, such taker-up shall receive of the said master or mistress, for his reward, the sum of Five Shillings, with reasonable charges. Sec. 15. *And be it further enacted by the authority aforesaid*, that no person shall employ or knowingly harbour, conceal or entertain another's servant or slave at his or her house or plantation without the master or owner's leave and consent, except in distress of weather or other extraordinary occasion or accident, under the penalty of Forty Shillings for every twenty four hours he or she shall entertain any such servant or slave, as afore said, and so in proportion for any lesser time." — O *Laws of the State of Delaware*, 215, 216.

72. South Carolina: — Regulation of slaves.

1740. *Statutes at Large, South Carolina*, III. 568.

73. North Carolina: — Entertainment of runaways, etc. [§ 3.]

1741. XXVII. Any person harbouring a runaway shall be prosecuted and compelled to pay the sum of twenty-five pounds or serve the owner of the slave or his assigns five years. If he actually carry away the slave, he shall be convicted of felony and suffer accordingly. XXVIII. Seven shillings and sixpence, Proclamation money, reward for taking up runaways. For every mile over ten, threepence. XXXIV. Runaways when taken up shall be whipped. XXXV. Constables must give a receipt for runaway. Any failure shall be fined twenty shillings, Proclamation money, to be paid the church warden. XXXVI. Sheriff who shall hold a runaway longer than the act directs shall forfeit five pounds. Sheriff who allows a runaway to escape is liable to action from the party grieved. XXXVIII. This article takes up the fees of the jailor, etc. — *Laws of North Carolina*, 89.

74. Virginia: — Ferriage of runaways.

1748, Oct. An Act for the Settlement and Regulation of Ferries, and for the Despatch of Public Expresses. VI. All constables and their assistants charged with conducting any runaway servant shall be passed ferry free. The ferriage shall then be paid by the owners of the runaways. — *Statutes at Large, Hening*, VI. 22.

75. South Carolina: Act additional to Act of 1740.

1751. *Statutes at Large of South Carolina*, III. 738.

76. Rhode Island: — Assistance of runaways.

1766-1798. An Act relative to Slaves, and to their Manumission and support. — Sec. 3. And be it further enacted, that if any person shall conceal any negro or mulatto slave, or shall in any manner assist such slave in escaping from the lawful authority of his or her master, the person so offending shall forfeit and pay the sum of three hundred dollars, to be recovered by action of debt, one moiety thereof to and for the use of the State, and the other moiety thereof to and for the use of the person who shall sue for the same. — *Laws of Rhode Island and Providence Plantations*, 607.

77. North Carolina: — Slave stealing.

1779. An Act to prevent the stealing of Slaves, or by Violence, Seduction, or any other Means, taking or conveying away any Slave or Slaves the Property of another, and for other Purposes therein mentioned. IV. And whereas many evil disposed Persons frequently entice or persuade Slaves (without any Intention to steal them) and Servants, to absent themselves from their Master or Mistress, and often times harbour and maintain runaway Servants and Slaves; *Be it therefore further enacted* by the authority aforesaid, that any Person or Persons who shall hereafter entice or persuade any Servant or Slave to absent him or herself from his or her Master or Mistress, or who shall harbour or maintain any runaway Servant or Slave, shall for every such Offence forfeit or pay to the Master or Mistress of such Servant or Slave, the sum of one hundred Pounds current money, to be recovered by Action of Debt, in any Jurisdiction having Cognizance thereof; and be further liable to the said master or mistress in an action for Damages, where in no Essoign, Injunction, Protection, or Wager of Law shall be allowed or admitted, notwithstanding any Law, Usage, or Custom to the contrary. — *Laws of North Carolina*, 371.

78. Connecticut: — Escape of negroes and servants.

No date given. An Act to prevent the Running away of Indian and Negro Servants. "Be it enacted by the Governour, Council, and Representatives, in General Court assembled, and by the Authority of the same, that whatsoever Negro or Indian Servant or Servants shall at any time after the publication hereof be found wandering out of the Town Bounds, or Place to which they belong, without a Ticket or Pass in writing under the Hand of some Assistant or Justice of the Peace, or under the Hand of the Master or Owner of such Negro or Indian Servant or Servants, shall be deemed and accounted to be Run-a-ways; and every person Inhabiting in this Colony, finding or meeting with any such Negro or Indian Servant or Servants, not having a Ticket as aforesaid, is hereby impowered to seize and secure him or them, and bring him or them before the next authority, to be examined and returned to his or their Master or Owner, who shall satisfy the charge accruing thereby; and all Ferrymen within this Colony are hereby required not to suffer any Indian or Negro Servant, without Certificate as aforesaid, to pass over their respective Ferrys, by assisting of them therein directly or indirectly, on penalty of paying a fine of Twenty Shillings for every such Offence to the County Treasury, to be levied on their estates upon non-payment, by warrant from any one Assistant or Justice of the Peace: And the like methods shall or may be used and observed as to Vagrant or Suspected Persons, found wandring from Town to Town, having no Certificate as aforesaid, who shall be seized and conveyed before the next Authority to be Examined and Disposed of according to Law: And if any Free Negroes shall travel without such Certificate or Pass, and be stopped, seized, or taken up, they shall pay all Charges arising thereby." — O *Acts and Laws of His Majesty's Province of Connecticut*, 87.

79. Connecticut: — Pursuit of runaways.

No date given. "It is also ordered, that when any servants shall runn from theire Masters, or any other inhabitants shall privately goe away with supition of ill intentions, It shall bee lawfull for the next Magistrate, or the constable and two of the chiefest inhabitants where no magistrate is, to press men and boates or pinnaces, at the publique charge, to persue such persons by sea or land, and bring them back by force of armes." — O *Colonial Records of Connecticut*, I. 539.

80. Pennsylvania: — Harboring fugitives.

Anno Regni Duodecimo Georgii Regis. [1726?] An Act for the better regulating of Negroes in this Province. "And be it further enacted by the Authority aforesaid, that no Person or Persons whatsoever shall Employ, or knowingly harbour, conceal, or entertain other Peoples Slaves at their Houses, Out-houses, or Plantations, without the Master or Owner's consent; excepting in Distress of weather or other Extraordinary Occasion, under the Penalty of Thirty Shillings for every twenty-four Hours he or they shall entertain or harbour him or them as aforesaid." — O *Province Laws of Pennsylvania*, 325.

APPENDIX B.

NATIONAL ACTS AND PROPOSITIONS RELATIVE TO FUGITIVE SLAVES. 1778–1854.

THIS Appendix contains all the important bills, acts, and treaties from the foundation of the Constitution to 1860. Many minor propositions may be found through the foot-notes to the text of Chapter II. The figures in brackets [ ] refer back to the text of the monograph.

1. Fugitive clause in treaty with the Delawares.
1778, Aug. 7. Art. IV. "And it is further agreed between the parties aforesaid, that neither shall entertain or give countenance to the enemies of the other, or protect in their respective States, criminal fugitives, servants, or slaves, but the same to apprehend, and secure and deliver to the State or States to which such enemies, criminals, servants, or slaves respectively belong." — *Statutes at Large*, VII. 14.

2. Fugitive clause in the treaty of peace. [§§ 13, 22.]
1782–83. 1782, Nov. 13. Provisional articles. 1783, Sept. 3. Definitive treaty. "His Britannic Majesty shall, with all convenient speed, and without causing any destruction, or carrying away any negroes or other property of the American inhabitants, withdraw all his armies, garrisons, and fleets from the said United States." — *Treaties and Conventions*, ed. of 1889, pp. 372, 378.

3. Fugitive clauses in Indian treaties. [§ 13.]
1784–86. 1784, Oct. 22. Treaty with the Six Nations, Art. I.
1785, Jan. 21. Treaty with the Wyandots, etc. Art. I. "All the prisoners white and black" taken by the Indians "shall be delivered up" or "restored." — *Statutes at Large*, VII. 15, 16.

4. Fugitive clause in King's ordinance. [§ 14.]
1785, April 6. Report of the Committee on Government of the Western Territory. "Provided that always, upon the escape of any person into any of the States described in the resolve of Congress of the twenty-third day of April, 1784, from whom labor or service is lawfully claimed in any one of the thirteen original States, such fugitive might be lawfully reclaimed and carried back to the person claiming his labor or service, this resolve notwithstanding." — *Papers of Old Congress*, XXI. 331, cited in *Bancroft, History of the United States (last Revision)*, VI. 133.

5. Fugitive clauses in Indian treaties. [§ 13.]
1785, Nov. 28. Treaty with the Cherokees, Art. I.
1786, Jan. 3. Treaty with the Choctaws, Art. I.
1786, Jan. 10. Treaty with the Chickasaws, Art. I.
Identical clauses. The Indians "to restore all the Negroes and all other property taken during the late war."

1786, June 31. Treaty with the Shawanees. Art. I. "All prisoners white and black taken in the late war from among the citizens of the United States by the Shawanee nation shall be restored." — *Statutes at Large*, VII. 18, 21, 25, 26.

6. Fugitive clause in Northwest Ordinance of 1787. [§ 14.]

1787, July 13. Art. VI. " There shall be neither slavery nor involuntary servitude in the said Territory, otherwise than in the punishment of crimes, whereof the party shall have been duly convicted; *provided*, always, that any person escaping into the same, from whom labor or service is lawfully claimed in any one of the original States, such fugitive may be lawfully reclaimed and conveyed to the person claiming his or her labor or service aforesaid." Read first time, July 11, 1787. Passed July 13, 1787. — O *Journals of Congress*, XII. 84, 92.

7. Fugitive clause in the Constitution. [§ 15.]

1787, Sept. 13. Art. IV. § 2. "No person held to service or labor in one State, under the laws thereof, escaping into another, shall, in consequence of any law or regulation therein, be discharged from such service or labor, but shall be delivered up on claim of the party to whom such service or labor may be due." — *Revised Statutes of the United States*, I. 18.

8. Clauses for returning fugitives in Indian treaties.

1789, Jan. 7. Treaty with the Wiandots, etc. Art. I. "The said nations agree to deliver up all the prisoners now in their hands (by what means soever they may have come into their possession)." — *Statutes at Large*, VII. 28.

1790–91. 1790, Apr. 7. Treaty with the Creeks. Art. III. "The Creek Nation shall deliver . . . all citizens of the United States, white inhabitants or negroes, who are now prisoners in any part of the said nation. And if any such prisoners or negroes should not be delivered on or before the first day of June next ensuing, the governor of Georgia may empower three persons to repair to the said nation, in order to claim and receive such prisoners and negroes." — *Statutes at Large*, VII. 35.

1791, July 2. Treaty with the Cherokees. Art. III. All prisoners to be yielded up on both sides. — *Statutes at Large*, VII. 36.

9. First Fugitive Slave Act.

1793, Feb. 12. *An Act respecting fugitives from justice and persons escaping from the service of their masters.*

"SECTION 1. *Be it enacted by the Senate and House of Representatives of the United States of America in Congress assembled*, That whenever the executive authority of any state in the Union, or of either of the territories northwest or south of the river Ohio, shall demand any person as a fugitive from justice, of the executive authority of any such state or territory to which such person shall have fled, and shall moreover produce the copy of an indictment found, or an affidavit made before a magistrate of any state or territory as aforesaid, charging the person so demanded, with having committed treason, felony or other crime, certified as authentic by the governor or chief magistrate of the state or territory from whence the person so charged fled, it shall be the duty of the executive authority of the state or territory to which such person shall have fled, to cause him or her to be arrested and secured, and notice of the arrest to be given to the executive authority making such demand, or to the agent of such authority appointed to receive the fugitive, and to cause the fugitive to be delivered to such agent when he shall appear : But if no such agent shall appear within six months from the time of the arrest, the prisoner may be discharged. And all costs or expenses incurred in the apprehending, securing, and transmitting such fugitive to the state or territory making such demand, shall be paid by such state or territory.

"SEC. 2. *And be it further enacted*, That any agent, appointed as aforesaid, who shall receive the fugitive into his custody, shall be empowered to transport him or her to the state or territory from which he or she shall have fled. And if any person or persons shall by force set at liberty, or rescue the fugitive from such agent while transporting, as aforesaid, the person or persons so offending shall, on conviction, be fined not exceeding five hundred dollars, and be imprisoned not exceeding one year.

" SEC. 3. *And be it also enacted*, That when a person held to labour in any of the United States, or in either of the territories on the northwest or south of the river Ohio, under the laws thereof, shall escape into any other of the said states or territory, the person to whom such labour or service may be due, his agent or attorney, is hereby empowered to seize or arrest such fugitive from labour, and to take him or her before any judge of the circuit or district courts of the United States, residing or being within the state, or before any magistrate of a county, city or town corporate, wherein such seizure or arrest shall be made, and upon proof to the satisfaction of such judge or magistrate, either by oral testimony or affidavit taken before and certified by a magistrate of any such state or territory, that the person so seized or arrested, doth, under the laws of the 'state or territory from which he or she fled, owe service or labour to the person claiming him or her, it shall be the duty of such judge or magistrate to give a certificate thereof to such claimant, his agent or attorney, which shall be sufficient warrant for removing the said fugitive from labour, to the state or territory from which he or she fled.

"SEC. 4. *And be it further enacted*, That any person who shall knowingly and willingly obstruct or hinder such claimant, his agent or attorney, in so seizing or arresting such fugitive from labour, or shall rescue such fugitive from such claimant, his agent or attorney when so arrested pursuant to the authority herein given or declared; or shall harbor or conceal such person after notice that he or she was a fugitive from labour, as aforesaid, shall, for either of the said offences, forfeit and pay the sum of five hundred dollars. Which penalty may be recovered by and for the benefit of such claimant, by action of debt, in any court proper to try the same; saving moreover to the person claiming such labour or service, his right of action for or on account of the said injuries - or either of them." — O *Statutes at Large*, I. 302-305.

10. Abstract of amendatory bill on fugitives. [§ 19.]

1801, Dec. 18. " The bill contemplates inflicting a penalty of five hundred dollars on any person harboring, concealing, or employing runaway slaves. Every person employing a black person, unless he had a certificate with a county seal to it, or signed by a justice of the peace, would be liable to the penalty."

1802, Jan. 15. A motion was made to strike out the second section of the bill, which would create therein and inflict the penalty for employing a person of color who has not a certificate of his freedom. Motion not carried. — *7 Cong. 1 Sess., Annals of Congress, H. of R.*, 423.

11. Restoration of slaves by Indian treaties. [§ 22.]

1814, Aug. 9. Treaty with the Creeks. Art. III. " The United States demand that a surrender be immediately made of all the persons and property taken from the citizens of the United States . . . to the respective owners." — *Treaties and Conventions.*

12. Fugitive slave clause in the Treaty of Ghent. [§ 22].

1814, Dec. 24. Art. I. " All territory, etc. shall be restored without delay, and without causing any destruction or carrying away any artillery, . . . or any slaves or other private property." — *Treaties and Conventions.*

13. Amendments proposed to Pindall's bill. [§ 20.]

1818, Jan. 29. " *Resolved*, That the said bill be referred to the committee to whom was referred the memorial of the annual meeting of the Society of Friends, of Baltimore, with instructions to inquire into the expediency of so amending the said bill as to guard more effectually against infringement of the rights of free negroes and other persons of color." Introduced by Mr. Rich. Resolution not accepted. — *House Journal 15 Cong. 1 Sess.*, 193; *Annals of Congress, 15 Cong. 1 Sess.*, 830.

To change the bill materially "by making judges of the State in which the apprentices, slaves, etc. are seized, the tribunal to decide the fact of slavery, instead of the judges of the States whence the fugitives have escaped." Introduced by Mr. Sergeant. Amendment not accepted. — *Annals of Congress*, 15 *Cong.* 1 *Sess.*, 830.

"Mr. Rich made several successive attempts to procure amendments to the bill, relaxing some of its provisions, which were successively negatived." — *Annals of Congress*, 15 *Cong.* 1 *Sess.*, 830.

14. Provision for delivery on executive requisition. [§ 20.]

1818, March 11. Mr. Daggett moved to strike out the following section of the bill: "Sec. 6. *And be it further enacted*, that whenever the Executive authority of any State in the Union, or of either of the Territories thereof, shall, for or in behalf of any citizen or inhabitant of such State or Territory, demand any fugitive slave of the Executive authority of any State or Territory, to which such slave shall have fled, and shall moreover produce a certificate, issued pursuant to the first section of this act, it shall be the duty of the Executive authority of the State or Territory to which such fugitive shall have fled to cause him or her to be arrested and secured, and notice of the arrest to be given to the Executive authority making such demand, or to the agent of such authority appointed to receive the fugitive, and to cause such fugitive to be delivered to the said agent, on the confine or boundary of the State or Territory in which said arrest shall be, and in the most usual and direct route to the place from whence the said fugitive shall have escaped; and the reasonable expense of such arrest, detention, and delivery of such fugitive shall be paid by the said agent." Amendment determined in the negative. — *Senate Journal*, 15 *Cong.* 1 *Sess.*, 227, 228; *Annals of Congress*, 15 *Cong.* 1 *Sess.*, 259.

15. Proposed limitation to four years. [§ 20.]

1818, May 10. Mr. Lacock moved to amend by adding the following: "Sec. -. *And be it further enacted* that this law shall be and remain in force for the term of four years, and no longer." The Senate being equally divided, the President determined the question in the affirmative. — *Senate Journal*, 15 *Cong.* 1 *Sess.*, 228; *Annals of Congress*, 15 *Cong.* 1 *Sess.*, 259.

16. Fugitive Slave clause in the Missouri Compromise. [§ 21.]

1820, March 19. The Missouri Compromise provided "that any persons escaping into the same, from whom labor or service is lawfully claimed in any State or Territory of the United States, such fugitive may be lawfully reclaimed, and conveyed to the person claiming his or her labor, or service, as aforesaid." — *Annals of Congress*, 16 *Cong.* 1 *Sess.*, 1469, 1587.

17. Investigation into the Pennsylvania Act. [§ 21.]

1820, April 3. Mr. Pindall introduced the following resolution: "*Resolved*, That the Secretary of State be instructed to procure and transmit to this House, as soon as practicable, a copy of such late act or acts of the Pennsylvania Legislature as prohibit or restrain the justices, aldermen, or other magistrates or officers of that State from interposing in the apprehension or surrender of fugitive slaves." — *House Journal*, 16 *Cong.* 1 *Sess.*, 371; *Annals of Congress*, 16 *Cong.* 1 *Sess.*, 1717.

Mr. Tarr moved to amend as follows: "Provided, any such act or acts shall have been passed." Resolution and amendment agreed to. — *House Journal*, 16 *Cong.* 1 *Sess.*, 371; *Annals of Congress*, 16 *Cong.* 1 *Sess.*, 1717.

1820, April 18. Ordered, That the letter from the Secretary of State with the Act of the Pennsylvania Legislature accompanying it, "be committed to the committee appointed 18th of March to inquire into the expediency of providing by law for reclaiming persons held to service or labor in one State, and escaping therefrom into another." — *House Journal*, 16 *Cong.* 1 *Sess.*, 427; *Annals of Congress*, 16 *Cong.* 1 *Sess.*, 1863.

18. Maryland resolutions protesting against Pennsylvanians. [§ 21.]

1821, Dec. 17. "Mr. Wright laid before the House an attested copy of a resolution passed by the General Assembly of the State of Maryland, complaining of the protection offered by the citizens of Pennsylvania to the slaves of the citizens of Maryland, who abscond and go into that State, and declaring that it is the duty of Congress to enact such a law as will prevent a continuance of the evils complained of; which resolution was referred to the Committee on the Judiciary." — *House Journal, 17 Cong. 1 Sess.*, 62 ; *Annals of Congress, 17 Cong. 1 Sess.*, 553.

19. Assumption of claims on Indians for fugitives. [§ 22.]

1832, May 9. Treaty with the Seminoles, Art. VI. "The Seminoles being anxious to be relieved from repeated vexatious demands for slaves and other property alleged to have been stolen and destroyed by them, so that they may remove unembarrassed to their new homes, the United States stipulate to have the same property investigated, and to liquidate such as may be satisfactorily established, provided the amount does not exceed seven thousand (7,000) dollars." — *Statutes at Large*, VII. 369.

20. Calhoun's resolution on the status of slaves on the high seas. [§ 24.]

1840, April 15. "*Resolved*, That a ship or vessel on the high seas, in time of peace, engaged in a lawful voyage, is, according to the laws of nations, under the exclusive jurisdiction of the State to which her flag belongs; as much so as if constituting a part of its own domain.

"*Resolved*, That if such ship or vessel should be forced by stress of weather, or other unavoidable cause, into the port, and under the jurisdiction of a friendly power, she and her cargo, and persons on board, with their property, and all the rights belonging to their personal relations, as established by the laws of the State to which they belong, would be placed under the protection which the laws of nations extend to the unfortunate under such circumstances.

"*Resolved*, That the brig Enterprise, which was forced unavoidably by stress of weather into Port Hamilton, Bermuda Island, while on a lawful voyage on the high seas from one port of the Union to another, comes within the principles embraced in the foregoing resolutions; and that the seizure and detention of the negroes on board by the local authority of the island, was an act in violation of the laws of nations, and highly unjust to our own citizens, to whom they belong." — *Cong. Globe, 26 Cong. 1 Sess.*, 327.

21. Woodbridge resolution on extradition of slaves. [§ 23]

1841, Dec. 22. Mr. Woodbridge submitted the following resolution, which was considered, and by unanimous consent agreed to.

"*Resolved*, That the Committee on Foreign Relations inquire into the expediency of entering into some arrangement with the Government of Great Britain, reciprocal in its provisions, for the arrest of fugitives escaping over the Northern or Western boundary of the United States, charged with the commission of any crime or crimes, and for the surrender of such fugitives upon reasonable requisition to the authorities of the State or province from which such fugitives may have fled: *Provided*, such arrangements do not comprehend cases of political offences merely, but be restricted to those which are in themselves criminal." No action taken. — *Senate Journal, 27 Cong. 2 Sess.*, 47 ; *Cong. Globe, 27 Cong. 2 Sess.*, 48.

22. Significant extracts from the Prigg decision. [§ 25.]

1842. "Upon this ground we have not the slightest hesitation in holding that, under and in virtue of the Constitution, the owner of a slave is clothed with entire authority, in every state in the Union, to seize and recapture his slave, whenever he can do it without any breach of the peace, or any illegal violence."

"The clause is found in the national Constitution, and not in that of any state. It does not point out any state functionaries, or any state actions to carry its provisions into effect. The states cannot, therefore, be compelled to enforce them; and it might well be deemed an unconstitutional exercise of the power of interpretation, to insist that the states are bound to provide means to carry into effect the duties of the national government nowhere delegated or intrusted to them by the Constitution."

"If this be so, then it would seem, upon just principles of construction, that the legislation of Congress, if constitutional, must supersede all state legislation upon the same subject; and by necessary implication prohibit it."

"As to the authority so conferred upon state magistrates, while a difference of opinion has existed, and may exist still on the point, in different states, whether state magistrates are bound to act under it; none is entertained by this Court that state magistrates may, if they choose, exercise that authority, unless prohibited by state legislation." — *16 Peters, Justice Story's Opinion*, 608.

23. Giddings's resolutions on the status of slaves on the high seas. [§ 24.]

1842, March 21. "Resolved, That when a ship belonging to the citizens of any State of this Union leaves the waters and territory of such State, and enters upon the high seas, the persons on board cease to be subject to the slave laws of such State, and thenceforth are governed in their relations to each other by, and are amenable only to, the laws of the United States.

"Resolved, That when the brig Creole, on her late voyage, for New Orleans, left the territorial jurisdiction of Virginia, the slave laws of that State ceased to have jurisdiction over the persons on board said brig, and such persons became amenable only to the law of the United States.

"Resolved, That the persons on board the said ship, in reserving their natural rights of personal liberty, violated no law of the United States, incurred no legal penalty, and are justly liable to no punishment." — *Cong. Globe, 27 Cong. 2 Sess.*, 324.

24. Benton's resolution on slaves escaping to Canada. [§ 23.]

1844, Jan. 29. Mr. Benton presented the following resolution: —

"*Resolved*, That the President be requested to communicate to the Senate the information, if any, which may be in the Department of State, in relation to slaves committing crimes and escaping from the United States to the British dominions since the ratification of the treaty of 1842, and the refusal of the British authorities to give them up. Also, that he communicate to the Senate the information, if any such is possessed by him, of the construction which the British government puts upon the said article in relation to slaves committing crimes in the United States and taking refuge in the British dominions." — *Congressional Record, 28 Cong. 1 Sess.*, 206.

25. Giddings's resolution for the abolition of the slave trade in the District of Columbia. [§ 28.]

1848, Jan. 17. Mr. Giddings described the seizure of a colored man employed as waiter in a colored boarding-house in Washington. He then offered the following resolution: —

"*Resolved*, That a select committee of five members be appointed to inquire into and report upon facts aforesaid; also as to the propriety of repealing such acts of Congress as sustain or authorize the slave trade in this District, or to remove the seat of the Government to some free State." Resolution laid on the table. — *House Journal, 30 Cong. 1 Sess.*, 250; *Cong. Globe, 30 Cong. 1 Sess.*, 179.

26. Hall's repeal resolution for the District of Columbia. [§ 28.]

1848, Feb. 28. Mr. Nathan K. Hall offered the following preamble and resolutions, which were read, and, debate arising thereon, it was laid over under the rule, viz.: —

"Preamble.... *Resolved*, That the Committee on the Judiciary be, and they are hereby, directed to report to this House with all convenient speed a bill repealing all laws of Congress, and abrogating, so far as they are operative or in force in the District of Columbia all the laws in the State of Maryland which authorize or require the courts, officers, or magistrates of the United States, or of the said District, within the District of Columbia to issue process for arrest, or commit to the jail of the said District any runaway or other slave or fugitive from service," etc. Resolution laid over under the rule. — *House Journal, 30 Cong. 1 Sess.*, 450, 453; *Cong. Globe, 30 Cong. 1 Sess.*, 390.

27. Giddings's resolution inquiring into the condition of the District of Columbia jail. [§ 28.]

1848, April 18. Mr. Giddings introduced the following resolution : —

" Whereas, more than eighty men, women, and children, are said to be now confined in the prison of the District of Columbia without being charged with crime or any impropriety other than an attempt to enjoy that liberty for which our fathers encountered toil, suffering, and death itself, and for which the people of many European governments are now struggling; And whereas said prison was erected, and is now sustained, by funds contributed by the people of the free as well as of the slave States, and is under the control of the laws and officers of the United States:

"And whereas, such practice is derogatory to our national character, incompatible with the duty of a civilized and Christian people, and unworthy of being sustained by an American Congress: Therefore, *Be it resolved*, That a select committee of five members of this body be appointed to inquire into and report to this House by what authority said prison is used for the purpose of confining persons who have attempted to escape from slavery, with leave to report what legislation is proper in regard to said practice. *Resolved, further*, that said committee be authorized to send for persons and papers." Objections being made, the motion was not received. — *Cong. Globe, 30 Cong. 1 Sess.*, 641.

28. Giddings's resolution on the jail in the District of Columbia. [§ 28.]

1848, April 21. Mr. Giddings visited the jail in the District of Columbia for the purpose of interviewing the persons confined there on charge of carrying away slaves from this District. He was then mobbed and his life endangered.

"*Resolved*, That a committee of five members be appointed to investigate and report to this House respecting the points alluded to in the above statement, and that said committee be authorized to send for persons and papers, and to sit during the session of the House."— *Cong. Globe, 30th Cong. 1 Sess.*, 664.

29. Meade's resolution on more effectual enforcement of the constitutional article on fugitive slaves. [§ 27.]

1849, Jan. 8. Mr. Meade moved that the rules be suspended to enable him to offer the following resolution : —

" Preamble. Whereas it is the duty of the Congress of the United States to enact all laws necessary to enforce such provisions of the Constitution as were intended to protect the citizens of the several States in their rights of property, and past experience has proved that laws should be passed by Congress to enforce the second section of the fourth article of the Constitution, which requires that persons held to labor in one State, escaping into another, shall be delivered up on claim of the party to whom such labor may be due; therefore, Resolved, That the Committee on the Judiciary is hereby instructed to report a bill to this House, providing effectually for the apprehension and delivery of fugitives from labor who have escaped, or may hereafter escape, from one State into another." Rules not suspended. — *House Journal, 30 Cong. 2 Sess.*, 213; *Cong. Globe, 30 Cong. 2 Sess.*, 188.

30. Legislative history of the Fugitive Slave Act. [Jan. 3 to Sept. 18, § 29.]

1850, Jan. 3. Mr. Mason of Virginia gave notice of his intention to introduce a bill.— *Cong. Globe*, 99.

Jan. 4 Senate bill No. 23 introduced by Mason, read twice, ordered printed, and referred to the Committee on the Judiciary. — *Senate Journal*, 54; *Globe*, 103.

Jan. 16. Bill reported favorably by Butler from the committee, ordered printed, and made a special order for Jan. 23 — *Senate Journal*, 88; *Globe*, 171; *Senate Reports*, I. No. 12.

Jan. 22. Debate begun. Mason offered an amendment which made the fine for any obstruction of the workings of the act one thousand dollars, and refused to allow the testimony of a fugitive. — *Globe*, 210.

Jan. 23, 24. Bill taken up and debated. — *Senate Journal*, 104, 110; *Globe*, 220, 228; *Globe App.* 79, 83.

Jan 28. Seward presented an amendment, which allowed the right of trial by jury, and punished judges who should disallow the writ of habeas corpus. — *Senate Journal*, 117; *Globe*, 233–237.

Jan. 29. Clay introduced, as a part of his compromise resolutions, a declaration that a more effective fugitive slave act should be passed. — *Senate Journal*, 118; *Globe*, 247.

Jan. 31. Mason offered a substitute for the bill already before the Senate. It was laid on the table, and ordered to be printed. — *Globe*, 270.

June 3. Webster brought in an amendatory bill. — *Senate Journal*, 370; *Globe*, 1111.

Aug. 15. The debate was again opened, and made the special order for Aug. 19 — *Senate Journal*, 560; *Globe*, 1588.

Aug. 19. Mason offered as an amendment a substitute for the bill already before the Senate. — *Senate Journal*, 564; *Globe*, 1605; *Globe App.*, 1582.

Dayton brought in an amendment which gave trial by jury. This was rejected. — *Senate Journal*, 564; *Globe App.*, 564.

Chase offered one of the same character, which was also rejected. — *Globe App*, 1589.

Winthrop brought in an amendment granting the protection of the habeas corpus. This was rejected. — *Senate Journal*, 565; *Globe App*, 1589.

Aug. 20. Mason's substitute was agreed to. — *Senate Journal*, 568; *Globe*, 1616; *Globe App.*, 1591.

An amendment to Mason's substitute was offered by Mr. Pratt. This gave the owner the right of suit against the United States for the value of the slave if not delivered. This was afterward amended by Mason and Pratt, and rejected, August 23. — *Senate Journal*, 570–573; *Globe*, 1636; *Globe App.*, 1609.

Aug 22. Underwood offered an amendment as a substitute, and Davis presented an amendment to Mason's bill striking out the clause providing compensation for escaped slaves. This was rejected. — *Senate Journal*, 573, 580; *Globe*, 1636; *Globe App.*, 1609, 1619.

Aug. 23. Amendments were offered to Underwood's amendment by Chase and Badger. Both were rejected. — *Senate Journal*, 575–580; *Globe App.*, 1619, 1623, 1625.

Another slight amendment by Chase was also rejected. — *Globe App.*, 1624.

Mason amended his bill by making the Marshal liable for the value of a slave who has escaped from his custody. — *Senate Journal*, 576; *Globe App.*, 1625.

An attempt to amend the bill by striking out the compensation for escaped slaves, and other slight changes, was made by Davis, and the amendment was accepted. — *Senate Journal*, 580; *Globe App.*, 1630.

Bill as amended was then ordered to be engrossed for the third reading. — *Senate Journal*, 581; *Globe*, 1647; *Globe App*, 1630.

Aug. 26. After changing the title to make it an act supplementary to that of 1793, the bill was passed, and sent to the House. — *Senate Journal*, 583; *Globe*, 1660.

Sept. 12. In the House it was read a first and second time by title. Thompson of Pennsylvania moved to put it on its passage, and moved the previous question, which he refused to withdraw, and which was carried — *House Journal*, 1289, 1448.

Stevens moved to lay it on the table, but the motion was lost, and the bill was ordered to a third reading. — *House Journal*, 1449.

The bill was passed, 109 to 75. — *House Journal*, 1451–1453; *Globe*, 1807.

It was returned to the Senate. — *Senate Journal*, 627; *Globe*, 1810.

Sept 14. The bill was signed by the presiding officer of the Senate. — *Senate Journal*, 629; *Globe*, 1815.

Bill signed by the Speaker of the House.— *House Journal,* 1457 ; *Globe,* 1812.
Sept. 16. Bill sent to the President, and signed by him Sept. 18. — *House Journal,* 1472, 1497 ; *Senate Journal,* 638, 648.

31. Second Fugitive Slave Act. [§§ 29, 30.]

1850, Sept. 18. "*An Act to amend, and supplementary to, the Act entitled 'An Act respecting Fugitives from Justice, and Persons escaping from the Service of their Masters,' approved February twelfth, one thousand seven hundred and ninety-three.*

"*Be it enacted by the Senate and House of Representatives of the United States of America in Congress assembled,* That the persons who have been, or may hereafter be, appointed commissioners, in virtue of any act of Congress, by the Circuit Courts of the United States, and who, in consequence of such appointment, are authorized to exercise the powers that any justice of the peace, or other magistrate of any of the United States, may exercise in respect to offenders for any crime or offence against the United States, by arresting, imprisoning, or bailing the same under and by virtue of the thirty-third section of the act of the twenty-fourth of September seventeen hundred and eighty-nine, entitled 'An Act to establish the judicial courts of the United States,' shall be, and are hereby, authorized and required to exercise and discharge all the powers and duties conferred by this act.

"SEC. 2. *And be it further enacted,* That the Superior Court of each organized Territory of the United States shall have the same power to appoint commissioners to take acknowledgments of bail and affidavits, and to take depositions of witnesses in civil causes, which is now possessed by the Circuit Court of the United States; and all commissioners who shall hereafter be appointed for such purposes by the Superior Court of any organized Territory of the United States, shall possess all the powers, and exercise all the duties, conferred by law upon the commissioners appointed by the Circuit Courts of the United States for similar purposes, and shall moreover exercise and discharge all the powers and duties conferred by this act.

"SEC. 3. *And be it further enacted,* That the Circuit Courts of the United States, and the Superior Courts of each organized Territory of the United States, shall from time to time enlarge the number of commissioners, with a view to afford reasonable facilities to reclaim fugitives from labor, and to the prompt discharge of the duties imposed by this act.

"SEC. 4. *And be it further enacted,* That the commissioners above named shall have concurrent jurisdiction with the judges of the Circuit and District Courts of the United States, in their respective circuits and districts within the several States, and the judges of the Superior Courts of the Territories, severally and collectively, in term-time and vacation; and shall grant certificates to such claimants, upon satisfactory proof being made, with authority to take and remove such fugitives from service or labor, under the restrictions herein contained, to the State or Territory from which such persons may have escaped or fled.

"SEC. 5. *And be it further enacted,* That it shall be the duty of all marshals and deputy marshals to obey and execute all warrants and precepts issued under the provisions of this act, when to them directed; and should any marshal or deputy marshal refuse to receive such warrant, or other process, when tendered, or to use all proper means diligently to execute the same, he shall, on conviction thereof, be fined in the sum of one thousand dollars, to the use of such claimant, on the motion of such claimant, by the Circuit or District Court for the district of such marshal; and after arrest of such fugitive, by such marshal or his deputy, or whilst at any time in his custody under the provisions of this act, should such fugitive escape, whether with or without the assent of such marshal or his deputy, such marshal shall be liable, on his official bond, to be prosecuted for the benefit of such claimant, for the full value of the service or labor of said fugitive in the State, Territory, or District whence he escaped: and the better to enable the said commissioners, when thus appointed, to execute their duties faithfully and efficiently, in conformity with the requirements of the Constitution of the United States and of this act, they are hereby authorized and empowered, within their counties respectively, to appoint, in writing under their hands, any one or more suitable persons, from time to time, to execute all such warrants and other process as may be issued by them in the lawful performance of their respective duties; with authority to such commissioners, or the persons to be appointed by them, to execute process as aforesaid, to summon and call to their aid the bystanders, or *posse comitatus* of the proper county, when necessary to insure a faithful observance of the clause of the Constitution referred to, in conformity with the provisions of this act; and all good citizens are hereby commanded to aid and assist in the prompt and efficient execution of this law, whenever their services may be required, as aforesaid, for that purpose; and said warrants shall run, and be executed by said officers, anywhere in the State within which they are issued.

"SEC. 6. *And be it further enacted*, That when a person held to service or labor in any State or Territory of the United States, has heretofore or shall hereafter escape into another State or Territory of the United States, the person or persons to whom such service or labor may be due, or his, her, or their agent or attorney, duly authorized, by power of attorney, in writing, acknowledged and certified under the seal of some legal officer or court of the State or Territory in which the same may be executed, may pursue and reclaim such fugitive person, either by procuring a warrant from some one of the courts, judges, or commissioners aforesaid, of the proper circuit, district, or county, for the apprehension of such fugitive from service or labor, or by seizing and arresting such fugitive, where the same can be done without process, and by taking, or causing such person to be taken, forthwith before such court, judge, or commissioner, whose duty it shall be to hear and determine the case of such claimant in a summary manner; and upon satisfactory proof being made, by deposition or affidavit, in writing, to be taken and certified by such court, judge, or commissioner, or by other satisfactory testimony, duly taken and certified by some court, magistrate, justice of the peace, or other legal officer authorized to administer an oath and take depositions under the laws of the State or Territory from which such person owing service or labor may have escaped, with a certificate of such magistracy or other authority, as aforesaid, with the seal of the proper court or officer thereto attached, which seal shall be sufficient to establish the competency of the proof, and with proof, also by affidavit, of the identity of the person whose service or labor is claimed to be due as aforesaid, that the person so arrested does in fact owe service or labor to the person or persons claiming him or her, in the State or Territory from which such fugitive may have escaped as aforesaid, and that said person escaped, to make out and deliver to such claimant, his or her agent or attorney, a certificate setting forth the substantial facts as to the service or labor due from such fugitive to the claimant, and of his or her escape from the State or Territory in which such service or labor was due, to the State or Territory in which he or she was arrested, with authority to such claimant, or his or her agent or attorney, to use such reasonable force and restraint as may be necessary, under the circumstances of the case, to take and remove such fugitive person back to the State or Territory whence he or she may have escaped as aforesaid. In no trial or hearing under this act shall the testimony of such alleged fugitive be admitted in evidence; and the certificates in this and the first [fourth] section mentioned, shall be conclusive of the right of the person or persons in whose favor granted, to remove such fugitive to the State or Territory from which he escaped, and shall prevent all molestation of such person or persons by any process issued by any court, judge, magistrate, or other person whomsoever.

"SEC. 7. *And be it further enacted*, That any person who shall knowingly and willingly obstruct, hinder, or prevent such claimant, his agent or attorney, or any person or persons lawfully assisting him, her, or them, from arresting such a fugitive from service or labor, either with or without process as aforesaid, or shall rescue, or attempt to rescue, such fugitive from service or labor, from the custody of such claimant, his or her agent or attorney, or other person or persons lawfully assisting as aforesaid, when so arrested, pursuant to the authority herein given and declared; or shall aid, abet, or assist such person so owing service or labor as aforesaid, directly or indirectly, to escape from such claimant, his agent or attorney, or other person or persons legally authorized as aforesaid ; or shall harbor or conceal such fugitive, so as to prevent the discovery and arrest of such person, after notice or knowledge of the fact that such person was a fugitive from service or labor as aforesaid, shall, for either of said offences, be subject to a fine not exceeding one thousand dollars, and imprisonment not exceeding six months, by indictment and conviction before the District Court of the United States for the district in which such offence may have been committed, or before the proper court of criminal jurisdiction, if committed within any one of the organized Territories of the United States; and shall moreover forfeit and pay, by way of civil damages to the party injured by such illegal conduct, the sum of one thousand dollars, for each fugitive so lost as aforesaid, to be recovered by action of debt, in any of the District or Territorial Courts aforesaid, within whose jurisdiction the said offence may have been committed.

"SEC. 8. *And be it further enacted,* That the marshals, their deputies, and the clerks of the said District and Territorial Courts, shall be paid, for their services, the like fees as may be allowed to them for similar services in other cases; and where such services are rendered exclusively in the arrest, custody, and delivery of the fugitive to the claimant, his or her agent or attorney, or where such supposed fugitive may be discharged out of custody for the want of sufficient proof as aforesaid, then such fees are to be paid in the whole by such claimant, his agent or attorney; and in all cases where the proceedings are before a commissioner, he shall be entitled to a fee of ten dollars in full for his services in each case, upon the delivery of the said certificate to the claimant, his or her agent or attorney; or a fee of five dollars in cases where the proof shall not, in the opinion of such commissioner, warrant such certificate and delivery, inclusive of all services incident to such arrest and examination, to be paid, in either case, by the claimant, his or her agent or attorney. The person or persons authorized to execute the process to be issued by such commissioners for the arrest and detention of fugitives from service or labor as aforesaid, shall also be entitled to a fee of five dollars each for each person he or they may arrest and take before any such commissioner as aforesaid, at the instance and request of such claimant, with such other fees as may be deemed reasonable by such commissioner for such other additional services as may be necessarily performed by him or them ; such as attending at the examination, keeping the fugitive in custody, and providing him with food and lodging during his detention, and until the final determination of such commissioner ; and, in general, for performing such other duties as may be required by such claimant, his or her attorney or agent, or commissioner in the premises, such fees to be made up in conformity with the fees usually charged by the officers of the courts of justice within the proper district or county, as near as may be practicable, and paid by such claimants, their agents or attorneys, whether such supposed fugitives from service or labor be ordered to be delivered to such claimants by the final determination of such commissioners or not.

"SEC. 9. *And be it further enacted,* That, upon affidavit made by the claimant of such fugitive, his agent or attorney, after such certificate has been issued, that he has reason to apprehend that such fugitive will be rescued by force from his or their possession before he can be taken beyond the limits of the State in which the arrest is made, it shall be the duty of the officer making the arrest to retain such fugitive in his custody, and to remove him to the State whence he fled, and there to deliver him to said claimant, his agent, or attorney. And to this end, the officer aforesaid is hereby authorized and required to employ so many persons as he may deem necessary to overcome such force, and to retain them in his service so long as circumstances may require. The said officer and his assistants, while so employed, to receive the same compensation, and to be allowed the same expenses, as are now allowed by law for transportation of criminals, to be certified by the judge of the district within which the arrest is made, and paid out of the treasury of the United States.

"SEC. 10. *And be it further enacted,* That when any person held to service or labor in any State or Territory, or in the District of Columbia, shall escape therefrom, the party to whom such service or labor shall be due, his, her, or their agent or attorney, may apply to any court of record therein, or judge thereof in vacation, and make satisfactory proof to such court, or judge in vacation, of the escape aforesaid, and that the person escaping owed service or labor to such party. Whereupon the court shall cause a record to be made of the matters so proved, and also a general description of the person so escaping, with such convenient certainty as may be; and a transcript of such record, authenticated by the attestation of the clerk and of the seal of the said court, being produced in any other State, Territory, or district in which the person so escaping may be found, and being exhibited to any judge, commissioner, or other officer authorized by the law of the United States to cause persons escaping from service or labor to be delivered up, shall be held and taken to be full and conclusive evidence of the fact of escape, and that the service or labor of the person escaping is due to the party in such record mentioned. And upon the production by the said party of other and further evidence if necessary, either oral or by affidavit, in addition to what is contained in the said record of the identity of the person escaping, he or she shall be delivered up to the claimant. And the said court, commissioner, judge, or other person authorized by this act to grant certificates to claimants of fugitives, shall, upon the production of the record and other evidences aforesaid, grant to such claimant a certificate of his right to take any such person identified and proved to be owing service or labor as aforesaid, which certificate shall authorize such claimant to seize or arrest and transport such person to the State or Territory from which he escaped: *Provided,* That nothing herein contained shall be construed as requiring the production of a transcript of such record as evidence as aforesaid. But in its absence the claim shall be heard and determined upon other satisfactory proofs, competent in law.

"Approved, September 18, 1850." — *Statutes at Large,* ix. 462-465.

32. McLanahan's resolution against repeal of the law of 1850.

1851, Jan. 13. Mr. McLanahan moved that the rules be suspended to enable him to introduce the following resolution, viz.: "*Resolved,* That it would be inexpedient and improper to repeal the law passed at the last session of Congress, entitled 'An act to amend, and supplementary to, the act entitled An act respecting fugitives from justice and persons escaping from the service of their masters,' approved Feb. 12, 1793." House refused to suspend the rules. — *House Journal, 31 Cong. 2 Sess.,* 139; *Cong. Globe, 31 Cong. 2 Sess.,* 226.

33. Clay's resolution on the Shadrach case, Boston. [§ 51.]

1851, Feb. 17. Mr. Clay submitted the following resolution, which lies over one day: "*Resolved,* That the President of the United States be requested to lay before the Senate, if not incompatible with the public interest, any information he may possess in regard to an alleged recent case of a forcible resistance to the execution of the laws of the United States in the city of Boston, and to communicate to the Senate under the above condition what means he has adopted to meet the occurrence, and whether, in his opinion, any additional legislation is necessary to meet the exigency of the case, and to more rigorously execute existing laws." Resolution adopted. — *Senate Journal, 31 Cong. 2 Sess.,* 187; *Cong. Globe, 31 Cong. 2 Sess.,* 580.

34. Bright's bill explanatory of law of 1850.

1851, Feb. 10. Mr. Bright obtained leave to bring in a bill (458) explanatory of the act approved 18th September in the year 1850, entitled, "An Act to amend, and supplemental to, the act entitled, 'An Act respecting fugitives from justice and persons escaping from the service of their masters,'" approved Feb. 12, 1793, which was read twice, and referred to the Committee on the Judiciary. — *Senate Journal, 32 Cong. 1 Sess.*, 162.

The bill is in the following terms: "*Be it enacted, etc.*, that all action and causes of action, and all proceedings instituted and to be instituted, for any violation of the provisions of said act respecting fugitives from justice and persons escaping from the service of their masters, approved the 12th February, 1793, may be instituted and prosecuted to final judgment and execution as if the said act of Sept. 18, 1850, had not been passed." — *Cong. Globe, 31 Cong. 2 Sess.*, 492.

35. Fitch's resolution affirming the Compromise.

1852, March 1. Mr. Fitch offered the following resolution: "*Resolved*, That we recognize the binding efficacy of the compromises of the Constitution, and believe it to be the intention of the people generally, as we hereby declare it to be ours individually, to abide such compromises, and to sustain the laws necessary to carry out the provisions for the delivery of fugitive slaves ordered, and that we deprecate all further agitation of questions growing out of that provision of the Constitution embraced in the acts of the last Congress known as the Compromise." — *House Journal, 32 Cong. 1 Sess.*, 408 ; *Cong. Globe, 32 Cong. 1 Sess.*, 659.

36. Jackson's resolution affirming the Compromise.

1852, March 22. "*Resolved*, That we recognize the binding efficacy of the compromises of the Constitution, and believe it to be the intention of the people generally, as we hereby declare it to be ours individually, to abide such compromises, and to sustain the laws necessary to carry them out, — the provision for the delivery of fugitive slaves, and the act of the last Congress for that purpose included, — and that we deprecate all further agitation of questions growing out of that provision, of the questions embraced in the acts of the last Congress known as the Compromise, and of questions generally connected with the institution of slavery as unnecessary, useless, and dangerous." Resolution, as amended by Mr. Hillyer below, agreed to. — *House Journal, 32 Cong. 1 Sess.*, 550 ; *Cong. Globe, 32 Cong. 1 Sess.*, 825.

37. Hillyer's finality resolution.

1852, April 5. Mr. Hillyer moved the following resolution: "*Resolved*, That the series of acts passed during the first session of the Thirty-first Congress, known as the compromise, are recorded as a final adjustment, and a permanent settlement of the questions there embraced, and should be maintained and executed as such." Resolution agreed to, April 6, 1852. — *House Journal, 32 Cong. 1 Sess.*, 548 ; *Cong. Globe, 32 Cong. 1 Sess.*, 979.

38. Chase's resolution of inquiry into payments under act of 1850.

1852, June 3. Mr. Chase submitted the following resolution: "*Resolved*, That the Secretary of the Interior be directed to communicate to the Senate statements, showing in detail the expenses incurred and claims made under the Act to amend and supplemental to the 'Act respecting fugitives from justice and persons escaping from the service of their masters,' distinguishing the expenses incurred and claimed by reason of prosecutions for treasons, alleged to have been committed in resistance of said act from expenses incurred and claimed by reason of other prosecutions for offending against said act, and for proceedings before and under orders made by committee." No action taken. — *Senate Journal, 32 Cong. 1 Sess.*, 450 ; *Cong. Globe, 32 Cong. 1 Sess.*, 1519.

APPENDIX C.

NATIONAL ACTS AND PROPOSITIONS RELATING TO FUGITIVE SLAVES.

(1860-1864.)

This Appendix is intended to contain references to all the resolutions, bills, and acts of Congress, relative to fugitives, from the beginning of the critical session of 1860-61 to the repeal of the acts in 1864. The resolutions for amendments to the Constitution have been collected by Mr. Herman V. Ames of the Harvard Graduate School, who has kindly selected out of the numerous amendments proposed in the last session of the Thirty-Sixth Congress those bearing upon this subject.

The single star (*) indicates a measure which passed one House: a double star (**) a measure which passed both Houses.

1. **President Buchanan's message.** [§ 86.]
1860, Dec. 4. Paragraph on the return of fugitive slaves: *Senate Journal, 36 Cong. 2 Sess.*, 18.
2. **Cochrane's Joint Resolution.** [§ 86.]
1860, Dec. 12. To amend the Constitution, for the return of fugitives: *House Journal, 36 Cong. 2 Sess.*, 61; *Cong. Globe*, 77.
3. **Morris's Resolution.** [§ 86.]
1860, Dec. 12. To amend the Fugitive Slave Law: *House Journal, 36 Cong. 2 Sess.* 63; *Cong. Globe*, 77.
4. **Leake's Joint Resolution.** [§ 86.]
1860, Dec. 12. Amendment to the Constitution: *House Journal, 36 Cong. 2 Sess.*, 65; *Cong. Globe*, 77.
5. **Cox's Resolution.** [§ 86.]
1860, Dec. 12. To amend the Fugitive Slave Law: *Senate Journal, 36 Cong. 2 Sess.*, 66; *Cong. Globe*, 77.
6. **Stevenson's Resolution.** [§ 86.]
1860, Dec. 12. To amend the Fugitive Slave Law: *House Journal, 36 Cong. 2 Sess.*, 67; *Cong. Globe*, 77.
7. **Niblack's Resolution.** [§ 86.]
1860, Dec. 12. To amend the Fugitive Slave Law: *House Journal, 36 Cong. 2 Sess.*, 69; *Cong. Globe*, 77.
8. **English's Joint Resolution.** [§ 86.]
1860, Dec. 12. Amendment to the Constitution on the return of fugitives: *House Journal, 36 Cong. 2 Sess.*, 68; *Cong. Globe*, 78.
9. **McClernand's Joint Resolution.** [§ 86.]
1860, Dec. 12. Amendment to the Constitution, on fugitive slaves: *House Journal, 36 Cong. 2 Sess.*, 68; *Cong. Globe*, 78.
10. **Hindman's Joint Resolution.** [§ 86.]
1860, Dec. 12. Amendment to the Constitution for the enforcement of the Fugitive Slave Law: *House Journal, 36 Cong. 2 Sess.*, 70; *Cong. Globe*, 79.

11. Kilgore's Resolution. [§ 86.]
1860, Dec. 12. To amend the Fugitive Slave Law: *House Journal, 36 Cong. 2 Sess.*, 70; *Cong Globe*, 78.

12. Johnson's Joint Resolution. [§ 86.]
1860, Dec. 13. Amendment to the Constitution for the return of fugitive slaves: *Senate Journal, 36 Cong. 2 Sess.*, 41; *Cong. Globe*, 83.

13. Crittenden's Joint Resolution. [§ 86.]
1860, Dec. 18. Amendment to the Constitution for payment for fugitive slaves: *Cong. Globe, 36 Cong. 2 Sess.*, 114.

14. Douglas's Joint Resolution. [§'86.]
1860, Dec. 24. Amendment to the Constitution for payment for fugitive slaves: *Senate Journal, 36 Cong. 2 Sess.*, 61; *Cong. Globe*, 183.

15. Florence's Joint Resolution.
1861, Jan. 15. Amendment to the Constitution for payment for fugitive slaves: *Cong. Globe, 36 Cong. 2 Sess.*, 378.

16. Morris's Joint Resolution.
1861, Jan. 23. Amendment to the Constitution on the return of fugitive slaves: *Cong. Globe, 36 Cong. 2 Sess.*, 527.

17. Douglas's Bill to amend the Fugitive Slave Laws. [§ 101.]
1861, Jan. 28. Introduced: *Cong. Globe, 36 Cong. 2 Sess.*, 586.

18. Florence's Joint Resolution.
1861, Jan. 28. Amendment to the Constitution against the obstruction of the Fugitive Slave Law by States: *Cong. Globe, 36 Cong. 2 Sess.*, 598.

19. Kellogg's Joint Resolution.
1861, Feb. 1. Amendment to the Constitution on the power of Congress over fugitive slaves: *Cong. Globe, 36 Cong. 2 Sess.*, 690.

20. Kellogg's Joint Resolution.
1861, Feb. 26. Same as above: *Cong. Globe, 36 Cong. 2 Sess.*, 1243.

21. Kellogg's Joint Resolution.
1861, Feb. 27. Similar to above: *House Journal, 36 Cong. 2 Sess.*, 410; *Cong. Globe*, 1259.

22. Peace Convention Amendment to the Constitution. [§ 85.]
1861, Feb. 27. Reported by select committee: *Senate Journal, 36 Cong. 2 Sess.*, 332, 637, *Cong. Globe*, 1254.

23. Clarence's Joint Resolution.
1861, Feb. 27. Amendment to the Constitution for payment for fugitive slaves: *Cong. Globe, 36 Cong 2 Sess.*, 1260.

24. Crittenden's Joint Resolution.
1861, Feb. 28. Amendment to the Constitution on the power of the States over fugitive slaves, etc.: *Cong. Globe, 36 Cong. 2 Sess.*, 1270.

* 25. Compromise Bill to amend the Fugitive Slave Act. [§ 87.]
1861, Mar. 1. Bill reported by the select committee of thirty-three for the amendment of the act for the rendition of fugitives from labor: *Cong. Globe, 36 Cong. 2 Sess.*, 1327. —— Mar. 1. Vallandigham's amendment to the above: *Cong. Globe, 36 Cong. 2 Sess.*, 1328. —— Mar. 1. Bill passed the House: *Cong. Globe, 36 Cong. 2 Sess.*, 1327, 1328. —— Mar. 2. Bill read in the Senate. *Cong. Globe, 36 Cong. 2 Sess.*, 1350.

26. Pugh's Joint Resolution.
1861, Mar. 2. Amendment to the Constitution on the return of fugitive slaves: *Senate Journal, 36 Cong. 2 Sess.*, 378; *Cong Globe*, 1368.

27. Johnson's Joint Resolution on the return of fugitives.
1861, Mar. 2. Amendment to the Constitution: *Senate Journal, 36 Cong. 2 Sess.*, 382; *Cong. Globe*, 1401.

28. Powell's Joint Resolution on the return of fugitive slaves.
1861, Mar. 2. Amendment to the Constitution · *Senate Journal, 36 Cong. 2 Sess.,* 384, *Cong. Globe,* 1404.

29. Lovejoy's Resolution against the return of fugitives by the Army. [§ 95.]
1861, July 9. Introduced: *House Journal, 37 Cong. 1 Sess.,* 653; *Cong. Globe,* 32.

30. Trumbull's confiscation Bill. [§ 90.]
1861, July 15. Introduced: *Senate Journal, 37 Cong 1 Sess.,* 42; *Cong. Globe,* 120.

** 31. Chandler's confiscation Act. [§ 90.]
1861, July 15. Introduced · *Senate Journal, 37 Cong. 1 Sess.,* 44; *Cong. Globe,* 120. —— July 22. Trumbull's amendment: *Senate Journal, 37 Cong. 1 Sess.,* 70; *Cong. Globe,* 218. —— July 22. Passed the Senate (yeas and nays not given): *Senate Journal, 37 Cong. 1 Sess.,* 71; *Cong. Globe,* 219. —— July 23. Senate bill introduced into the House and referred: *House Journal, 37 Cong. 1 Sess.,* 136; *Cong. Globe,* 231. —— Aug. 2. Reported with amendment in the House: *House Journal, 37 Cong. 1 Sess.,* 197; *Cong. Globe,* 409. —— Aug. 3. Committee amendments: *House Journal, 37 Cong. 1 Sess.,* 232; *Cong. Globe,* 431. —— Aug 3. Passed the House (yeas 60, nays 48): *House Journal, 37 Cong. 1 Sess.,* 235; *Cong. Globe,* 431. —— Aug 5. Passed the Senate as amended in the House: *Senate Journal, 37 Cong. 1 Sess.,* 178; *Cong. Globe,* 434. —— Aug. 6. Bill signed by the President: *Senate Journal, 37 Cong. 1 Sess.,* 195; *Cong. Globe,* 454.

32. Wilson's Joint Resolution for discharge of fugitives from the Washington jail. [§ 97.]
1861, Dec. 4. Introduced and referred: *Senate Journal, 37 Cong. 2 Sess.,* 24; *Cong. Globe,* 12.

* 33. Wilson's Resolution on repeal of the black code in the District of Columbia. [§ 97.]
1861, Dec. 4. Introduced and agreed to: *Senate Journal, 37 Cong. 2 Sess.,* 22; *Cong. Globe,* 12.

* 34. Clarke's Resolution on persons in Washington jail.
1861, Dec. 4. Introduced and agreed to: *Senate Journal, 37 Cong 2 Sess.,* 22; *Cong. Globe,* 12.

35. Lovejoy's Bill to prevent return by the Army. [§ 95.]
1861, Dec. 4. Introduced: *House Journal, 37 Cong. 2 Sess.,* 16, *Cong. Globe,* 34.

* 36. Sumner's Resolution on Army orders relating to fugitive slaves.
1861, Dec. 4. Introduced and agreed to: *Senate Journal, 37 Cong. 2 Sess.,* 19; *Cong. Globe,* 9.

37. Trumbull's Confiscation Bill.
1861, Dec. 5. Introduced and read twice: *Senate Journal, 37 Cong. 2 Sess.,* 27; *Cong. Globe,* 10.

* 38. Fessenden's Resolution on the Washington jail. [§ 97.]
1861, Dec. 9. Introduced: *House Journal, 37 Cong 2 Sess.,* 54; *Cong. Globe,* 36. —— Dec. 9. Aldrich's amendment: *Cong. Globe, 37 Cong. 2 Sess.,* 36. —— Dec. 9. Lovejoy's amendment: *Cong. Globe, 37 Cong. 2 Sess.,* 36. —— Dec. 9. Passed as amended: *Cong Globe, 37 Cong., 2 Sess.,* 36.

39. Bingham's Resolution on the Washington jail. [§ 97.]
1861, Dec. 9. Introduced and referred: *House Journal, 37 Cong. 2 Sess.,* 52; *Cong. Globe,* 35.

40. Morrill's confiscation Joint Resolution. [§ 91.]
1861, Dec. 11. Introduced and referred: *Senate Journal, 37 Cong. 2 Sess.,* 36; *Cong. Globe,* 49.

*41. Hale's Resolution on the slaves of rebels. [§ 95.]
1861, Dec. 16. Introduced and agreed to: *Senate Journal, 37 Cong. 2 Sess.,* 45; *Cong. Globe,* 88.

42. Wilson's Bill for emancipation in the District of Columbia. [§ 98.]
1861, Dec. 16. Introduced and read twice: *Senate Journal, 37 Cong. 2 Sess.,* 47; *Cong. Globe,* 89 —— Dec. 19. Referred: *Cong. Globe,* 37 *Cong. 2 Sess.,* 153. [See No. 54.].

*43. Sumner's Resolution against the surrender of fugitives by the Army. [§ 95.]
1861, Dec. 18. Introduced and agreed to: *Senate Journal, 37 Cong. 2 Sess.,* 130; *Cong. Globe,* 130.

44. Lovejoy's confiscation and emancipation Resolution. [§§ 91, 95.]
1861, Dec. 20. Introduced and laid on the table: *Senate Journal, 37 Cong. 2 Sess.,* 106; *Cong. Globe,* 158.

*45. Julian's Resolution to amend the Fugitive Slave Law. [§ 95.]
1861, Dec. 20. Introduced and adopted: *House Journal, 37 Cong. 2 Sess.,* 103; *Cong. Globe,* 158.

46. Shank's Resolution on the return of fugitives by the Army. [§ 95.]
1861, Dec. 20. Introduced and referred: *House Journal, 37 Cong. 2 Sess.,* 102, 124; *Cong. Globe,* 158, 172.

*47. Wilson's Resolution for articles of war. [§ 95.]
1861, Dec. 20. Introduced: *House Journal, 37 Cong. 2 Sess.,* 103; *Cong. Globe,* 158.
—— Dec. 23. Adopted: *Senate Journal, 37 Cong. 2 Sess.,* 109, 114; *Cong. Globe,* 159, 168.

48. Wilson's Bill on the arrest of fugitives by the officers of the Army and Navy. [§ 95.]
1861, Dec. 23. Introduced: *Senate Journal, 37 Cong. 2 Sess.,* 167; *Cong. Globe,* 161, 209. —— 1862, Jan. 7. Committee Amendments: *Senate Journal, 37 Cong. 2 Sess.,* 88; *Cong. Globe,* 207. [See No. 53.]

49. Howe's Bill for repeal of the Fugitive Slave Act of 1850. [§ 101.]
1861, Dec. 26. Introduced: *Senate Journal, 37 Cong. 2 Sess.,* 74; *Cong. Globe,* 177.

50. Davis's confiscation Bill.
1861, Dec. 30. Introduced and referred: *Senate Journal, 37 Cong. 2 Sess.,* 75; *Cong. Globe,* 178.

**51. Grimes's Act on criminal justice in the District of Columbia [§ 97.]
1861, Dec. 30. Introduced: *Senate Journal, 37 Cong. 2 Sess.,* 75; *Cong. Globe,* 182. ——1862, Jan. 6. Reported: *Cong. Globe, 37 Cong. 2 Sess.,* 199. —— Jan. 10. Committee amendments: *Senate Journal, 37 Cong. 2 Sess.,* 98; *Cong. Globe,* 264. —— Jan. 10 Powell's amendment: *Senate Journal, 37 Cong. 2 Sess.,* 98, 109; *Cong. Globe,* 264, 319. —— Jan. 14. Pearce's two amendments: *Senate Journal, 37 Cong. 2 Sess.,* 109; *Cong. Globe,* 319. —— Jan. 14. Ten Eyck's amendment: *Senate Journal, 37 Cong. 2 Sess.,* 109, *Cong. Globe,* 320. —— Jan. 14. Harlan's amendment. *Cong. Globe, 37 Cong. 2 Sess.,* 320. —— Jan. 14. Clark's amendment: *Cong. Globe, 37 Cong. 2 Sess.,* 320. —— Jan 14. Saulsbury's amendment: *Senate Journal, 37 Cong. 2 Sess.,* 109; *Cong. Globe,* 320. —— Jan. 14. Clark's amendment: *Cong. Globe, 37 Cong. 2 Sess.,* 321. —— Jan. 14. Passed the Senate (yeas 31, nays 4): *Senate Journal, 37 Cong. 2 Sess.,* 109; *Cong. Globe,* 321.

52. Trumbull's Bill for the confiscation of property of rebels and to free the slaves of rebels. [§ 91.]
1862, Jan. 15. Reported from the Senate Committee on Judiciary: *Senate Journal, 37 Cong. 2 Sess.,* 113; *Cong. Globe,* 334. [See No. 57.]

53   Amendments to Wilson's Bill on Army and Navy officers. [§ 95.]
1862, Jan. 16. [See No. 48.] Collamer's amendment: *Senate Journal, 37 Cong. 2 Sess.*, 116; *Cong. Globe*, 358. —— Jan. 16. Saulsbury's amendment: *Senate Journal, 37 Cong. 2 Sess*, 116; *Cong. Globe*, 358. —— Jan. 16. Rice's amendment to Saulsbury's amendment: *Cong. Globe, 37 Cong. 2 Sess.*, 359.

54.   Wilson's District of Columbia Bill. [§ 98.]
1862, Feb. 12. [See No. 41.] Reported: *Cong. Globe, 37 Cong. 2 Sess.*, 785.

* 55.   Wilson's Resolution on the management of the Washington jail.
1862, Feb. 18. Introduced and agreed to: *Senate Journal, 37 Cong. 2 Sess.*, 217; *Cong. Globe*, 861.

56.   Wilson's Bill to repeal the black code in the District of Columbia.
[§ 98.]
1862, Feb. 24. Introduced and referred: *Senate Journal, 37 Cong. 2 Sess.*, 263; *Cong. Globe*, 917.

57.   Amendments to the confiscation Bill. [§ 91.]
1862, Feb. 25. [See No. 52.] Trumbull's amendment: *Senate Journal, 37 Cong. 2 Sess.*, 239; *Cong. Globe*, 942. —— Feb. 25. Sumner's amendment: *Senate Journal, 37 Cong. 2 Sess.*, 239; *Cong. Globe*, 946. —— Feb. 27. Davis's substitute: *Cong. Globe, 37 Cong. 2 Sess.*, 986. [See No. 59.]

**58.   Blair's Act prohibiting return by the Army. [§ 95.]
1862, Feb. 25. Introduced: *Senate Journal, 37 Cong. 2 Sess.*, 358; *Cong. Globe*, 955. —— Feb. 25. Bingham's amendment: *House Journal, 37 Cong. 2 Sess.*, 358; *Cong. Globe*, 955. —— Feb. 25. Passed the House (yeas 95, nays 51): *House Journal, 37 Cong. 2 Sess.*, 265; *Cong. Globe*, 958. —— Mar. 10. In the Senate; Davis's amendment. *Senate Journal, 37 Cong. 2 Sess.*, 285; *Cong. Globe*, 1142. —— Mar. 10. Saulsbury's amendment · *Senate Journal, 37 Cong. 2 Sess.*, 284; *Cong. Globe*, 1142. —— Mar. 10. MacDougall's amendment: *Senate Journal, 37 Cong. 2 Sess.*, 284; *Cong. Globe*, 1142. —— Mar. 10. Saulsbury's amendment: *Senate Journal, 37 Cong. 2 Sess.*, 284; *Cong. Globe 37 Cong. 2 Sess.*, 1142. —— Mar 10. Passed the Senate (yeas 29, nays 9). *Senate Journal, 37 Cong. 2 Sess.*, 285; *Cong. Globe*, 1142. —— Mar. 14. Approved by the President: *Cong. Globe, 37 Cong. 2 Sess.*, 1243.

59.   Harris's confiscation Bill. [§ 91.]
1862, Mar. 14. Introduced and referred: *Senate Journal, 37 Cong. 2 Sess.*, 304; *Cong Globe*, 1228. [See No. 63.]

60.   Report of House Judiciary Committee on confiscation.
1862, Mar. 30. Adverse to all bills referred by the House: *Cong. Globe, 37 Cong. 2 Sess.*, 1303. [See No. 64.]

61.   Wilson's Resolution on the return of fugitives by the Army and Navy.
1862, Apr. 3. Introduced: *Senate Journal, 37 Cong. 2 Sess.*, 361; *Cong. Globe*, 1546. [See No. 70.]

* 62.   Bill for the abolition of slavery in the District of Columbia.
[§ 98.]
1862, Apr. 3. Passed the Senate: *Cong. Globe, 37 Cong. 2 Sess.*, 1648. [See No. 65.]

63.   Sherman's Amendment to Harris's confiscation Bill.
1862, Apr. 10. [See No. 59.] Introduced: *Cong. Globe, 37 Cong. 2 Sess.*, 1652. [See No. 67.]

64.   Wilson's Bill to amend the Fugitive Slave Act. [§ 101.]
1862, Apr. 11. Introduced: *Senate Journal, 37 Cong. 2 Sess.*, 385; *Cong. Globe*, 1624. —— Apr. 14. Harris's amendment: *Cong. Globe, 37 Cong. 2 Sess.*, 1652. —— Apr. 14. Grimes's amendment. *Senate Journal, 37 Cong. 2 Sess.*, 393, 439; *Cong. Globe*, 1692.

*65. Bill for the abolition of slavery in the District of Columbia. [§ 98.]
1862, Apr. 16. [See No. 62.] Passed the House: *Cong. Globe, 37 Cong. 2 Sess.*, 1686. Approved by the President.

66. Lovejoy's Bill on return of fugitives by the Army. [§ 95.]
1862, Apr. 16. Reported adversely from the Committee on Judiciary in the House: *Cong. Globe, 37 Cong. 2 Sess.*, 1682.

67. Harris's confiscation Bill. [§ 91.]
1862, Apr. 16. [See No. 63.] Reported from the Senate Committee on Judiciary: *Senate Journal, 37 Cong. 2 Sess.*, 400 ; *Cong. Globe, 37 Cong. 2 Sess.*, 1678. —— Apr. 22. Walton's amendment: *Cong. Globe, 37 Cong. 2 Sess.*, 1771. —— Apr. 22. Porter's amendment: *Senate Journal, 37 Cong. 2 Sess.*, 703; *Cong. Globe*, 1767, 1772. —— Apr. 22. Bingham's amendment: *Cong. Globe, 37 Cong. 2 Sess.*, 1767.——Apr. 22. Col. lamer's amendment: *Cong. Globe, 37 Cong. 2.Sess.*, 1782, 1895. —— Apr. 24. Motion to recommit: *Senate Journal, 37 Cong. 2 Sess.*, 434; *Cong. Globe*, 1856, 1886. [See No. 71.]

68. House confiscation Bill. [§ 91.]
1862, Apr. 23. A Select Committee raised in the House: *House Journal, 37 Cong. 2 Sess.*, 602 ; *Cong. Globe*, 1788, 1820.

69. Eliot's confiscation and emancipation Bill. [§ 91.]
1862, Apr. 30. Introduced: *House Journal, 37 Cong. 2 Sess.*, 625; *Cong. Globe*, 1886. [See No. 73.]

70. Saulsbury's amendment of Wilson's Resolution.
1862, May 1. [See No. 61.] Introduced: *Senate Journal, 37 Cong. 2 Sess.*, 439 ; *Cong. Globe*, 1894.

71. Harris's confiscation Bill recommitted. [§ 91.]
1862, May 6. [See No. 67.] Wilson's amendment of Collamer's amendment: *Senate Journal, 37 Cong. 2 Sess.*, 450; *Cong. Globe*, 1954. —— May 6. Final vote: *Senate Journal, 37 Cong. 2 Sess.*, 450; *Cong. Globe*, 1954, 1965.

72. Clark's confiscation Bill. [§ 91.]
1862, May 14. Reported: *Senate Journal, 37 Cong. 2 Sess.*, 476; *Cong. Globe*, 2112. —— May 14. Discussed but not acted upon: *Cong. Globe, 37 Cong. 2 Sess.*, 2163, 2188, 2219, 2842.

73. Confiscation and emancipation Bill. [§ 91.]
1862, May 14. [See No. 69.] Reported in the House: *House Journal, 37 Cong. 2 Sess.*, 683 ; *Cong. Globe*, 2128. [See No. 75.]

74. Sumner's Resolution on fugitive slaves.
1862, May 22. Introduced: *Senate Journal, 37 Cong. 2 Sess.*, 520 ; *Cong. Globe*, 2275. —— May 23. Grimes's amendment: *Senate Journal, 37 Cong. 2 Sess.*, 523 ; *Cong. Globe*, 2306. —— May 26. Walton's emancipation bill amendment: *Cong. Globe, 37 Cong. 2 Sess.*, 2362, 2363.

75. Emancipation Bill.
1862, June 4. [See No. 73.] Recommitted: *House Journal, 37 Cong. 2 Sess.*, 799 ; *Cong. Globe*, 2561. [See No. 76.]

76. Julian's Bill to repeal the Fugitive Slave Act. [§ 101.]
1862, June 9. Introduced with a resolution: *House Journal, 37 Cong. 2 Sess.*, 826 ; *Cong. Globe*, 2623.

77. Colfax's Resolution demanding trial by jury for fugitives.
1862, June 9. Introduced: *House Journal, 37 Cong. 2 Sess.*, 828 ; *Cong. Globe*, 2624.

*78. Bill for emancipation of fugitives from disloyal masters. [§ 91.]
1862, June 17. [See No. 75.] Reported in the House: *House Journal, 37 Cong. 2 Sess.*, 874 ; *Cong. Globe*, 2764. —— June 18. Eliot's substitute: *House Journal, 37 Cong. 2 Sess.*, 282 ; *Cong. Globe*, 2793. —— June 18. Emancipation bill passed the

House (yeas 82, nays 54) : *Cong. Globe, 37 Cong. 2 Sess.*, 2793. —— June 23. Clark's Senate amendment to Eliot's substitute : *Cong. Globe, 37 Cong. 2 Sess.*, 2879, 2996. —— June 28. Trumbull's Amendment : *Cong. Globe, 37 Cong. 2 Sess.*, 2999, 3006.

**79. Progress of the confiscation Bill. [§ 91.]
1862, June 28. Passed the Senate (yeas 28, nays 13): *Senate Journal, 37 Cong. 2 Sess.*, 726. —— July 11. Report of Conference Committee adopted by the House : *House Journal, 37 Cong. 2 Sess.*, 1045; *Cong. Globe*, 3267. —— July 12. Report of Conference Committee adopted by the Senate : *Senate Journal, 37 Cong. 2 Sess.*, 814; *Cong. Globe*, 3275. —— July 17. Approved by the President : *Cong. Globe, 37 Cong. 2 Sess.*, 3403.

80. Bills for the repeal of the Fugitive Slave Act. [§§ 101-103.]
1863, Feb. 8. Ten Eyck's report on Wilson's repeal bill: *Cong. Globe, 37 Cong. 3 Sess.* —— Dec. 14. Stevens's repeal bill: *House Journal, 38 Cong. 1 Sess.*, 43 ; *Cong. Globe*, 19. —— Dec. 14. Julian's repeal bill: *House Journal, 38 Cong. 1 Sess.*, 43 ; *Cong. Globé*, 20. —— Dec. 14. Ashley's repeal bill: *House Journal, 38 Cong. 1 Sess.*, 43 ; *Cong. Globe*, 29. —— 1864, Feb 8. Sumner's repeal bill: *Senate Journal, 38 Cong. 1 Sess.*, 133 ; *Cong. Globe*, 521. —— Feb. 8. Spalding's repeal bill : *House Journal, 38 Cong. 1 Sess.*, 235 ; *Cong. Globe*, 526. —— Feb. 29. Sumner's bill reported : *Senate Journal, 38 Cong. 1 Sess.*, 196 ; *Cong. Globe*, 864. [See No. 84.]

81. Saulsbury's substitute on the validity of personal liberty laws in the States, etc.
1864, Apr. 8. Joint resolution for an amendment to the Constitution : *Senate Journal, 38 Cong. 1 Sess.*, 311 ; *Cong. Globe*, 1489.

82. Discussion of the repeal of the Fugitive Slave Law. [§ 101.]
1864, Apr. 19. [See No. 80.] Sherman's amendment: *Senate Journal, 38 Cong. 1 Sess.*, 348 ; *Cong. Globe*, 1710, 1714. —— Apr. 19. Henderson's amendment to Sherman's amendment : *Cong. Globe, 38 Cong. 1 Sess.*, 1710. —— Apr. 19. Saulsbury's amendment : *Senate Journal, 38 Cong. 1 Sess.*, 348, 621 ; *Cong. Globe*, 1715, 3191. —— Apr. 19. Hale's amendment to Saulsbury's amendment : *Senate Journal, 38 Cong 1 Sess.*, 358 ; *Cong. Globe*, 1782. —— Apr. 21. Howard's amendment : *Senate Journal, 38 Cong. 1 Sess.*, 358 ; *Cong. Globe*, 1782. [See No. 81.]

**83. Act repealing the Fugitive Slave Acts. [§§ 101-104.]
1864, June 6. [See No. 82.] Hubbard's repeal resolution : *House Journal, 38 Cong. 1 Sess.*, 749. —— June 6. House substitute for repeal bill, reported by the Committee on Judiciary : *House Journal, 38 Cong. 1 Sess.*, 755 ; *Cong. Globe*, 2774. —— June 13. Passed House (yeas 82, nays 57) : *House Journal, 38 Cong. 1 Sess.*, 503 ; *Cong. Globe*, 2920. —— June 15. Referred in the Senate : *Senate Journal, 38 Cong. 1 Sess.*, 561 ; *Cong. Globe*, 2963. —— June 23. Saulsbury's amendment : *Senate Journal, 38 Cong. 1 Sess.*, 621 ; *Cong. Globe*, 1864. —— June 23. Johnson's amendment : *Senate Journal, 38 Cong. 1 Sess.*, 621 ; *Cong. Globe*, 3191. —— June 23. Passed the Senate : *Senate Journal, 38 Cong. 1 Sess.*, 621 ; *Cong Globe*, 3191. —— June 28. Signed by the President : *House Journal, 38 Cong 1 Sess.*, 931 ; *Cong. Globe*, 3360.

APPENDIX D.

LIST OF IMPORTANT FUGITIVE SLAVE CASES.

No attempt has been made to present a full list of cases, but only such as had especial influence on the public mind, or such as illustrate some special phase of the question.

1. New Netherlands and Hartford controversy. [§ 11.]
1646. Escapes from both colonies: *Winthrop, History of New England,* 383; *Moore, Notes on History of Slavery in Massachusetts,* 28; *Doyle, English in America,* I. 391.

2. Escape to Manhattan. [§ 7.]
1659. Four men escaped from New Amsterdam: *New York Colonial Manuscripts,* XIII. 238; *Documentary History of N. Y. Colony,* II. 556 (Ch. I. p. 4).

3. Escape of white servants to Cape May. [§ 9.]
1661. Virginian white colonists escape: *New York Colonial Manuscripts,* XIII. 346.

4. Escape to the Indians. [§ 8.]
The negro servants of the Governor of Virginia: *New York Colonial Manuscripts,* II. 637.

5. Escape from English to French. [§ 11.]
1748. Negro servant escapes from English to Canada: *New York Colonial Manuscripts,* X. 209.

6. Crispus Attucks. [§ 5.]
1750, Oct. Escaped from Framingham, Mass.: *Boston Gazette, Oct. 2, 1750; Liberator, Mar. 16, 1860; Nineteenth Anniversary of Boston Massacre, W. C. Neil, Address; Williams, History of the Negro Race in America,* I. 330.

7. Glasgow. [§ 12.]
Slave freed in Glasgow: *Mass. Historical Society Collections, Third Series,* IX. 2.

8. Shanley v. Haney. [§ 12.]
1762. Slave freed in England: *Quincy, Reports of Cases,* 96.

9. Somersett case. [§ 12.]
1772. England will not return a fugitive slave: *Moore, Slavery in Mass.,* 117; *Cobb, Historical Sketch of Slavery,* 163; *Goodell, Slavery and Antislavery,* 44-52; *Hurd, Law of Freedom and Bondage,* I. 189-193; *Broom, Constitutional Law,* 6-119; *Howells, State Trials,* XX. 1; *Tasswell-Langmead, English Constitutional History,* 300, *n.*

10. Ship Friendship, case of. [§ 5.]
1770. Harbored a slave: *Moore, Slavery in Mass.,* 117.

11. John. [§ 17.]
1778. Free negro kidnapped in Pennsylvania: *Am. State Papers,* I. 39; *Cong. Globe, 31 Cong. 1 Sess., Appendix,* 1585.

[124]

12. Quincy's case. [§ 34.]

1793. First case in Boston after 1793: *Edw. C. Learned, Speech on The New Fugitive Slave Law, Chicago, Oct. 25, 1850; Whittier, Prose Works,* II, 129, *A Chapter of History; Goodell, Slavery and Antislavery,* 232; *Boston Atlas, Oct. 15, 1850.*

13. Washington's slave. [§ 35.]

1796, Oct. President Washington demanded a slave from Portsmouth, N. H.: *Magazine of American History, Dec., 1877,* p. 759; *Charles Sumner, Works,* III. 177.

14. North Carolina fugitives. [§ 19.]

1796. *Annals of Congress,* 1796-7, p. 2015, 1801-2, p. 343.

15. Columbia case.

1804. General Boude defends a runaway: *Smedley, Underground Railroad,* 26.

16. Solomon Northup. [§ 38.]

1808. Kidnapping at Saratoga, N. Y.: *Solomon Northrup, Autobiography.*

17. Williams case.

1815. Claimed as a fugitive in Philadelphia: *Greeley, American Conflict,* I. 216.

18. Prigg case. [§ 27.]

1832. *16 Peters,* 539; *Report of Case of Edward Prigg, Supreme Court, Pennsylvania; Cobb, Historical Sketch of Slavery; Bledsoe, Liberty and Slavery,* 355; *Clarke, Antislavery Days,* 69; *Hurd, Law of Freedom and Bondage,* II. 456-492; *Wilson, Rise and Fall of the Slave Power,* I. 472-473; *Von Holst, Constitutional History,* III. 310-312.

19. Kidnapping of Jones. [§ 37.]

1836. Kidnapping in New Jersey: *Liberator, Aug. 6, 1836.*

20. Chickasaw rescue. [§ 42.]

1836. Rescue of two colored women on brig Chickasaw: *Liberator, Aug. 6, 1836.*

21. Schooner Boston case. [§ 47.]

1837. Georgia and Maine controversy: *Wilson, Rise and Fall of the Slave Power,* I. 473. *Niles's Register,* LIII. 71, 72, LV. 356; *Senate Journal,* 1839-40, pp. 235-237; *Senate Doc., 26 Cong. 1 Sess.,* Vol. V. Doc. 273.

22. Philadelphia. [§ 43.]

1838. Attempted rescue: *Liberator, March 16, 1838.*

23. Escape of Douglass. [§§ 68, 75.]

1838. Escape of Frederick Douglass: *Life and Times of Douglass; Williams, Negro Race in America,* II. 59, 422; *Wilson, Rise and Fall of the Slave Power,* I. 501, 502.

24. Isaac Gansey case. [§ 47.]

1839. Virginia and New York controversy: *U. S. Gazette, Case of Isaac, Judge Hopkinson's speech; Wilson, Rise and Fall of the Slave Power,* I. 474; *Seward, Works,* II. 449-518; *Von Holst, Constitutional History,* II. 538-540; *Senate Documents, 27 Cong. 2 Sess.,* Vol. II. Doc. 96.

25. Van Zandt case. [§ 50.]

1840. Prosecution for aiding escape: *Wilson, Rise and Fall of the Slave Power,* I. 475; *T. R. Cobb, Historical Sketch of Slavery,* 207.

26. Oberlin case. [§ 50.]

1841 (about). *Liberator, May 21, 1841.*

27. Thompson case.

1841, July. Prosecution for aiding escapes: *Thompson, Prison Life and Reflections; Wilson, Rise and Fall of the Slave Power,* II. 69; *Goodell, Slavery and Antislavery,* 440.

28. Latimer case. [§ 44.]

1842. Famous fugitive slave case, Boston: *Liberator, Oct. 25, Nov. 11, Nov. 25, 1842, Feb. 3, 7, 17, 1843, and Aug. 16, 1844; Law Reporter, Latimer case; Eleventh Annual Report of Mass. Antislavery Society; Mass. House Journal, 1843,* pp. 72, 158; *Mass. Senate Journal, 1843,* p. 232; *Wilson, Rise and Fall of the Slave Power,* I. 477.

29. Goin case.
1844. Attempted seizure of fugitive: *Liberator, April 19, 1844.*
30. Thomas case.
1844. Seizure in Marietta, Penn.: *Liberator, June 14, 1844.*
31. Walker case. [§ 50.]
1844. Prosecution for aiding escapes: *Trial and Imprisonment of Jonathan Walker, Liberator, Aug. 16, 31, Sept. 6, 13, Oct. 18, 25, and Dec. 27, 1844, Aug. 8, 15, and July 18, 1845.*
32. Smithburg.
1845. Battle between whites and ten runaways: *Liberator, June 27, 1845.*
33. Kirk case.
Between 1845 and 1849. Unsuccessful attempt to capture George Kirk in New York: *Wilson, Rise and Fall of the Slave Power*, II. 52. *Supplement to New York Legal Observer*, containing report of case, Boston Public Library.
34. Brig Ottoman. [§ 45.]
1846. Unsuccessful attempt to rescue slave on brig: *Wilson, Rise and Fall of the Slave Power*, II. 54.
35. Kennedy case. [43.]
1847. Riot in Carlisle, Penn.: *Liberator, Sept. 10, 27, 1847; Congressional Globe, 1860-61*, pp. 801, 802, 908.
36. Slaves on board Brazilian ship.
1847. Attempt to rescue: *Wilson, Rise and Fall of the Slave Power*, II. 53; *Liberator, Aug. 20, 1847.*
37. Ohio and Kentucky controversy. [§ 48]
1848. Controversy on account of extradition demanded: *Liberator, July 14, 1848.*
38. South Bend case.
1847, Oct. 9. Fugitives discharged on trial in Michigan: *South Bend Fugitive Slave case.*
39. Brig Wm. Purrington.
1848. Escape from: *Liberator, Dec. 31, 1848.*
40. Drayton and Sayres. [§ 50.]
1848. Prosecution for aiding escapes: *Wilson, Rise and Fall of the Slave Power*, II. 104.
41. Crafts escape. [§ 69.]
1848. Escape of William and Ellen Crafts: *Liberator, Nov. 1, 1850; Still, Underground Railroad*, 368; *Wilson, Rise and Fall of the Slave Power*, II. 325.
42. Washington case. [§ 39.]
Between 1840-1850: *Liberator, May 26, 1848.*
43. Hamlet case. [§ 53.]
1850. Rendition in N. Y.: *Fugitive Slave Bill, its History and Unconstitutionality, with an Account of the Seizure of James Hamlet*, 3; *Wilson, Rise and Fall of the Slave Power*, II. 304.
44. Gannett case.
1850, Oct. 18. Alleged fugitive discharged in Philadelphia: *Wilson, Rise and Fall of the Slave Power*, II. 326; *May, Fugitive Slave Law and its Victims*, 8.
45. Gibson case.
1850, Dec. 21. Rendition of an innocent man: *Wilson, Rise and Fall of the Slave Power*, II. 327; *May, Fugitive Slave Law and its Victims*, 8; *Still, Underground Railroad*, 349.
46. Case in Pennsylvania.
1851, Jan. House of colored man entered by force: *Liberator, Jan. 10, 1851.*

47. Sims case. [§ 54.]

1851. Rendition in Boston: *Liberator, April 17 and 18, 1851; Daily Morning Chronicle, April 26, 1851; Twentieth Annual Report of Mass. Antislavery Society, 1855*, p. 19; *Wilson, Rise and Fall of the Slave Power*, II. 333; *New England Magazine, June, 1890; May, Fugitive Slave Law and its Victims,* 16; *Trial of Sims, Arguments by R. Rantoul, Jr. and C. G. Loring ; C. F. Adams, Richard Henry Dana,* I. 185-301.

48. Shadrach case. [§ 57.]

1851, Feb. Rendition in Boston: *Liberator, Feb. 21, May 30, 1851 ; Cong. Globe, 31 Cong. 2 Sess., Appendix,* 238, 295, 510; *Von Holst,* III. 21; *May, Fugitive Slave Law and its Victims,* 10; *Wilson, Rise and Fall of the Slave Power,* II. 329; *New England Magazine, May, 1890 ; Boston Traveller, Feb. 15, 1851 ; Boston Courier, Feb. 17, 1851 ; Washington National Era, Feb. 27, 1851; Statesman's Manual,* III. 1919.

49. Christiana case. [§ 60.]

1851, Sept. Riot in Christiana: *Parker's account, The Freedman's Story, T. W. Higginson, Atlantic Monthly, Feb. and March, 1866 ; U. S.* v. *Hanway, Treason,* 247 *Smedley, Underground Railroad,* 105, 107, 130, 223 ; *May, Fugitive Slave Law,* 14; *Lunsford Lane,* 114; *Wilson, Rise and Fall of the Slave Power,* II. 324; *History of the Trial of Castner Hanway and others for Treason ; N. Y. Tribune, Sept. 12, 1851, and Nov. 26 to Dec. 12 ; Greeley, American Conflict,* I. 215; *National Antislavery Standard, Sept. 18, 1851 ; Lowell Journal, Sept. 19, 1851 ; Boston Daily Traveller, Sept. 12, 1851; Still, Underground Railroad,* 348.

50. Miller. [§ 61.]

1851, Nov. Mr. Miller murdered: *Liberator, Feb. 4, 1853 ; Lunsford Lane,* 113; *May, Fugitive Slave Law,* 15 ; *Wilson, Rise and Fall of the Slave Power,* II. 324.

51. Jerry case. [§ 58.]

1851, Oct. Rescue in Syracuse, N. Y.: *Liberator, Oct. 10 to 17, 1851 ; Life of Gerrit Smith,* 117; *Trial of H. W. Allen,* 3; *Wilson, Rise and Fall of the Slave Power,* II. 327.

52. Parker rescue.

1851, Dec. 31. Rescue by Mr. Miller: *Wilson, Rise and Fall of the Slave Power,* II. 324; *May, Fugitive Slave Law and its Victims,* 15; *Liberator, 1853, Feb. 4 ; Lunsford Lane,* 113.

53. Brig Florence

1853. Rescue of slave on board by Mr. Bearse : *Bearse, Reminiscences of Fugitive Slave Days in Boston,* 34.

54. Lewis case.

1853. Escape of Lewis from trial: *Liberator, Oct. 28, 1853.*

55. Glover case.

1854. Joshua Glover rescued by a mob at Milwaukee : *Wilson, Rise and Fall of the Slave Power,* 444 ; *Liberator, April 7, 24, 1854.*

56. Bath.

1854. Escape to Canada from ship from Florida: *Liberator, Oct. 6, 1854.*

57. Burns case. [§ 55.]

1854. Rendition in Boston: *Liberator, May, June, 1854, Aug.- 22, 1861 ; Kidnapping of Burns, Scrapbook collected by Theo. Parker ; Personal Statement of Mr. Elbridge Sprague, N. Abington ; Accounts in Boston Journal, May 27, 29, 1854 ; Daily Advertiser, May 26, 29, June 7, 8, July 17 ; Traveller, May 27, 29, June 2, 3, 6, 10, July 15, 18, Oct. 3, Nov. 29, Dec. 5, 7, 1854, April 3, 4, 10, 11, 1855 ; Evening Gazette, May 27, 1854 ; Worcester Spy, May 31 ; Argument of Mr. R. H. Dana ; May, Fugitive Slave Law and its Victims,* 256 ; *Clarke, Antislavery Days,* 87; *Wilson, Rise and Fall of the*

Slave Power, II. 435, *Steveys, History of Anthony Burns*; *Greeley, American Conflict* I. 218, *New York Tribune*, May 26, 1854; *Liberator, June 2, 9, 16, 1854; Von Holst* VI. 62, *Garrisons' Garrison*, II. 201, III. 409; *C. F. Adams, Dana*, I. 262-330.

58. Garner. [§ 56.]

1856. Rendition of a family in Ohio : *Liberator, Feb. 8, 22, 29, 1856 ; May, Fugitive Slave Law and its Victims*, 37 ; *Lunsford Lane*, 119; *Greeley, American Conflict*, I. 219; *Lalor's Cyclopædia*, I. 207 ; *Wilson, Rise and Fall of the Slave Power*, II. 446, 447.

59. Williamson case.

1856, Jan. Prosecution for aiding fugitives; *Wilson, Rise and Fall of the Slave Power*, II. 448; *May, Fugitive Slave Law and its Victims*, 9, 34; *Annual Report of American Antislavery Society, N. Y.*, May 7, 1856, p. 24; *Narrative of the Facts in the Case of Passmore Williamson, Penn. Antislavery Society.*

60. Johnson case.

1856, July 16. Rescue of slave on ship from Mobile : *Liberator, July 18, 1856*.

61. Gatchell case.

1857, Jan. Rendition of Philip Young : *Chambers, Slavery and Color ; Fugitive Slave Law, Appendix*, 197.

62 Oberlin-Wellington case. [§ 59.]

1858. Rescue at Wellington : *Liberator, Jan. 28, April 29, May 6, June 3, June 10, 1859 ; Shepherd, Oberlin-Wellington Rescue ; Lunsford Lane*, 179; *Anglo-African Magazine (Oberlin-Wellington Rescue)*, 209; *May, Fugitive Slave Law and its Victims*, 108.

63. John Brown's Raid. [§ 62.]

1858. Raid in Missouri: *Sanborn, Life and Letters of John Brown*, 420; *Von Holst, John Brown*, 104.

64. Nalle case.

1859, April 28. Rescue of Charles Nalle by a mob: *Bradford, Harriet, the Moses of her People, Appendix*, 143 ; *Liberator, May 4, 1830.*

65. Anderson case. [§ 23]

1860. Extradition case between U. S. and Canada: *Liberator, Dec. 3, 1860; Pamphlets on Anderson Case, Boston Public Library; Life of Gerrit Smith*, 15; *Liberator, Jan. 22, 1861*.

66. Wisdom case. [§ 91.]

1861. Rendition by army officers : *Liberator, July 19, 1861.*

67. Major Sherwood's servant. [§ 91.]

1861. Rendition ordered in army : *Liberator, July 19, 1861.*

68. Norfolk case.

1863. Kidnapping by N. Y. Volunteers: *Liberator, March 27, 1863.*

69. Archer Alexander.

1863. Fugitive during the war : *Archer Alexander.*

APPENDIX E.

BIBLIOGRAPHY OF FUGITIVE SLAVE CASES AND FUGITIVE SLAVE LEGISLATION.

1. Sources of information.
2. Libraries.
3. Secondary works.
4. Biographies.
5. Original sources.
6. Slave autobiographies.
7. Records of trials.
8. Speeches.
9. Reminiscences.
10. Reports of societies.
11. Periodicals and newspapers.
12. Materials bearing on legislation.
13. Alphabetical list of works.

1. Sources of information.

There are many sources from which material for a study of fugitive slaves may be gathered. Almost any work upon the slavery question touches sooner or later upon this topic, and the difficulties arise rather from the amount of the literature which must be examined than from lack of information. No formal bibliography of the subject, or of any phase of it, has been found; it has therefore been necessary to go through a large body of material, and to sift out references which bear upon the subject.

2. Libraries.

The labor has been much facilitated by the completeness and convenient arrangement of the literature bearing upon slavery in the libraries of Cambridge and Boston. The Harvard College Library possesses two unique collections of slavery pamphlets, one the bequest of Charles Sumner, the other the gift of Colonel T. W. Higginson; and the Card Catalogue of the Library is a comprehensive guide to a large alcove of other books. The great collections of the Boston Public Library have also been made accessible by the full Card Catalogue of that Library. The Boston Athenæum has also furnished valuable material; and in the Massachusetts State Library is an excellent set of State Statutes, which has been freely used. I have not been able to consult the antislavery collection of the Cornell Library at Ithaca.

3. Secondary works.

The material upon fugitive slaves, as upon any topic, may be divided into two classes, secondary and original. The general and local histories which come under the first class have been of good service as guides to further investigation. *The Rise and Fall of the Slave Power in America*, by *Henry Wilson*, takes up the whole question of slavery in a thorough manner, and devotes special attention to the debates in Congress. Though long and ill-arranged, it is comprehensive and trustworthy. Unfortunately, the work is not provided with foot-notes. *Williams's History of the Negro Race*, and *Greeley's American Conflict*, are other surveys of the whole subject. For a discussion of political forces and constitutional questions, *Von Holst* is the best authority, while *Hurd*, besides enumerating the statutes from colonial times down, considers the subject with great clearness from a judicial point of view, describes many cases, and in foot-notes gives references to others.

Studies of colonial slavery are found in *Lodge's English Colonies in America* and *Doyle's English in America.* Several special essays have been printed on slavery in Massachusetts; *Deane's* and *Moore's Notes on Slavery,* and *Washburn's Extinction of Slavery in Massachusetts.* Little attention is in any of these works given to fugitive slaves.

To another class belong books descriptive of the institution of slavery. *Mrs. Frances Kemble* wrote about life on a Southern plantation before the war, and the *Cotton Kingdom* and other volumes by *Frederick Law Olmsted* give many interesting details, and furnished me with much material for the chapter on Fugitives and their Friends.

4. Biographies.

Biographies of antislavery men are likely to contain information on fugitive slave cases. The *Life of Isaac T. Hopper* is full of accounts of his ways of aiding flight, and for the same reason the *Life of Gerrit Smith* is exceedingly interesting. Birney's *Life of James G. Birney* deals little with fugitives. The biographies of Mrs. Lydia Maria Child, Arthur and Lewis Tappan, John Brown, Garrison, Phillips, and the Grimké sisters, may also be mentioned. Others, like those of Jonathan Walker, L. W. Paine, Daniel Drayton, captain of the schooner Pearl, W. L. Chaplin, Work, Burr, and Thompson, and the recently published *Life of Rev. Calvin Colman,* relate simply the stories of trials and imprisonments for aiding fugitives, and are often more in the nature of original than secondary sources.

5. Original sources.

Very early in the preparation of this work it became evident that no writer had systematically examined and compared the legislation of the Colonies and States, or searched the records of Congress, or looked for contemporary accounts of any considerable number of escapes. I was therefore obliged to search for such original material as was within my reach. Doubtless some important books and pamphlets have escaped me, and an examination of other collections would enlarge the bibliography; but the effort has been made to exhaust the literature of the subject, except in newspapers.

6. Slave autobiographies.

Out of the great variety of original sources containing descriptions of slave life and escapes, the autobiographies of the slaves themselves are the most interesting, and often the saddest. The Rev. James Freeman Clarke says, in his Antislavery Days: "Even now, when it is all over, the flesh creeps and the blood curdles in the veins at the accounts of the dreadful cruelties practised on slaves in many parts of the South. I would advise no one to read such histories to-day unless his nerves are very well strung." *Frederick Douglass* has given us two books, one written before slavery was abolished, and a fuller account afterward, when it was no longer imprudent to reveal the whole story of his escape. Many of these lives were published by antislavery people, who wished by such means to rouse the North. Such are the stories of *Box Brown, Peter Still, Archy Moore, Solomon Northrup, Lunsford Lane,* and others, most of which have been quoted above.

7. Records of trials.

Much descriptive detail can often be found in the published reports of trials. A volume is devoted to the Oberlin-Wellington case, and several volumes have been published on the Burns trial. For the Prigg and Hanway cases, and others of importance, the records of the Supreme Court and lower courts have been consulted. Most of the important cases were tried in State courts or before commissioners, and the only reports are fugitive pamphlets, of which many have been consulted and cited.

8. Speeches.
In the study of public sentiment and for the weighing of argument the speeches of *Phillips, Sumner, Seward, Giddings, Webster, Mann, Rantoul, Loring*, and others, are of the greatest value. They often throw light upon obscure cases, and the fugitive slave stories brought in as illustrations have sometimes led to the discovery of interesting and forgotten cases.

9. Reminiscences.
A valuable aid in reconstructing in the mind the conditions of the slavery struggle are the reminscences of participants. *Rev. James Freeman Clarke's Antislavery Days* and *Mr. Parker Pillsbury's* book have been helpful in these chapters. A pamphlet by *Mr. Austin Bearse* describes the Fugitive Slave Laws in Boston, and relates the work of the Vigilance Committee in protecting escaped negroes. The books of *Still, Smedley,* and *Coffin*, on the workings of the Underground Railroad, are composed chiefly of reminiscences, and have furnished many essential facts.

10. Reports of societies.
The reports of the various antislavery societies, especially of those of Massachusetts and Pennsylvania, have also been examined with profit as to the work among the refugees in Canada, etc. For the colonial period the publications of the Massachusetts and New York Historical Societies are exceedingly important, and have been freely drawn upon.

11. Periodicals and newspapers.
Not much has been gathered from periodicals. *Poole's Index* was used and occasionally something of importance was discovered. Thus *The Freedman's Story* in the *Atlantic Monthly* has furnished one of the most striking of the stories about resistance to escapes. Such articles are few, and occur long after the slavery period, when such disclosures were no longer unpopular. The *Magazine of American History* contains several articles. Among newspapers, the *Liberator* is without doubt the most complete record of the extreme antislavery sentiment toward the fugitive slave laws and their workings. Each case as it occurs is fully commented upon, and in addition there is each week a column or two of atrocities, and among them stories of fugitives are often given. The Harvard College Library contains a complete file, which I have examined; and references to the Liberator are therefore frequent throughout the work. The colonial newspapers are of little value, except for the conclusions which may be drawn from the advertisements for runaways. Newspapers of that time were so limited in scope, that an affair so unimportant to them as a fugitive slave case would scarcely appear.

12. Materials bearing on legislation.
The materials for the study of colonial legislation must be gathered from many sources. The best collection of them in Boston may be found at the State Library. In some colonies there are carefully edited series of volumes chronologically arranged, but in others the records have been but irregularly printed. The laws of New Netherlands and of early New York are easily accessible in well printed volumes of a recent date. For the Southern States, the Hening edition of the Virginia Statutes at Large is clear, and covers a long period. There is also the Cooper collection for South Carolina, Bacon's series for Maryland, Iredell's edition of South Carolina Statutes, and Leaming and Spicer for New Jersey. There are of course many others, but these comprise the most important.

From the beginning of the Constitutional period, the proceedings of Congress may be followed as minutely as desired. An outline of the proceedings is given in the Journals of the Senate and House, while for a fuller account and reports of speeches the Annals of Congress and Congressional Debates to 1837, and the Congressional Globes from 1833 to 1863, furnish ample material. Information in regard to the number and personnel of the House is most readily gathered from Poore's Congressional Directory.

13. **Alphabetical list of works.**

This list includes all the books and articles which have been of service in preparing the monograph, except a few of the general histories.

Adams, Charles Francis, Jr. Richard Henry Dana: a Biography. 2 vols. Boston, 1890.

Allen, H. W. Trial of U. S. Deputy Marshal for Kidnapping, etc. Syracuse, 1852.

Antislavery Almanacs, miscellaneous collection of, in the Library of Harvard College.

Antislavery Pamphlets, miscellaneous collection of, unsuitable for binding, in the Library of Harvard College.

Antislavery Societies, Annual Reports of.

Amherstburg Quarterly Mission Journal, Amherstburg, Canada West.

Ball, J. P. Mammoth Pictorial Tour of the United States, compiled for a Panorama. Cincinnati, 1855.

Bayard, James. A Brief Exposition of the Constitution of the United States. Philadelphia, 1845.

Bearse, Anthony. Remembrances of Fugitive Slave Law Days in Boston. Boston, 1880. pp. 41.

Birney, J. G. Examination of the Decision of the Supreme Court of the United States in the Case of Strader, Gorman, and Armstrong *vs.* Christopher Graham, 1850. Cincinnati, 1851. pp. 47.

Bledsoe, Albert T. An Essay on Liberty and Slavery. Philadelphia, 1887. pp. 383.

Bowditch, H. I. To the Public. [Defence of his conduct in the case of Latimer against the charges of J. B. Gray.] Boston, 1842. pp. 11.

Bowditch, W. I. The Rendition of Anthony Burns. Boston, 1854. pp. 40.

————. The United States Constitution a Pro-slavery Instrument. New York, 1855. pp. 12.

Bowen, C. W. Arthur and Lewis Tappan, a Paper read at the Fiftieth Anniversary of the New York City Antislavery Society, Oct. 2, 1883. New York, 1883. (?) pp. 116.

Bowen, F. Fugitive Slaves. In *North American Review,* LXXI. 252. (July, 1850.)

Boston Slave Riot and Trial of Anthony Burns. Boston, 1854.

Brown, W. W. Narrative of a Fugitive Slave. Boston, 1848. pp. 144.

Bump, O. F. Notes of Constitutional Decisions, being the Digest of the Provincial Interpretations of the Constitution of the United States, etc. New York, 1878.

Canada Mission, 7th Annual Report of. Rochester, N. Y.

Case of William R. Chaplin, etc. Boston, 1851. pp. 54.

Chambers, William. American Slavery and Color: London, 1857.

Chase, S. P. Reclamation of Fugitive Slaves from Service, an Argument for the Defendant, submitted to the Supreme Court of the United States at December Term, 1840, in Case of W. Jones *vs.* John Van Zandt. Cincinnati, 1847. pp. 108.

Child, Lydia Maria. The Duty of Disobedience to the Fugitive Slave Act (an Appeal to the Legislators of Mass.). Boston, 1860. pp. 36.

————. Isaac T. Hopper (a True Life). Boston, 1853. pp. 120.

————. Letters of Lydia Maria Child. Boston, 1883.

Clarke, James Freeman. Antislavery Days. New York, 1884.

Clarke, Lewis and Milton, Narrative of the Sufferings of, among the Slaveholders of Kentucky. Boston, 1848. pp. 144.
Cobb, T. R. Historical Sketch of Slavery. Philadelphia, 1836.
Coffin, L. (President of Underground Railroad). Reminiscences of a Lifetime spent in Behalf of the Slave. Cincinnati, 1876.
Constitutional Provision, The, respecting Fugitives from Justice, and the Act of Congress, Sept. 18, 1850. Boston, 1852.
Cooley, Thomas M. The General Principles of Constitutional Law in the United States of America. Boston, 1880. pp. 376.
Daggs (Ruel) *vs.* **Elihu Frazier et als.** Fugitive Slave Case, Southern Division of Iowa. Burlington, 1850. pp. 40.
Deane, Charles, and Moore. Slavery in Massachusetts. Connecticut, 1877.
Desty, Robert. Constitution of the United States, with Notes by Robert Desty, etc. San Francisco, 1887.
Douglass, Frederick. Narrative of his Life. Written by himself. Boston, 1845.
———. Life and Times of Frederick Douglass. Hartford, 1881-82.
Drayton, Daniel. Personal Memoirs of, for four years and four months (a prisoner for charity's sake in Washington Jail), including Narrative of Voyage and Capture of Schooner Pearl. New York, 1855.
Drew, Benjamin. North Side View of Slavery, or Narrative of a Refugee in Canada, with an Account of the History of the Colored Population in Upper Canada. Boston, 1856.
Eliot, W. G. The Story of Archer Alexander from Slavery to Freedom. Boston, 1885.
Elliott, Chas. W. The New England History, from the Discovery of the Continent by the Northmen, A. D. 986, to the Period when the Colonies declared their Independence, A. D. 1776. 2 vols. New York, 1857.
Friend, By A. The Experiences of Thomas Jones, who was for forty-three years a Slave. Boston, 1850.
Frothingham, O. B. Life of Gerrit Smith. A Biography. New York, 1878. pp. 381.
Fugitive Slave Bill enacted by U. S. Congress, and approved by President Fillmore, Sept. 8, 1850. Boston, 1854. pp. 7.
Fugitive Slaves. In *Democratic Review*, XXVIII. 57 (April, 1851).
Furness, W. H. The Moving Power. A Discourse delivered in the First Congregational Unitarian Church in Philadelphia, Feb. 9, 1851, after the occurrence of a Fugitive Slave Case. Philadelphia, 1851.
Garrison, Wendell Phillips, and Garrison, Francis Jackson. William Lloyd Garrison, 1805-1879: the Story of his Life, told by his Children [Wendell Phillips Garrison and Francis Jackson Garrison]. 4 vols., 8vo. New York, 1885.
Giddings, J. R. The Exiles of Florida, or Crimes committed by our Government against Maroons who fled from South Carolina, etc. Columbus, O., 1858.
Goodell, William. Views of American Constitutional Law in its Bearings upon American Slavery. 2d ed. Utica, N. Y., 1845.
Goodloe, D. R. The Southern Platform, or Manual of Southern Sentiments on the Subject of Slavery. Boston, 1858.
Gray, A. F. (?) Letter to W. H. Seward touching the Surrender of certain Fugitives from Justice. New York, 1841.
Great Britain. British Documents, Parliament of Great Britain, Correspondence respecting Case of Fugitive Slave Anderson. London, 1861.
Greeley, Horace. The American Conflict; a History of the Great Rebellion, 1860-65; its moral and political Phases, with the Drift and Progress of America respecting Human Slavery from 1776. 2 vols., 8vo. Hartford, 1864.

Green, William (formerly a slave), Narrative of Events in the Life of. Written by himself. Springfield, 1853. pp. 23.

Hawkins, W. G. Lunsford Lane, or Another Helper from North Carolina. Boston, 1863.

Helper, H. R. The Impending Crisis in the South, and How to Meet it. New York, 1860. pp. 420.

Henson, Josiah. Life of J. Henson, formerly a Slave, now an Inhabitant of Canada, as narrated by himself.

Hildreth, R. The Slave, or Memoirs of Archy Moore. Boston, 1840

Hopper, I. T. Thomas Cooper. New York, 1837.

Hossack, John. Speech of John Hossack, convicted of Violation of the Fugitive Slave Law, before Judge Drummond of the United States District Court, Chicago, Ill. New York, 1860. pp. 12.

Howe, S. G. Refugees from the South in Canada West. Report to Freedman's Inquiry Committee. Boston, 1864.

Hurd, J. C. The Law of Freedom and Bondage. 2 vols. New York, 1858, 1862.

———. Topics of Jurisprudence connected with the Condition of Freedom and Bondage. New York, 1856. pp. ix, 113.

Hurd, R. C. Treatise on the Right of Personal Liberty, and on the Writ of Habeas Corpus, and Practice connected with it, with a View of the Law of Extradition of Fugitives. Albany, 1858.

Joliffe, John. In the Matter of George Gordon's Petition for Pardon. John Joliffe's Argument for Petitioner. Cincinnati, 1862.

Kane, Judge. District Court of the United States for the Eastern District of Pennsylvania. United States of America, ex relatione Wheeler, *vs.* Williamson. Opinion of Judge Kane, Oct. 12, 1855. Philadelphia, 1855. pp. 20.

Kemble, Frances Anne. Journal of a Residence on a Georgian Plantation in 1836-39. New York, 1863.

Kent, J. Commentaries on American Law. 4 vols. Boston, 1884.

Kidnapping. *African Observer*, May, 1837.

Kingsbury, Harmon. The Fugitive Slave Bill, its History and Unconstitutionality: with an Account of the Seizure and Enslavement of James Hamlet and his subsequent Restoration to Liberty (with Appendix). New York, 1850.

Larned, E. C. Argument on the Trial of Joseph Stout, indicted for rescuing a Fugitive Slave from a United States Deputy Marshal at Ottawa, Ill., Oct. 20, 1859, delivered March 12 and 13, 186-. Chicago, 186-. pp. 43.

———. The new Fugitive Slave Law. Speech of E. C. Larned, Chicago, Oct. 25, 1850. Chicago, 1850.

Latimer Case. From the *Law Reporter*, March, 1843. Boston, 1843. pp. 10.

Letter to His Excellency, William H. Seward, Governor of the State of New York, touching the Surrender of certain Fugitives from Justice. New York, 1841. pp. 101.

Lord, J. C. The Higher Law in its Application to the Fugitive Slave Bill. Buffalo, 1851.

Madison, James. The Constitution a Pro-slavery Compact. New York, 1844.

Mann, Horace. Fugitive Slave Law. Boston, 1851.

Massachusetts Senate. Various Documents. Senate, 1851, No. 89 (examination of Sims Case).

May, S. J. American Antislavery Society. The Fugitive Slave Law and its Victims. New York, 1856, 1861.

———. Catalogue of Antislavery Publications in America, 1750-1830.

Moore, G. H. Notes on the History of Slavery in Massachusetts. New York, 1866.

Narrative of Facts in the Case of Passmore Williamson. Philadelphia, 1855.

Narrative of Solomon Northrup, a Citizen of New York, kidnapped in Washington in 1844, and rescued in 1853 from a Cotton Plantation near Red River, Louisiana. Cincinnati, H. W. Derby.

Needles, Edward. Historical Memoir of the Pennsylvania Society for Promoting the Abolition of Slavery. Philadelphia, 1848.

New York Court of Appeals, Report of the Lemmon Slave Case. New York, 1861. pp. 446.

New York Legal Observer, Supplement to, containing Report of the Case In the Matter of George Kirk, a Fugitive Slave, heard before J. W. Edmunds, Circuit Judge; also the Argument of John Jay, Counsel for the Slave. New York, 1844. pp. 20.

Oberlin-Wellington Rescue. *New Englander*, XVII. 686.

Olmsted, F. L. The Cotton Kingdom. 2 vols. New York, 1861.

Paine, Byron, and **Smith, A. D.** Unconstitutionality of the Fugitive Slave Act. Argument of A. D. Smith. Milwaukee, 1854. pp. 35.

· **Paine, L. W.** Six Years in a Georgia Prison. Narrative of L. W. Paine, who suffered Imprisonment for aiding Slaves to escape from that State after he had fled from Slavery. Boston, 1852.

Parker, Joel. Personal Liberty Laws (State of Massachusetts) and Slavery in the Territories (Case of Dred Scott). Boston, 1861. pp. 97.

Parker, Theodore. Anthony Burns. [Collection made and arranged in the form of a scrap-book by Theodore Parker, whose Autograph and Manuscript it contains.] Boston Public Library.

Peabody, Andrew Preston. [Address before the New England Historic-Genealogical Society, May 6, 1891.]

Peabody, E. Narratives of Fugitive Slaves. *Christian Examiner*, XLVII. 61.

Phillips, Wendell. Argument of Wendell Phillips, Esq., against Repeal of the Personal Liberty Laws before the Committee of the Legislature, Tuesday, January 29, 1861. Boston, 1861.

———. No Slave Hunting in the Old Bay State, before Committee on Federal Relations, H. R., Thursday, Feb. 17, 1859. Boston, 1859.

———. Speech in the House of Representatives of Massachusetts before the Committee on Federal Relations [against the recapture of fugitive slaves]. Boston, 1859.

Pickard, Mrs. K. E. R. The Kidnapped and the Ransomed. Personal Reflections of Peter Still and his Wife Vina after Forty Years of Slavery. Syracuse, New York, 1856.

Pierce, E. L. Remarks of E. L. Pierce before the Committee of the Legislature of Massachusetts on the General Statutes relating to Personal Liberty, at their Hearing of Feb. 1, 1861. Boston, 1861.

Pomeroy, J. N. An Introduction to the Constitutional Laws of the United States. Boston, 1868.

Poole, W. F. Sketch of Antislavery Opinion before Year 1800. An Essay read before the Cincinnati Literary Club, Nov. 16, 1872. Cincinnati, 1873.

Randolph, Peter, an emancipated slave. Sketches of Slave Life. Boston, 1855. pp. 82.

Rantoul, Robert. Speech at Lynn, April 3, 1852, on the Fugitive Slave Law. Speech in Congress on June 11, 1852, on the Constitutionality of the Fugitive Slave Law.

Rendition of Fugitive Slaves. Acts of 1793 and 1850, and Decisions of the Supreme Court sustaining them. The Dred Scott Case. 1860. pp. 15.

Refugees' Home Society, Report of Committee. Winsor, 1852. pp. 8.

Report of the Trial of Castner Hanway for Treason, etc. Philadelphia, 1852. pp. 275.

Report of the Case of Edward Prigg against the Commonwealth of Pennsylvania in Superior Court. Philadelphia, 1842.

Roper, Moses, Narrative of the Adventures and Escape of, from American Slavery. Philadelphia, 1838. pp. 89.

Sergeant, Thomas. On Constitutional Law. Philadelphia, 1830.

Seward, W. H. John Van Zandt, etc., Argument for Defendant by W. H. Seward. Albany, 1847. pp. 40.

Sherman, H. Slavery in the United States; from the Establishment of the Confederation to the present Time. Hartford, 1860. pp. 60.

Shipherd, J. R. History of Oberlin-Wellington Rescue. Boston, 1859.

Smedley, R. C., M. D. History of the Underground Railroad in Chester and neighboring Counties of Pennsylvania. Lancaster, Pa., 1883. pp. 395.

Smith, Gerrit. Argument on the Fugitive Slave Law, June, 1852, on the Trial of H. W. Allen for Kidnapping. Syracuse. pp. 32. No date.

South Bend Fugitive Slave Case, The. (John Ames *vs.* L. B. Newton.) New York. pp. 24.

Spooner, L. A Defence for Fugitive Slaves against the Acts of Congress of Feb. 12, 1793, and Sept. 18, 1850. Boston, 1850. Pam.

Stearns, Charles. Narrative of Henry Box Brown, who escaped from Slavery enclosed in a Box three feet long and two wide. Boston, 1849.

Stearns, Charles. The "Fugitive Slave Law of the United States."

Stevens, C. E. Anthony Burns (a Fugitive Slave). A History. Boston, 1856.

Still, W. The Underground Railroad. Philadelphia, 1872.

Stroud, G. M. Sketch of Laws relative to Slavery in the several States of the United States of America. Philadelphia, 1827. pp. 128.

Sumner, Charles. Fugitive Slaves. *Brownson*, XI. 487 (October, 1854).

Tappan, Arthur. The Life of. New York, 1870.

Thomas, B. F. A few Suggestions to a Friend upon Personal Liberty Laws and Secession (so called), in a Letter to a Friend. Boston, 1861.

Thompson, George. Prison Life and Reflections, Narrative of Trial, Imprisonment, etc. of Work, Burr, and Thompson for aiding Slaves to Liberty. Hartford, 1849.

———. The Negroes' Flight from American Slavery to British Freedom. 1849. pp. 16.

Watson, Henry. Narrative of Henry Watson, a Fugitive Slave. Written by himself. Boston, 1848. pp. 48.

Weld, S. D. American Slavery as it is: Testimony of Thousands of Witnesses. New York, 1839.

Wesley, Rev. J. The Rev. J. W. Loguen as a Slave and as a Freeman. Syracuse, New York, 1859.

Weston, G. M. Progress of Slavery in the United States. Washington, 1857.

White Slave, The: Or Memoirs of a Fugitive. Boston, 1852. pp. 408.

Whittier, John G. The Writings of John G. Whittier. Boston, 1888-89. 7 vols. 12mo.

Wigham, E. Antislavery Cause in America and its Martyrs. London, 1863.

Wilcox, A. The Powers of the Federal Government over Slavery. Baltimore, 1862. pp. 23.

Willey, Rev. Austin. History of the Antislavery Cause in State and Nation. Portland, 1886. pp. xii, 503.

Wilson, Henry. History of the Antislavery Measures in the 37th and 38th United States Congresses. Boston, 1865.

―――――. History of the Rise and Fall of the Slave Power in America. 3 vols. Boston, 1875-1877.

Williams, George W. History of the Negro Race in America. 2 vols. New York, 1883.

Wisconsin Supreme Court. Unconstitutionality of the Fugitive Slave Act. Decision in Case of Booth and Bycraft. Milwaukee, 1855.

INDEX.

ABOLITION, in the D. C., 82, 98, 121 (No. 62), 122 (No. 65); of the slave trade in the D. C., 25. See also Antislavery, Emancipation.
Abolitionists, known to slaves, 53; efforts on the Underground Railroad, 64. See also Antislavery.
Acorn, ship, 44.
Act, first fugitive slave, 105, 106 (No. 9); second fugitive slave, 112-115 (No. 31); Grimes, 120 (No. 51); Blair, 121 (No. 58); repealing fugitive slave act, 123 (No. 83). See also Bill.
Adams, ——, against fugitive slave bill, 21.
Adams, J. Q., in Treaty of Ghent Convention, 25; presented petitions, 40.
Advertisement, of runaways, 4; colonial, 5; later, 56, 80; of probable place of refuge of an habitual runaway, 57.
Albany, escapes from, 8, 97, 98 (No. 50).
Aldrich, amendment, 121 (No. 58).
Alexander, Archer, 128 (No. 69).
Alien and Sedition Acts, absorb attention, 20.
Allen, Henry W., tried for kidnapping, 49.
Amendments to the Constitution, 86, 87.
Amsterdam, banishes runaway colonists, 92 (No. 15).
Anderson case, 25, 26, 128 (No. 65).
Antislavery men, biographies of, 132 (No. 4).
Antislavery reminiscences, 131 (No. 9).
Antislavery sentiment, rise of, 35.
Antislavery societies, character of work, 38; reports of, 131 (No. 10).
Apprentices, fugitive, 91 (No. 9), 95 (No. 39).
Arbitration, in Creole case, 27.
Army officers, arrests by, 79.

Arrest, negro liable to, 55; by army officers, 79.
Articles of Confederation, fugitive slave clause in, 7, 13, 91 (No. 8).
Articles of war, resolution on, 120 (No. 47); bill for an additional, 79.
Artis, Jordan, advertisement of, 56.
Ashley, repeal bill, 83, 123 (No. 80).
Athenæum, Boston, 129 (No. 2).
Attorneys, to defend fugitives, 66; forbidden to act, 69.
Attucks, Crispus, escape of, 5, 124 (No. 6).

BADGER, on fugitive slave bill, 32.
Bahamas, treatment of fugitives in, 24, 26.
Bass, aids S. Northrup, 37.
Batchelder, James, death of, 46.
Bath, escape from, 127 (No. 56).
Bell, Governor. See Ohio.
Benton Resolution, 109.(No. 24).
Bermudas, treatment of fugitives in, 26.
Bill, for a new fugitive slave law, reported, 17-21, 24; 28-29; character of, 1802, 19, 20; principles of, 1818, 20-21; for amending, 21-22; on Maryland resolutions, 24; Douglas's, 118 (No. 17); Lovejoy's, 119 (No. 35), 122 (No. 66); Wilson's, 120 (Nos. 42, 48), 122 (Nos. 54, 56); Howe's, 120 (No. 49); Davis's 120 (No. 50), 121 (No. 57); confiscation, 122 (Nos. 68, 72, 73, 79); abolition, 121, 122 (Nos. 62, 65); Harris's, 121 (No. 59), 122 (Nos. 67, 71); Clarke's, 122 (No. 72); Julian's, 120 (No. 45), 122 (No. 76); emancipation, 122 (Nos. 73, 75), 122, 123 (No. 78); repeal, 123 (No. 80); Stevens's, 123(No. 80); Ashley's, 123 (No. 80); Sumner's, 123 (Nos. 80, 83); Spalding's, 123 (No. 80);

(139)

House substitute, 123 (No. 83). See also Acts.
Bingham, ——, on Blair bill, 79, 80; resolutions, 81, 119 (No. 39); amendments, 121 (No. 58), 122 (No. 67).
Black Code, in the D. C., resolution on, 119 (No. 33); bill to repeal, 121 (No. 56).
Blair, ——, bill, 79, 80; Act, 121 (No. 58).
Blake, ——, introduces repeal bill, 73.
Boston massacre, Attucks killed in, 5, 6.
Boston, schooner, case of, 41, 125 (No. 21).
Boucher, Rev. John, on Washington's education, 2.
Bound servants, escape from Virginia, 9.
Bourne, ——, appointed on committee, 17.
Bowditch, H. I. See Latimer Journal.
Boyle, ——, Brigadier General in Sherwood case, 78.
Bright, ——, Explanatory Bill, 116 (No. 34).
Brown, on repeal bill, 86.
Brown, John, in Missouri and Kansas, 51; plan of, 51; effect of raid, 84; case, 128 (No. 63).
Brown, Mary, demands arrest of Hamlet, 43, 44.
Browne, William, story of escapes, 9.
Browne, William, a runaway, 57.
Buchanan, James, presidential message of, 72, 117 (No. 1).
Burnett, Governor, conference with Indians, demands slave, 8.
Burns, Anthony, arrest and trial, 45, 55, 127; use of court house in his case, 68, (No. 57).
Butler, ——, proposition on fugitive slave clause, 14; on fugitive slave bill, 32; reports fugitive slave bill, 110 (No. 30).
Butler, General B. F., on "contrabands," 74.

CALHOUN, Resolution, 27, 108 (No. 20).
California, sanctions rendition, 67.
Calvert, appointed on committee, made chairman, 17.
Cape May, escapes to, 124 (No. 3).

Carlisle, fugitive slave case in, 39.
Cases, legal, change in character of, 34; classification of, 35; principle of selection of, 43.
Certificate, evidence for conviction, 7.
Chandler, Zachary, introduces confiscation bill, 75; confiscation act, 119 (No. 31).
Chase, S. P., on fugitive slave law, 32; on payments under law of 1850, 116 (No. 38); offers amendments, 111 (No. 30).
Cherokees. See Treaty.
Chickasaws. See Treaty.
Chickasaw case, 38, 39, 125 (No. 20).
Christiana case, 50, 51, 127 (No. 49); influence traced, 50, 51.
Choctaws. See Treaty.
Clarence, ——, joint resolution, 118 (No. 23).
Clark, ——, reports confiscation bill, 76; substitute, 77; resolution, 119 (No. 34); amendments, 120 (No. 51); 122, 123 (No. 78); confiscation bill, 122 (No. 72).
Clarke, J. F., quoted, 43, 46, 58, 62.
Clay, Henry, see Gallatin, provision on fugitives, 30; on Shadrach case, 48, 115 (No. 33); amendment, 111 (No. 30).
Cochrane, joint resolution, 117 (No. 2).
Colfax, Schuyler, resolution, 122 (No. 77).
Collamer, ——, amendments, 121 (No. 53); 122 (No. 67).
Colonial regulation, began early, 2; cases, 1-12; legislation, 89-103.
Colonists, runaway, 92 (No. 15).
Colony, of fugitives, 57.
Columbia, case in, 125 (No. 15).
Comet case, 26.
Commissioners, of United Colonies, complain of fugitives, 10; duty of, 31.
Committee, for a new fugitive slave law, 17; on the fugitive slave law, 17-23, 27; on Maryland resolution, 24; to prevent outrages, 41; conference, 77; amendments by, 119 (No. 31), 120 (Nos. 48, 51); on judiciary, instructed, 29; report a fugitive slave law, 29.
Compromise, resolution affirming, 116 (No. 35); fugitive slave act, 118 (No. 25).
Conferences, between Indians and the Governor of New York, 8.

Confiscation, of slaves of rebels, 74; report on, 121 (No. 60); bill, 75, 76; amendments, 75; provisions extended, 75, 76; presented, 75, 76; act approved by President, 77; Trumbull's, 119 (Nos. 30, 37), 120 (No. 52); Chandler's, 119 (No. 31); Davis's, 120 (No. 50); coupled with emancipation, 120 (No. 44), 122 (Nos. 69, 73); amendments to, 121, (No. 57), 123 (Nos. 67, 71); Harris's, 121, 122 (Nos. 59, 63, 67, 71); Clark's, 122 (No. 72); progress of, 123 (No. 79); Morrill's joint resolution, 119 (No. 40).

Congress, action of, from 1847 to 1850, 28, 29.

Connecticut, legislation in, 4; in the New England confederation, 7; offers reward, 8; emancipation in, 13; Personal Liberty Laws in, 65, 66, 69; servants in, 91 (No. 9); against runaways, 100 (No. 67), 103 (Nos. 78, 79).

Constitution, fugitive slave clause in, 16, 105 (No. 7); defended slavery, 16; amendments proposed, 118 (No. 22).

Constitutional Convention, fugitive question in, 14, 15.

Contrabands, origin of term, 74.

Convention, in Treaty of Ghent, 25. See also Constitutional Convention.

Conviction of a fugitive, evidence necessary, 18, 19.

Cooledge, N., in Latimer case, 39.

Court, Commissioners, how chosen, 30. See also Conviction, Trials.

Court-house assaulted, 49, 58.

Cowden, Colonel, in Wisdom case, 78.

Cox, ——, resolution, 117 (No. 5); on repeal bill, 84.

Crafts, William and Lucy, escape of, 59, 60, 126 (No. 41).

Creek Indians, escapes to, 8; treaty with, 24; restoration clause in treaty, 106 (No. 11).

Creole, case of, 27.

Crittenden, joint resolution, 118 (Nos. 13, 24).

Curtis, Commissioner, 44.

Curtis, Judge, trial of, 46.

DAGGET amendment, 20, 107 (No. 14);
Dana, R. H., defends Burns, 46.
Daniel, offered for sale, 57.
Davis, amendment, 111 (No. 30); bill, 120 (No. 50); substitute bill, 121 (No. 57); amendments, 121 (No 58).
Davis, Charles G., in Shadrach case, 47 48.
Dayton amendment, 111 (No. 30).
Debate, on fugitive slave clause in the constitution, 14, 15; on fugitive slave bill, 17-20; on the slave trade, 20; on the fugitive slave act, 20, 22; on the admission of Missouri, 23; on slavery in the D. C., 29; on the fugitive slave law of 1850, 31-33.
De Bere, John, in Shadrach case, 47.
Delaware, regulation of servants and slaves, 101 (No. 70).
Delawares, fugitive slave clause in treaty, 104 (No. 1).
Diggs, S. T. P., in Anderson case, 26.
Dismal Swamp, refuge for fugitive, 57.
District of Columbia, slavery in, 29; repeal of jail laws in, 80, 82; Grimes's bill, 81, 82; debate on abolition of slavery in, 82; resolution on repeal of the Black Code in, 119 (No. 33); bill for emancipation in, 120 (No. 42); act on criminal justice in, 120 (No. 51); bill, 121 (No. 54); bill to repeal Black Code in, 121 (No. 56); bill for the abolition of slavery in, 121, 122 (Nos. 62, 65).
Drayton, ——, Captain, aids fugitives, 42.
Drayton and Sayres, case of, 42; 126 (No 40).
Douglass, Frederick, method of escape, 58, 64, 125 (No. 23).
Douglas, Stephen A., joint resolution, 118 (No. 14).
Dutch Colonies, along the coast, 1; regulations on fugitives, 2, 4; legislation in, 6. See also New Amsterdam, New Netherlands.

EAST JERSEY, against fugitives, 2, 3, 95, 96 (No. 41); against runaways, 96 (No. 45).
Eldridge, Captain, of brig Chickasaw, 38, 39.

Eliot, ——, introduces confiscation bill, 76; bill, 122 (No. 69); substitute bill, 122 (No. 78).

Elton, Governor, action in fugitive slave case, 10.

Emancipation, in Great Britain, 26; resolutions on, 76; in the District of Columbia, 120 (No. 42); bill, 122 (No. 75); coupled with confiscation, 120 (No. 44); 122 (Nos. 69, 73); of fugitives from disloyal masters, bill for, 122 (No. 78).

Emancipation proclamation, effect of, as a war measure, 77.

Encomium, case of, 24.

England. See Great Britain.

English, ——, joint resolution, 117 (No. 8).

English colonies, 1. See Colonies.

Enterprise, case of, 24.

Escape, by ferries, 4, 5; methods of investigation of, 53; methods of, 53; motives for, 54; to the woods, 56, 57; to the North, 57; by laundry work, 58; by coach, 58, 59; by passports, 63, 75; general effect of, 64; from English to French, 124 (No. 5). See also Fugitives, Runaways.

Extradition, no system of, in the colonies, 9.

FALSE TESTIMONY, punished, 70.

Faneuil Hall, mass meetings in, 40, 45, 55.

Fee, of commissioners, 30.

Felons, runaway apprentices, 90 (No. 4).

Felony, when guilty of, 69.

Ferries, escapes by, 4, 5.

Fessenden, ——, requests investigation of the District of Columbia jail, 81, 119 (No. 38).

Fitch, ——, resolutions affirming the Compromise, 116 (No. 35).

Florence, ——, joint resolutions, 118 (Nos. 15, 18).

Florida, escapes to, 8; Seminole trouble in, 25.

Fortress Monroe, contrabands at, 74.

French colonies, interval of unpopulated country south, 1; refuse to return fugitives, 11.

Free negroes, penalty for harboring fugitives, 4; condition of, 27.

Free States, difficulty of transporting slaves across, 36.

Friendship, ship, case of, 6, 126 (No. 10).

Frontiers, places of refuge, 25.

Fugitive apprentices, act applies to, 18. See also servants.

Fugitives, evidence to convict, 19; status on the high seas, 26; penalty for harboring, 31, 103 (No. 80); pursuit interfered with, 38; length of journeys, 57, 58; disguised as whites, 58, 59; how conducted on the underground railroad, 61; in loyal slave states, 77, 78; typical cases of, during the war, 78; arrests of, by civil officers, advertisement of, 80; entertainment of, 90 (No. 6); against, 91 (Nos. 11, 12); resolution for the discharge of, 119 (No. 32); bill to prevent return of, 119 (No. 35); resolution against the return of, 120 (Nos. 43, 46); bill on the arrest of, by army and navy officers, 120 (No. 48); act to prohibit return by the army, 121 (No. 58); resolution on the return of, by the army and navy, bill on the return of, by the army, resolution demanding trial by jury for, 121, 122 (Nos. 61, 66, 77); bill for the emancipation of fugitives from disloyal masters, 122, 123 (No. 78). See also Runaways, Escapes; see Table of Contents.

Fugitive Slaves, appeal for, 19; status of question from 1823 to 1847, 22, 25; resolutions on, 78; question discussed, 78, 79; arrest by army officers, 79; resolutions on the return of, resolution on army orders on, 119 (Nos. 28, 36); resolution on, 122 (No. 74); sources of information on, general histories of, 129 (Nos. 1, 3); secondary sources of information on, original sources of information on, autobiographies of, records of trials of, periodicals and newspapers upon, 129–131 (Nos. 3, 5, 6, 7, 11); materials for study of legislation upon, 131, 132 (No. 12). See also Escapes, Fugitives, Runaways, and Table of Contents.

Fugitive Slave Act, first (1793), 16, 17; first called for, 17; necessity of the act, 17; passed the Senate, passed the House, 17; signed by the President, 18; text, 105, 106 (No. 9); followed earlier examples, 17, 18; status of opinion on, 17, 18; remained inoperative, 16, 17; to enforce the, 110 (No. 29).

Fugitive Slave Act, second (1850), attempts to secure, 21, 24; secured, 29, 30; introduced by Mason, 29, 110 (No. 30); Webster proposes, 111 (No. 30); substitute offered, 111 (No. 30); passed Congress, 29, 30; necessity of, urged, 31; arguments for, 31, 32; arguments against, 32, 33; provisions of, 30, 31; text of, 112 (No. 31); unpopularity of, 43, 51; no moral foundation, 43; declared unconstitutional, 71; non-execution of, 72; resolution to amend, 120 (No. 45).

Fugitive Slave Acts repealed (1864), repeal urged, 72; status of, 83; early propositions, 83; discussion, 83; repeal bill, 83; passed, 85; repeal bill discussed, 84–86; bill to amend, 118 (No. 25); repeal bills, 120 (No. 49), 122 (No. 76), 126 (Nos. 80, 82); repeal bill passes, 86; text of, 86, 87; 124 (No. 83).

Fugitive Slave Bill of 1818, passed the House, 20–22; title of, 22; failure in the Senate, 23.

Fugitive Slave Cases. See Table of Contents.

Fugitive Slave Clause, in the New England Articles of Confederation, 7; in the Constitution, 14–16; in the Treaty of Ghent, 24, 106 (No. 12).

Fugitive Slave Controversy, educating effect of, recapitulation of, 87, 88.

Fugitive Slave Legislation, opposed by Northern States, 28; inadequacy of, proved, 28; necessity of more stringent, 26, 28; proposition for new, 29; must be carried out, 42; new element in, 66; in 1860, 71; resistance to, declared felony, 72, 73; propositions to repeal or amend, 73; after emancipation proclamation, 77.

GALLATIN, ALBERT, in Treaty of Ghent, 25.
Gannett, case of, 126 (No. 44).
Gansey, Isaac, case of, 125 (No. 24).
"Gap Gang," aid kidnappers, 50.
Gardiner, ———, commissioner in Hamlet case, 43, 44.
Garner, Margaret, flight and seizure, 47.
Garner, Robert, flight and seizure, 47.
Garner, Simeon, flight and seizure, 47; case 128 (No. 58).
Garrett, Thomas, trial and fine, reward offered for, 63.
Gatchell case, 128 (No. 61).
Georgia, difficulty in recovery of fugitives in, 8; Governor of, demands fugitives from justice, 41.
Gibson case, 126 (No. 45).
Giddings resolution, 29, 109 (Nos. 23, 25); resolution, 110 (Nos. 27, 28).
Glasgow, freedom case in, 12, 124 (No. 7).
Glocester, given jurisdiction over runaways, 93 (No 24).
Glover case, 127 (No. 55).
Goin case, 126 (No. 29).
Gorsuch, Edward, claims a fugitive, 50.
Grahame, Thomas, in freedom case, 12.
Grayson, ———, on fugitive slave clause, 15.
Great Britain, status of fugitives in, 11, 12; diplomatic relations, 11, 12; encouragement of fugitives, 24, 25; pays indemnity, 26. See also England.
Great Dismal Swamp, refuge for runaways, 57.
Grey, James B., demands a fugitive, 39.
Grimes, criminal justice bill, 81; act, 120 (No. 51); amendments, 121 (No. 64), 122 (No. 74).

HALE, ———, resolution, 79, 120 (No. 41); amendment, 123 (No. 82).
Hall, ———, resolution, 29, 109 (No. 26).
Hamlet, James, case, 43, 44, 126 (No. 43).
Hannum, Captain, in Ottoman case, 40.
Hanway, Castner, in Christiana case, 50, 51.
Harlan, ———, amendment, 120 (No. 51).
Harris, ———, introduces confiscation bill,

76; confiscation bill, 121 (No. 59), 122 (Nos. 67, 71); amendment, 121 (No. 64).
Hartford, fugitive harbored in, 10; treaty of, ratified, 91 (No. 14); controversy with New Netherlands, 124 (No. 1).
Harvard College, Library of, 129 (No. 2).
Henderson amendment, 123 (No. 82).
Hepburne, Judge, in Kennedy case, 39.
Higginson, T. W., in Burns case, 45, 46.
Hilliard, Mrs. G. S., harbors a fugitive, 64.
Hillyer, ——, finality resolution, 116 (No. 37).
Hindman, ——, proposition, 72; joint resolution, 117 (No. 10).
- Holmes, ——, on the fugitive slave bill, 22.
Howard, ——, amendment, 123 (No. 82).
Howe, ——, repeal bill, 83, 120 (No. 49).
Hubbard, ——, on repeal bill, 84, 85; resolution, 123 (No. 83).

ILLINOIS, no full personal liberty law in, 67.
Immigration, into Missouri, 23.
Impeachment, ground for, 69.
Imprisonment of a runaway, 56.
Indented Servants. See Servants.
Indiana, personal liberty law in (1824), 65, 67.
Indians, received fugitives in the wilderness, 1; as slaves, 2; as slave hunters, 8; conferences with, 8; escapes to, 9. See Chickasaws, Choctaws, Creeks, Delawares, Seminoles.
Intercolonial cases, early agreements as to fugitives, 1, 2; agreement between the Dutch and English, 7; difficulty of arranging regulations, 7; first contained in Articles of Confederation, 7; dependent upon intercolonial feeling, 9; case of escape of slaves, 11.
Interferences and rescues, 38.
International cases, earliest, 10; relations unsettled, 9, 10; regulations under the Articles of Confederation, 12, 13.
Interstate relations, affected by Prigg decision, 41.

Iowa, personal liberty laws in, 67.
Iredell, on fugitive slave clause, 15.
Isaac, case of, 41, 124 (No. 24).

JACKSON, ——, resolution, 116 (No. 36).
Jager, Cornelis Herperts de, escape of servants of, 6, 7.
Jail, in the District of Columbia, resolution on, 80; denied to fugitives, 80, 81, 110 (Nos. 27, 28). See District of Columbia.
Jails, State, not to be used, 40, ; denied to fugitives, 47; denial constitutional, 70; use forbidden, 69. See also Personal Liberty Bill.
Jefferson, Thomas, proposition, 13.
John case, 17, 124 (No. 11).
Johnson, on committee, 17; joint resolution, 118 (Nos. 12, 27); amendment, 124 (No. 83).
Johnson Case, 128 (No. 60).
Jones, George, case, 36, 37, 125 (No. 19).
Julian, George W., repeal bills, 83, 122 (No. 76), 123 (No. 80); resolution, 120 (No. 45).
Jury trial, not admitted, 7; disuse of, 66.

KANSAS, personal liberty laws in, 67, 70.
Kellogg, ——, joint resolution, 118 (Nos. 19, 20, 21).
Kennedy case, 39, 126 (No. 35).
Kentucky, resolutions, 25; petition of Legislature, 28; demands extradition of abettors of fugitives, 41; controversy with Ohio, 126 (No. 37).
Kidnapping, suggests new fugitive slave law, 17; from 1793 to 1850, 27; in border States, 27; character of cases, 36; enlists sympathy, 60; regulations against, 82.
Kilgore, resolution, 73, 118 (No. 11).
King, ——, on repeal bill, 84.
Kirk case, 126 (No 33).
Kline, Marshal, demands assistance, 50,

L'AMISTAD case, 27.
Latimer, George, case of, 39, 125 (No. 28); effect, 68; daily journal, 40.

Leake, ——, joint resolution, 117 (No. 9).
Le Screux, slave on, 11.
Lewis case, 127 (No. 54).
Lewis, Elijah, prosecution of, 50, 51, 127 (No. 49).
Liberator, kidnapping case in, 82. See Newspapers.
Liberty, love of, by slaves, 54.
Liberty Party, convention of, 49.
Libraries, use of, 129 (No. 2).
Lincoln, President, preliminary proclamation, 77; final emancipation proclamation, 77.
List, counsel in Shadrach case, 47.
Loring, Ellis Gray, in Shadrach case, 47; Crafts taken to house of, 60.
Louisiana, escape of slaves from, 23.
Lovejoy, bills, 78, 79, 119 (No. 35), 122 (No. 66); resolutions, 119 (No. 29), 120 (No. 44); amendment, 119 (No. 38).

MADISON, on fugitive slave clause, 15.
Maine, Governor of, refuses to surrender fugitives from justice, 41; personal liberty law in, 69.
Malbronne, Ensign de, loses servant, 11.
Mallory, ——, on Blair bill, 79; on repeal, 84.
Manhattan, escape to, 6, 124 (No. 2).
Mansfield, Lord. See Somersett case.
Market women, on Underground Railroad, 63.
Maryland, regulations on fugitives, 3; offers reward, 7; letter from, to New Netherlands, 10, 11; fugitives escape from, 10, 11; resolution, 24; resolutions debated, 24, 107 (No. 18); offers reward for Thomas Garrett, 63; regulations against runaways, 90 (No. 4), 91 (Nos. 11, 12), 93 (Nos. 26, 28), 94 (No. 31), 95 (Nos. 38, 40).
Mason, of Massachusetts, on the fugitive slave bill, 22.
Mason, of Virginia, fugitive slave bill, 29, 30, 110 (No. 30); amendment, 29; argument, 31.
Massachusetts Bay, regulation against transportation of apprentices and servants, 99 (No. 63); on the capture of servants in, 89 (No. 2); regulation of free negroes, 98 (No. 53).
Massachusetts Colony, first law as to fugitives, 4; in the New England Confederation, 7; emancipation in, 13; first fugitive slave case in, 35.
Massachusetts State, Governor of, advised, 68; personal liberty law, 66, 67, 68; no recovery of fugitives in, 71.
May, S. J., in "Jerry" case, 49.
McClernand, ——, 117 (No. 9).
McHenry, "Jerry," case, 48, 49, 127 (No. 51).
McLanahan, ——, resolution, 115 (No. 32).
Meade, ——, proposition, 29; resolution, 110 (No. 29).
Meionaon, mass meetings in, 45.
Merrill, Amos B., in Latimer case, 39.
Mexico, as a place of refuge, 25.
Michigan, personal liberty laws in, 67, 70.
Miller, in kidnapping case, 51, 127 (No. 50).
Miner, Jo, advertisement of, 80.
Minnesota, personal liberty law in, 67.
Missouri, admission of, 23; Anderson case in, 26; Governor of, offers reward for John Brown, 51.
Missouri Compromise, fugitive slave clause in, 23, 107 (No. 16); period of, 23.
Mob, provisions against, 31.
Morgan, Margaret. See Prigg Case.
Morrill, ——, resolution, 119 (No. 40).
Morris, cutter, in Burns case, 46, 55.
Morris, ——, substitute reported, 83; on repeal bill, 85; resolution, 117 (No. 3); joint resolution, 118 (No. 16).
Morris, John B., demands a fugitive slave, 39.
"Moses." See Harriet Tubman.
Murray, ——, motion, 19.

NALLE CASE, 128 (No. 64).
Nassau, fugitives in, 27.
Negroes, ignorance of, 57; regulation of, 100 (No. 65); against escape of, 103 (No. 78); petition of a soldier, 20; free, how affected, 21; regulation of, 98 (No. 53). See also Fugitives.

New Amsterdam, escape of servants from, 67; trial at, 9. See also New Netherlands.
New England, regulations as to fugitives, 4.
New England Confederation, composition of, 7, 8; articles of, 91 (No. 8).
New Hampshire, legislation in, 4, 99 (No. 61); personal liberty laws in, 67, 69.
New Haven, in the New England Confederation, 7.
New Jersey, regulations on fugitives, 3, 94 (No. 32), 95 (No. 39), 96 (No. 42); sanctions rendition, 67; slaves, 98 (No. 55); white servants, 98 (No. 56).
New Netherlands, legislation in, 4; on fugitive slave cases, 11; regulations against runaways, 89 (No. 1), 89, 90 (No. 3), 90 (No. 5), 91 (Nos. 10, 14), 92 (No. 19); Quakers, 93 (No. 29); controversy with Hartford, 126 (No. 1). See also Dutch Colonies.
New York, regulation on fugitives, 8, 97 (No. 50), 98 (No. 51), 99 (No. 59); Governor of, in Solomon Northrup case, 37, 38; refusal to return abettors of fugitives, 41; personal liberty laws, 66, 69, 70; slaves, 97 (No. 49); prevention of insurrections, 101 (No. 68); kidnapping in, 82.
Niblack, ——, resolution, 117 (No. 7).
Nicholson, on committee, 20.
Norfolk, kidnapping cases in, 82, 128; (No. 68).

OBERLIN CASE, 38, 125 (No. 26).
Oberlin-Wellington, rescue, 49, 50, 128 (No. 62).
Officers, return of fugitives by army and navy, 121 (No. 53).
Ohio, fugitives protected in, 23; refusal to return abettors of fugitives, 41; personal liberty law, 67, 70.
Olmsted, F. L., quoted, 56.
"Omnibus Bill," fugitive slave provision in, 30.
Ordinance of 1787, for the Northwest Territory, 13, 14; confirmed, 16.
Ottoman case, 40, 126 (No. 34).

PARKER, THEODORE, speaks on Burns' case, 45; indicted for riot, 46; protects William and Lucy Crafts, 59, 60.
Parker, William, in Christiana case, 50.
Pass, necessity of, 55.
Patrols, duty of, 55.
Patroons, runaways from, 89 (No. 1).
Peace Convention, amendment, 118 (No. 22).
Pearl, carries fugitives, 42.
Penalties for escape, 31; for violating personal liberty laws, 67.
Pennsylvania, emancipation in, 13; Governor of, in "John" case, 17; act of, reported, 23, 107 (No. 17); fugitives abetted in, 24; personal liberty laws in, 66, 69; regulation of servants, 97 (No. 48); regulation of negroes, 100 (No. 65); harboring of fugitives, 103 (No. 80); case in, 126 (No. 46).
Pennsylvania Society for the Abolition of Slavery, efforts in behalf of "John," 17; petition of, 21; efforts of, 28.
Pensacola, Walker embarks from, 42.
Personal Liberty Laws, passed, 28; character of, 65; before the Prigg decision, 65; between the Prigg decision and the Second Fugitive Slave Law, 66; occasioned by the law of 1850, 66, 67; change in character, 66; table of, 67; distribution among States, 67; report on, 68; effect of, 70, 102; constitutionality of, 70; obstruction by, 71; repeal urged, 72; resolution against, 72; Saulsbury substitute on, 123 (No. 81).
Petition of North Carolina negroes, 19; of free negroes, 20; of a free colored soldier, 20; of the Pennsylvania Abolition Society 21; from the Kentucky Legislature, 28; to remove jailer and sheriff in Latimer case, 40; for an amendment to the Constitution, 40; for a new personal liberty law, 68.
Philadelphia, constitutional convention sits in, 14; attempted rescue in, 39, 125 (No. 22).
Phillips, Wendell, speeches on Latimer case, 40; addresses mass meeting, 45;

speaks on Burns' case, 45; indicted for riot, 46.
Pierce, Franklin, President, sends executive message, 48; issues proclamation, 48.
Pindall, on revision of the fugitive slave act, 21; made chairman of committee, 21; amendatory bill, 106 (No. 10).
Pine Grove Plantation, probable refuge, 57, 66.
Pinkney, Gen. C. C., on the fugitive slave clause, 14.
Plymouth, in the New England Confederation, 7.
Pomeroy, ——, on confiscation bill, 76.
Porter, ——, amendment, 122 (No. 67).
Potter, R. J., advertisement by, 80.
Powell, ——, on District of Columbia jail, 81; joint resolution, 119 (No. 28); amendment, 120 (No. 51).
Pratt, ——, amendment, 111 (No. 30).
Priggs *vs.* Pennsylvania case, 27, 28, 125 (No. 18); consequences of, 66; extracts from, 108 (No. 22).
Proclamation, by West India Company, 10; on Shadrach case, 48; emancipation, 77.
Prosecutions, carried on, 42; after "Jerry" rescue, 49; of Oberlin-Wellington rescuers, 50; of Wendell Phillips, 46.
Protection papers, use of, 58.
Pugh, George H., joint resolution, 118 (No. 26).
Purrington, brig William, 126 (No. 39).
Purvis, Robert, connection with Underground Railroad, 63.

QUAKERS, arrange station on the Underground Railroad, 60; fugitives hidden by, 61; refused admision to New Netherlands, 93 (No. 29).
Quincy, Josiah, account of first fugitive slave case in the North, 35, 125 (No. 12).

RAIDS, upon plantations, 56.
Rantoul, Robert, Jr., in Sims case, 44.
Read, ——, on committee, 17.
Redemptioners, described, 2; cases of, 2; case of running away with negroes, 3.
Refuge, place of, 57.
Rendition, a duty, 7. See also Fugitives.
Rescue, first case of, 35.
Resolution, by Maryland Legislature, 23, 24; on relations with Canada, 25; Kentucky, 25; on fugitives on the high seas, 26; Giddings, 29; against the return of Latimer, 40; to base representation on free persons, 40; Georgia Legislature, 41; on arrests by army officers, 79; Fitch, 116 (No. 35); Jackson, 116 (No. 36); Hillyer, 116 (No. 37); Chase, 116 (No. 38); Cochrane's joint, 117 (No. 2); Morris, 117 (No. 3); Leake, 117 No. 4); Cox, 117 (No. 5); Stevenson, 117 (No. 6); Niblack, 117 (No. 7); English joint, 117 (No. 8); McClernand joint, 117 (No. 9); Hindman, 117 (No. 10); Kilgore, 118 (No. 11); Johnson's joint, 118 (Nos. 12, 27); Crittenden's joint, 118 (No. 13); Douglas's joint, 118 (No. 14); Florence, 118 (Nos. 15, 18); Morris's joint, 118 (No. 16); Kellogg's joint, 118 (Nos. 19, 20, 21); Clarence's joint, 118 (No. 23); Crittenden's joint, 118 (No. 24); Pugh's joint, 118 (No. 26); Powell's joint, 119 (No. 28); Lovejoy's, 119 (No. 29); Wilson's 119 (Nos. 32, 33), 120 (No. 47), 121 (No. 55), 121 (No. 61); Clark, 119 (No. 34); Sumner, 119 (No. 36); Fessenden, 119 (No. 38); Bingham, 119 (No. 39)'; Morrill's confiscation joint, 119 (No. 40); Hale, 120 (No. 41); Sumner, 120 (No. 43), 122 (No. 74); Lovejoy, 120 (No. 44); Julian, 120 (No. 45); Shank, 120 (No. 46); Colfax, 122 (No. 77); Hubbard's repeal, 123 (No. 83).
Revolution, did not change condition of slave, 13.
Reward, offered by Missouri, 51; by United States, 52; by colonies, 7, 8.
Rhode Island legislation, 4; emancipation, 13; personal liberty law, 66, 67, 69; regulation of ferries in, 98 (No. 57).

Rice, ——, amendment, 121 (No. 53).
Rice, John, kidnapped, 49.
Rich, on the fugitive slave bill, 21.
Riker, Richard, in Jones case, 37.
Riley, ——, United States commissioner, 47.
Rotch, aids escape, 6.
Runaways, regulations against, 6, 7, 8; easily regulated, 7; the habitual, 57; methods pursued, 58; harboring upon a ship, 58; regulations against, 89 (Nos. 1, 3), 90 (Nos. 4, 7), 92 (No. 17), 93 (Nos. 24, 25, 27), 94 (Nos. 31, 33), 95 (No. 40), 98 (No. 52), 99 (No. 61), 100 (No. 6); entertainment of, 91 (No. 10), 92 (No. 16), 93 (No. 29), 94 (No. 37), 102 (No. 73); second offence, how punished, 91 (No. 13); hue and cry after, 92 (No. 18); from the Dutch, 93 (No. 21); apprehension of, 93 (No. 22); English, 93 (No. 23); in Glocester, 93 (No. 24); apprehension of, 95 (Nos. 35, 38); capture rewarded, 95 (No. 37); prevention of, 96 (No. 42); to Canada, 97, 98 (No. 50); trade with, inhibited, 97 (No. 47); against ferriage of, 98 (No. 57), 102 (No. 4); minor, 99 (No. 61); pursuit of, 103 (No. 79).
Russia, Emperor of, arbitration by, 25.

SAULSBURY, amendments, 120 (No. 51), 121 (Nos. 53, 58), 122 (No. 70), 123 (Nos. 81, 82, 83).
Savannah Georgian, advertisement in, 57, 66.
Secrecy, observed by fugitives, 63.
Sedgwick, ——, on committee, 17.
Seizure, of North Carolina negroes, 19. See also Arrest, Kidnapping Cases.
Seminoles, steal slaves, 24; trouble, 25; United States claims on, 108 (No. 19).
Sergeant, ——, on the fugitive slave bill, 22.
Servants, English, 93 (Nos. 25, 28); an act concerning, 99 (No. 60); regulation of, 98 (No. 56), 101 (No. 70), 101 (No. 71); fugitive, 91 (No. 9), 92 (No. 19), 93 (No. 21), 94 (No. 32), 95 (Nos. 39, 41), 96 (No. 45), 100 (No. 67), 103 (No.

78); how to know a, 92 (No. 20). See also Fugitives, Runaways.
Sewall, Samuel E., counsels fugitives, 39, 47.
Seward, W. H., amendments, 29, 111 (No. 30).
Shadrach case, 47, 48; personal liberty laws tested, 68; Clay's resolution on, 115 (No. 33); case, 127 (No. 48).
Shank, ——, resolution, 120 (No. 46).
Shanley vs. Haney case, 124 (No. 8).
Shaw, Chief Justice, in Latimer case, 39.
Shell, O. P., advertises a runaway, 56.
Sheriff, power of, 31.
Sherman, John, amendments, 86, 123 (No. 82).
Sherman, Roger, on the fugitive slave clause, 14; on committee, 18.
Sherwood, Major, case of servant of, 78, 128 (No. 67).
Ship, refuge for runaways, 58; slave on Brazilian, 126 (No. 36).
Ship-masters, Dutch, rewarded, 93 (No. 21).
Sims, Thomas M., case, 44; brigade, 44; courthouse used as jail, 68; case, 126 (No. 44).
Slaves, conditions of life, 55; Mother's Farewell, extract from, 54; stealing of, 102 (No. 77); abolition of trade in, 21; status of, in England, 24; question of damages, 31; must wear livery, 55; new conditions surround, 73; regulation of, 97 (No. 49), 98 (Nos. 54, 55), 99, 100 (Nos. 60, 64), 100 (No. 67), 101 (No. 70), 101, 102 (Nos. 71, 72); extradition of, 108 (No. 21); status on the high seas, 108 (No. 20), 109 (No. 23); of the Dutch, escape to the English, 7; escape to the forest, 7, 8; of rebels, resolutions on, 73; bill to free, 120 (No. 52).
Slaveholder, demand for legislation, 14; basis of, argued, 16; complaints of, 20.
Slave-hunters, how received, 62; insurrections to prevent, 101 (No. 68).
Slavery, condition in the colonies, 11; interests advanced, 16; justification of, 16; extinction of, 35; attacked in

Congress, 74; abolition in the District of Columbia, 82, 121, 122 (Nos. 62, 65); studies of the institution of, 129 (No. 3); studies of colonial, 129 (No. 3); speeches upon, 131 (No. 8).
Smith, ——, on fugitive slave law, 21, 22.
Smith, Gerrit, in Anderson case, 26; in "Jerry" rescue, 49.
Smithburg case, 126 (No. 32).
Society for the Abolition of Slavery. See Pennsylvania.
Somersett case, 12, 124 (No. 9).
Soulé, ——, on the fugitive slave bill, 31, 32.
South Bend Case, 126 (No. 38).
South Carolina, regulations on fugitives, 3; difficulty in recovering fugitives, 8; constitutional convention in, 14; regulations against runaways, 96 (No. 43), 97 (No. 47), 99, 100 (Nos. 58, 62, 64); regulation of slaves, 98 (No. 54), 100 (No. 64),101 (No. 69), 102 (No. 77).
Southern States, complain of Underground Railroad, 64.
Spalding, ——, repeal bill, 83, 123 (No. 80).
Spanish colonies, interval of unpopulated country south, 1.
Sprague, E., 46.
State Jails. See Jails.
State Officers, power discussed, 20, 22; forfeiture of office, 69; forbidden to act, 66, 69.
St. Augustine, escapes to, 8.
St. Luc, Sieur de la Corne, negro servant of, 11.
Staunton, General, in Sherwood case, 78, 94.
Stevens, ——, repeal bill, 83, 123 (No. 80); motion of, 111 (No. 30).
Stevenson, ——, resolution, 117 (No. 6).
Stewart, ——. See Somersett Case.
Story, Justice, decision in Prigg case, 28.
Stuyvesant, Governor, in fugitive slave case, 10.
Sumner, Charles, in Drayton case, 42; resolutions, 79; repeal bills, 83, 85, 124 (No. 80), resolutions, 119 (No. 36), 120 (No. 43), 120 (No. 74); amendment, 121 (No. 57).

Suttle, Charles F., in Burns case, 45.
Swain, John, suit for slave, 5.
Swamps, as a refuge, 56, 57.
Swan, Captain, in Wisdom case, 78.
Swedish colonies, along the coast, 1; regulations on fugitives, 2.
Syracuse, "Jerry" rescue in, 48.

TAYLOR, ——, on committee, 18.
Ten Eyck, ——, amendment, 120 (No. 51); report of, 123 (No. 80).
Thomas case, 126 (No. 30).
Thompson, ——, case, 125 (No. 27).
Treaty, of Hartford, fugitive slave clause in, 91 (No. 14); of 1783, 104 (No. 2); with Indian tribes, 12, 13, 16, 17, 24, 104 (Nos. 1, 3, 5), 105 (No. 8), 106 (Nos. 11, 12), 108 (No. 19); of Ghent, 24, 106 (No. 12); proposed with Great Britain, 25.
Tremont Temple, mass meetings in, 45.
Trial, by jury, not admitted, in first act, 19; objected to, 22; denied, 31; proposed, 73; resolution demanding, 122 (No. 77).
Trumbull, confiscation bill, 75, 119 (Nos. 30, 37); bill, 120 (No. 52); amendments, 119 (No. 31), 121 (No. 57), 122 (No. 78).
Tubman, Harriet, account of, 62.
Tukey, Marshal, in Sims case, 44.
Turc, escape of, 9.

UNDERGROUND RAILROAD, beginnings of, 27; how regarded by the South, 31; methods south of the Ohio, 47; use of, by John Brown, 51; incident at, 54; description of, 60; rise and growth, 60, 61; stations on, described, 61; methods pursued, 61; extent of system, 60, 61; origin of name, 61; in the South, 61; in the North, 61; colored agents on, 61, 62; prosecution of agents, 63; formal organization, 63; market women as helpers, 63.
Underwood, ——, amendment, 111 (No. 30).
United Colonies, treaty with New Netherlands, 91 (No. 14).

United States, reward offered for John Brown, 51, 52; in Seminole trouble, 24; in Anderson case, 26. See also Acts, Bills, Fugitives, Resolutions Runaways.
United States Hotel, slave hunters at, 60, 69.

VALLANDIGHAM, C. L., amendment, 118 (No. 25).
Van Zandt, aids fugitive, 42, 125 (No. 25).
Vermont, personal liberty laws in, 66, 67, 69.
Vigilance committee organized, 38; in "Jerry" rescue, 48.
Villeinage, ceased in England, 11.
Virginia, regulations on fugitives, 3; rewards the recovery of a fugitive, 7, 8; slaves escape, 8; constitutional convention in, 15; Governor of, action in "John" case, 17; demands arrest of abettors of a fugitive, 41; regulation against the entertainment of fugitives, 90 (No. 6); regulations against runaways, 90 (No. 7), 91 (No. 13), 92 (Nos 16, 17, 18, 20), 93 (Nos. 22, 25, 27, 30), 94 (No. 33), 95 (Nos. 35, 37), 98 (No. 52); reward for the capture of runaways, 93 (No. 21), 95 (No. 36); on English runaways, 93 (No. 22); in county of Glocester, 93 (No. 24); repeal law, 96 (No. 44); amends law, 96 (No. 48); amended, 100, (No. 66); against ferriage of runaways, 102 (No. 74).

WALKER, JONATHAN, aids fugitives, 42, 126 (No. 31).
Walton, ———, amendment, 122 (Nos. 67, 74).
Washington, President, asks for the return of a fugitive, 35, 125 (No. 13).
Washington case, 38, 126 (No. 42).

Washington, jail, resolutions on, 119 (Nos. 32, 34, 38, 39), 121 (No. 55). See also Jail.
Webster, Daniel, in Creole case, 27; introduces bill, 111 (No. 30).
Wellington. See Oberlin-Wellington.
West India Company, regulation of, 2; execution of regulation 6, 7; ordinance of, 89 (No. 1).
Whipping, motive for flight, 54.
Whipple, ———, in kidnapping case, 35, 36.
White, ———, on committee, 17.
White slaves. See Redemptioners, Servants.
Whitman, ———, on the fugitive slave bill 20, 22.
Williams case, 125 (No. 17).
Williamson case, 128 (No. 59).
Wilkins, Frederick. See Shadrach.
Wilson, ———, on Butler's proposition, 14, 15.
Wilson, Henry, on confiscation, 75; bills, 82, 120 (Nos. 42, 48), 121 (Nos. 54, 56); resolutions, 79, 80, 119 (Nos. 32, 33), 120 (No. 47), 122 (Nos. 55, 61); amendment, 123 (No. 71).
Winthrop, ———, amendment, 111 (No. 30).
Winthrop, Governor John, in fugitive slave case, 10, 11.
Wisconsin, personal liberty laws in, 67, 70; Supreme Court decision, 71.
Wisdom case, 78, 128 (No. 66).
Woodbridge resolutions, 25, 108 (No. 21).
Woods, as a refuge, 1, 56.
Wright, ———, presents Maryland Resolution, 24.
Writ, of habeas corpus, in Somersett case, 12; allowed, 22; advisability of, 20, 22; refused, 26; issued, 38, 39; of personal replevin, sworn out, 39.

YULEE, on the fugitive slave law, 32.

www.ingramcontent.com/pod-product-compliance
Lightning Source LLC
Chambersburg PA
CBHW030308170426
43202CB00009B/921